Ultimate Full-Stack Web Development with MERN

Design, Build, Test and Deploy Production-Grade Web Applications with MongoDB, Express, React and NodeJS

Nabendu Biswas

www.orangeava.com

First published: December 2023

Published by: Orange Education Pvt Ltd, AVA™

Address: 9, Daryaganj, Delhi, 110002

ISBN: 978-81-19416-42-4

www.orangeava.com

Dedicated To

My wife Shikha and My Son Hriday

About the Author

Nabendu Biswas is a full-stack JavaScript developer and has been working in the IT industry for the past 19 years with some of the world's top development firms and investment banks, including J.P. Morgan, Oracle, and L&T Infotech.

He is a passionate tech blogger and YouTuber with an active following on both platforms, where he teaches everyone to be a web developer. Currently, he works as an Architect in an IT firm in Bhopal. Additionally, he is the author of seven books focusing on topics such as Gatsby, MERN, TypeScript, GraphQL, and React Firebase, all of which are available on Amazon.

About the Technical Reviewer

Samarth is a seasoned Full Stack Developer with over 5 years of experience in software development, specializing in multiple technology stacks, including the popular MERN (MongoDB, Express.js, React, Node.js) stack. His career journey has been marked by a diverse range of projects across industries such as Community-based apps, Legal, Crypto/Blockchain, Ed-Tech, HealthCare, and IOT.

Samarth is widely recognized for his expertise in creating solutions to real-world problems through innovative software development, with a specific focus on JavaScript and React. His commitment to improving the world through technology is a driving force in his work, and his comprehensive experience in diverse industries demonstrates his ability to deliver value in a variety of contexts.

Outside of software development, Samarth's interests include science and philosophy, reflecting his diverse set of passions and interests.

Acknowledgements

There are a few people I want to thank for the continued and ongoing support during the writing of this book. First and foremost, I would like to thank my wife for continuously encouraging me to write the book. I could have never completed this book without her support.

I am also grateful to the courses and the companies that supported me throughout the learning process of web development. Thank you for the all hidden support you provided.

My gratitude also goes to the team at Orange AVA for being supportive enough and providing me with quite a long time to finish and publish the book.

Preface

This book covers all the top technologies in the JavaScript ecosystem: MongoDB, ExpressJS, ReactJS and NodeJS. With these technologies, we can create a completely functional web application that includes frontend, backend and database.

We will build a fairly large production-ready app in this book. Here, we will first learn to set up the frontend with React, then create the backend APIs with NodeJS and Express. The backend will be connected to our database which is MongoDB. We will learn to use authentication in our project by implementing JWT. We will also learn to test both frontend and backend using the Unit testing framework of Jest. Finally, we will learn how to deploy both frontend and backend with ease to use free apps.

After going through the book, the readers will be able to create any MERN app with ease and can also modify the project in the book to create other apps.

Chapter 1: This book will begin with an introduction to all technologies related to MERN (MongoDB, Express, React and NodeJS) followed by a complete project overview of the app, which we are going to build in this book. We will also cover the backend setup required for the same.

Chapter 2: This chapter covers the creation of an Express app. We will create our first routes and controllers in this chapter. We will also learn about error handling.

Chapter 3: This chapter covers connecting to the MongoDB database and creating a model in our backend app. We will also start creating routes for our task app.

Chapter 4: This chapter deals with the implementation of JWT authentication and also the implementation of hashing passwords.

Chapter 5: This chapter covers the implementation of Auth middleware and protecting routes. Here, we will learn how to allow only authorized users to access certain routes.

Chapter 6: This chapter deals with the creation of frontend in ReactJS. We will also cover the setup for React Router version 6 in the project, which is used for navigation in React. We will also create the Register and Login pages on the frontend.

Chapter 7: This chapter covers the implementation of Redux, with the latest slice in the frontend. We will also set up a reducer for the registration form.

Chapter 8: This chapter deals with the login and logout functionalities with Redux.

Chapter 9: This chapter covers the creation of a dashboard in ReactJS. We will also learn how to restrict the dashboard to authorized users.

Chapter 10: This chapter covers the implementation of thunk in tasks and also fetching tasks from the server. It also completes our app, in which we display and delete tasks.

Chapter 11: This chapter covers the testing of the frontend. We will test the frontend created in React using Jest and React Testing Library.

Chapter 12: This chapter deals with the testing of the backend. We will test the backend created in NodeJS using Jest.

Chapter 13: This chapter covers the deployment of both frontend and backend using freely available services.

Get a Free eBook

We hope you are enjoying your recently purchased book! Your feedback is incredibly valuable to us, and to all other readers looking for great books.

If you found this book helpful or enjoyable, we would truly appreciate it, if you could take a moment to leave a short review with a 5 star rating on Amazon. It helps us grow, and lets other readers discover our books.

As a thank you, we would love to send you a free digital copy of this book, and a **30%** discount code on your next cart value on our official websites:

www.orangeava.com

www.orangeava.in (For Indian Subcontinent)

☑ **Here's how:**

Leave a review for the book on Amazon.

Take a screenshot of your review, and send an email to **info@orangeava.com** (it can be just the confirmation screen).

Once, we receive your screenshot, we will send you the digital file, within 24 hours.

Thank you so much for your support – it means a lot to us!

Downloading the code bundles and colored images

Please follow the link to download the
Code Bundles of the book:

https://github.com/ava-orange-education/Ultimate-Full-Stack-Web-Development-with-MERN

The code bundles and images of the book are also hosted on
https://rebrand.ly/bde02d

In case there's an update to the code, it will be updated on the existing GitHub repository.

Errata

We take immense pride in our work at **Orange Education Pvt Ltd,** and follow best practices to ensure the accuracy of our content to provide an indulging reading experience to our subscribers. Our readers are our mirrors, and we use their inputs to reflect and improve upon human errors, if any, that may have occurred during the publishing processes involved. To let us maintain the quality and help us reach out to any readers who might be having difficulties due to any unforeseen errors, please write to us at :

errata@orangeava.com

Your support, suggestions, and feedback are highly appreciated.

DID YOU KNOW

Did you know that Orange Education Pvt Ltd offers eBook versions of every book published, with PDF and ePub files available? You can upgrade to the eBook version at **www.orangeava.com** and as a print book customer, you are entitled to a discount on the eBook copy. Get in touch with us at: **info@orangeava.com** for more details.

At **www.orangeava.com**, you can also read a collection of free technical articles, sign up for a range of free newsletters, and receive exclusive discounts and offers on AVA™ Books and eBooks.

PIRACY

If you come across any illegal copies of our works in any form on the internet, we would be grateful if you would provide us with the location address or website name. Please contact us at **info@orangeava.com** with a link to the material.

ARE YOU INTERESTED IN AUTHORING WITH US?

If there is a topic that you have expertise in, and you are interested in either writing or contributing to a book, please write to us at **business@orangeava.com**. We are on a journey to help developers and tech professionals to gain insights on the present technological advancements and innovations happening across the globe and build a community that believes Knowledge is best acquired by sharing and learning with others. Please reach out to us to learn what our audience demands and how you can be part of this educational reform. We also welcome ideas from tech experts and help them build learning and development content for their domains.

REVIEWS

Please leave a review. Once you have read and used this book, why not leave a review on the site that you purchased it from? Potential readers can then see and use your unbiased opinion to make purchase decisions. We at Orange Education would love to know what you think about our products, and our authors can learn from your feedback. Thank you!

For more information about Orange Education, please visit **www.orangeava.com**.

Table of Contents

CHAPTER 1

Getting Started with MERN and Setup

Introduction

This chapter talks about the basic principles of MERN and REST API. We will talk about the technology stack behind MERN and also the way REST API works. Here, we will also do a complete project overview. We are going to learn about the complete project, which we are going to create in this book. Beside this, we are also going to do the basic setup of the backend part of the application. Here, we are going to set up the NodeJS application.

Structure

In this chapter, we are going to discuss the following topics:

- MERN
- REST APIs
- Complete Project Overview
- Setting up a NodeJS Application

About MERN

MERN stands for MongoDB, Express, React, and NodeJS. It is one of the most popular stacks for creating full-stack apps. Now, full-stack apps are fully functional apps in which we create both the frontend and the backend.

Traditionally, creating the backend and frontend are tasks for two different teams. But with startups coming into picture, a lot of companies have the complete app created by a single team.

Before the creation of NodeJS in 2009, most of the backend programming was done in Java. But with the creation of NodeJS, a lot of companies started using NodeJS in the backend.

The reason is that they can have a JavaScript engineer build the frontend in ReactJS, and the backend in NodeJS. Both ReactJS and NodeJS are JavaScript libraries and are coded using common JavaScript.

We will learn about each tech in MERN and its usage in the MERN stack.

MongoDB

The M in MERN stands for MongoDB. Now, MongoDB is a NoSQL database that stores the data in BSON format. The full form of BSON is Binary JSON and it is quite similar to JSON (JavaScript Object Notation).

It is an object which contains key-value pairs. The strings should be in double quotes, which is similar to JSON. But BSON also contains types like datetime.

A sample BSON document from a MongoDB database is as follows:

```
{
  "_id": {
      "$oid": "646c4c0b3ed1bed3064c20e2"
  },
  "company": "JP Morgan",
  "position": "Architect",
  "jobType": "full-time",
  "createdBy": {
      "$oid": "6450b1cbfb52c1a172e790e2"
  },
  "createdAt": {
      "$date": {
      "$numberLong": "1684245010932"
      }
  },
  "updatedAt": {
      "$date": {
```

```
        "$numberLong": "1684245010932"
        }
    },
    "__v": {
        "$numberInt": "0"
    }
}
```

MongoDB is totally different from traditional Relational databases, which store data in rows and tables. There are also complex relations between tables, which is not required in MongoDB.

MongoDB is a very fast database, with data stored as BSON. Therefore, it is used in most modern web-apps, like an e-commerce site or ride-sharing app. These apps are less concerned about the success of a transaction, like banking apps.

They are more concerned about getting millions of concurrent connections and handling them. Here, MongoDB excels as a NoSQL database, which makes it so popular in the MERN stack.

Express

The E in MERN stands for Express. Now, Express or ExpressJS is not a JavaScript framework but a NodeJS framework, which in turn is a JavaScript backend framework.

Now, NodeJS is used for a variety of backend tasks, including socket programming. But the major task of a backend language, which is to create API endpoints, can also be done in NodeJS.

We will learn more about the REST API in the next section. But they are basically a bridge between the database and the frontend. Writing API endpoints is the main feature of Express.

But why do we need Express, when we also have NodeJS to write API endpoints? The answer is that it is easier to write API code in Express than in Vanilla NodeJS.

So, when Express was created in 2010, it always started to be used with NodeJS for API development.

Following is the express code for a GET API. Here, we are first importing the express in our app. Then we are using it. Next, we are creating the home route '/' with the simple **app.get()** function.

Lastly, we are listening at port 8000.

```
const express = require('express');
const app = express();

app.get('/', (req,res) => {
        res.send('Welcome to Express');
});

app.listen(8000, () =>  console.log(`Server is up on port 8000`));
```

Once we run the app and goto http://localhost:8000 from our browser, we will get **Welcome to Express** text.

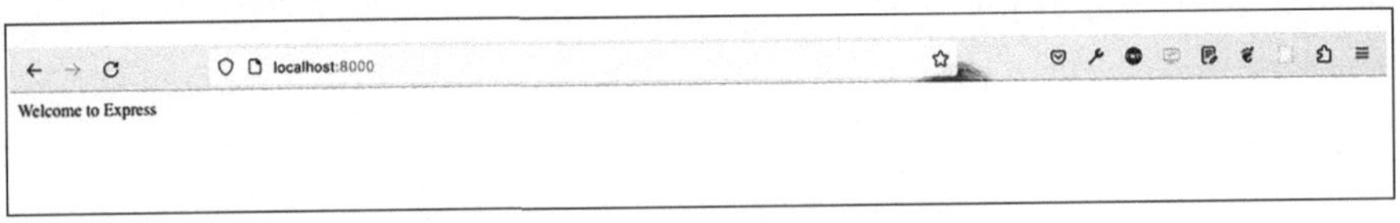

***Figure 1.1**: Express app on browser*

ReactJS

The R in MERN stands for ReactJS. ReactJS is the world's most popular JavaScript Library/Framework. It is just a small JavaScript Library, but way more popular than the JavaScript Framework of Angular.

Almost all major sites on this planet have frontend as ReactJS or some part in ReactJS. It powers Facebook, Instagram, Netflix, Airbnb, BBC, Paypal, Reddit, and almost every other web-app on this planet.

ReactJS was released in 2013 by Facebook, and before that AngularJS was released in 2010, by Google. Angular powers most of Google web-apps and many corporate apps also.

But even after a late release, ReactJS became the de facto library for startups and most companies due to its ease of learning in comparison to Angular. Being a small library, a lot of major tasks like routing and global state management are done by external packages.

But due to its popularity, ReactJS has more than 200,000 open source packages available. You can find a package for everything, from creating beautiful forms to drag drop packages.1

Sites made with ReactJS are very fast, even with extreme loads. The best examples are Facebook, Instagram, and Netflix. This power of ReactJS comes from using Virtual DOM instead of the real DOM.

The DOM manipulation is generally slow, so ReactJS changes the Virtual DOM at first. Later, it changes the DOM behind the scene.

Code written in ReactJS uses a special syntax called JSX (JavaScript XML). In ReactJS, we basically combine the HTML and JavaScript file into one file, called the JSX file.

In ReactJS, we divide the project into small, manageable components. This also helps to divide a large project into different teams. Following is the code for a simple Greet component.

Here, we are receiving data from a Parent component. This is called props. And after that, we are showing it using html. Notice that in a js extension file, we are directly showing html. This kind of file gets converted using the in-built Babel and web-pack to HTML, CSS and JavaScript code because the browser only understands them and not ReactJS.

```
import React from 'react'


const Greet = (props) => {
      const {lang, children} = props;

      return (
      <>
            <h1>Greet from {lang}</h1>
            <p>{children}</p>
      </>
      )
```

```
}

export default Greet
```

NodeJS

The N in MERN stands for NodeJS. It's a backend scripting language created for writing backend code. It allows you to write backend code using JavaScript.

NodeJS was created in 2009 by Ryan Dahl. It uses the famous V8 engine of Chrome, which is used to run JavaScript on the browser. But NodeJS runs JavaScript outside the browser and runs on all Windows, Linux, Unix, and MacOS machines.

It can handle a lot of concurrent connections, which is around 70,000 requests per second. When a web-app becomes popular, more users connect to it, and hence the load on the server increases.

NodeJS is the second-fastest backend language after Java, which can handle 1 million requests per second. So, NodeJS can be easily used in medium-level apps which get less than or equal to 70,000 requests per second.

NodeJS can be used in all kinds of backend programming; from creating API endpoints to creating real-time apps with socket programming. Further API programming can be done using ExpressJS.

The following is a small piece of code from socket programming. This kind of programming is used to create messaging apps like WhatsApp.

In this kind of app, we need to use a socket library. After that, the server creates the connections between different clients which emits messages from other clients through it.

```
const socketio = require('socket.io')

io.on('connection', socket => {
      socket.on('join', ({ username, room }, callback) => {
      const { error, user } = addUser({ id: socket.id, username, room
})
      if(error) return callback(error)
```

```
        socket.join(user.room)
        socket.emit('message', generateMsg('Admin','Welcome to the Chat
App!'))
        callback()
        })
})

server.listen(port, () => console.log(`Server is up on port ${port}`))
```

Other Popular stacks beyond MERN

There are two other popular stacks beyond MERN. These stacks use the same backend technologies and database. Only the frontend technology gets changed.

These are MEAN (MongoDB, Express, Angular, NodeJS) and MEVN (MongoDB, Express, VueJS, NodeJS). In these stacks, the other two popular JavaScript frontend frameworks of Angular and VueJS are used.

REST APIs

REST APIs, also known as RESTful endpoints, are the way the modern internet works in most cases. In the Internet, there is a client which nowadays is mostly a browser or a mobile app.

All web-apps like Facebook, Instagram, Netflix or mobile apps get the data from a database. But they don't read the data directly from a database. They interact with a middleware through HTTP (HyperText Transfer Protocol) protocol, using these predefined RESTful endpoints.

There are four basic REST APIs - POST, GET, PUT, and DELETE. They are used to perform the CRUD (Create, Read, Update, Delete) operation on a database.

As shown in *Figure* 1.2, the client machine sends REST API requests and then gets back the response from the database. The REST APIs are created using languages like NodeJS, Spring Boot (Java), C# .NET, and many others.

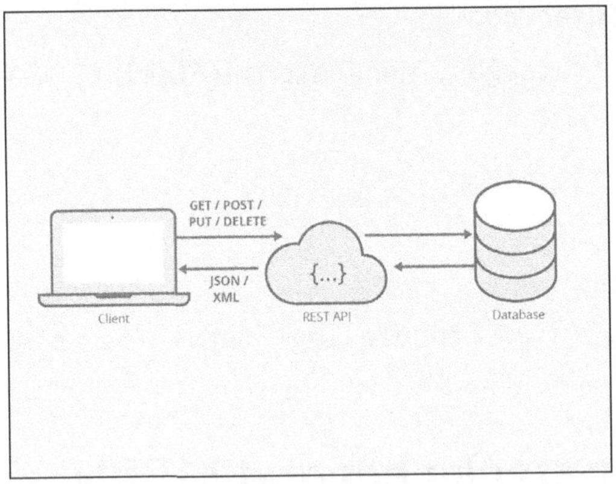

Figure 1.2: REST API

Next, we will look into each REST API endpoint in detail.

POST

The POST API is used to implement the Create operation in CRUD. It is one of the most used REST APIs, which we use from the moment we start using a web-app.

The first time you go to a social media web-app like Facebook, it asks you to register. Now, you enter your name, age, and other details in a form and hit the Register button.

The data will be sent through a POST API to the Facebook database and will be stored there. Next, once we log in, we will create a new post and hit the post button on Facebook.

Again, the POST API will come into picture and send the data to Facebook server. So, whether you purchase some products on Amazon and hit the buy button or upload some photos on Instagram, a POST API comes into picture and sends the data to the respective database.

The data is sent to the backend server in JSON format. The JSON (JavaScript Object Notation) format is similar to JavaScript objects. But here, double strings are mandatory for strings.

A sample POST API, JSON data for an e-commerce purchase is shown here:

```
[ "userID": 23,
  "username": "Keshav",
```

```
  {
      "id": 1,
      "qty": 2,
      "price": 109.95
  },
      {
      "id": 11,
      "qty": 3,
      "price": 119.95
  }
]
```

GET

The GET API is used to implement the Read operation in CRUD. It is the most commonly used API in the world.

Continuing with the Facebook example from POST, when you go to Facebook for the first time, you see a lot of posts. These posts are read from a database through the GET API.

Whether you are scrolling through your Instagram feed, or browsing through Amazon products, or checking articles on Medium, the GET API comes into picture. It reads all the data from the database and shows it in the frontend.

The data is received from the REST APIs in JSON format. Following is a sample JSON data received from an e-commerce site. Notice that most of the time the data is an array of objects. This is the case because arrays are easy to iterate and objects can store data about the items.

After receiving this data, it is the responsibility of the frontend developer to iterate over it and show it on the website. So, this is how you see those beautiful items on the Amazon home page or structured articles on the Medium home page.

Also, when we click a particular item on Amazon or a post on Medium, another GET API is done for that individual item to get all the data.

```
[
```

```
{
      "id": 1,
      "title": "Fjallraven",
      "price": 109.95,
      "description": "Your perfect pack for everyday use and walks in
the forest.",
      "image": "https://fakestoreapi.com/img/81fPKd-2AYL._AC_SL1500_.
jpg",
  },
  {
      "id": 2,
      "title": "Mens Casual T-Shirts ",
      "price": 22.3,
      "description": "Slim-fitting style, contrast raglan long sleeve",
      "image": "https://fakestoreapi.com/img/71-3HjGNDUL._AC_SY879._
SX._UX._SY._UY_.jpg",
  },
  {
      "id": 3,
      "title": "Mens Cotton Jacket",
      "price": 55.99,
      "description": "great outerwear jackets for Spring/Autumn/Winter,
suitable for many occasions.",
      "image": "https://fakestoreapi.com/img/71li-ujtlUL._AC_UX679_.
jpg",
  }
]
```


PUT

The PUT API is used to implement the Update operation in CRUD. It is used when some existing data needs to be updated.

Continuing with the Facebook example, after we create some posts. We might need to edit a post due to some mistakes So, we click the edit and make the changes.

Again we hit the post button and the update is done. But for the update to happen in the database the exact identification of the post is required. Each post contains a unique id, as in the GET example we can see the unique id for each item.

So, the PUT API sends the id along with the data to be updated to the backend server, which in turn updates the exact data in the database.

The following is a sample PUT API json, where we update our small post. Note that the id is mandatory here, since this will be used to update the correct post in the database.

```
{
    "id": 101,
    "title": "ReactJS tutorials",
    "description": "ReactJS is the most popular JavaScript frontend library."
}
```

DELETE

The DELETE API is used to implement the Delete operation in CRUD. This API is used when we want to delete data from the database.

Continuing with the Facebook example, after we create some posts. Suppose, we want to delete one of our Facebook posts, then we hit the delete button on the post.

Now, to delete the post, we just need to send the id of the post to the Facebook server. The Delete API only needs the id to be sent to the backend server, and it gets deleted from the database.

Alternatives to REST API

In the past few years, two alternatives have emerged to the REST API. One is the tool of Firebase, in which the frontend directly interacts with the database without any need for a middleware written in language like NodeJS.

Here, instead of API endpoints we have some boiler plate code which directly does the CRUD operations. But Firebase is not as popular as REST endpoints created using backend languages.

Another technology is GraphQL, which is gaining a lot of momentum for the past two years. It also has an endpoint but we can get selective data from the database. Let's consider in the GET example, where we want only the title and price for all items.

If we are using REST then we either need to write this logic in the frontend after receiving all data or we need to create a new endpoint. But this can be easily achieved through GraphQL query.

Sample GraphQL query to achieve the same. With this query, we will only receive the title and price for each item.

```
{
  items {
       title
       price
  }
}
```

Complete Project Overview

In this book, we are going to create a complete MERN project. This will be a task app in which we will be able to add our daily tasks.

The frontend will be made in ReactJS, and we will also do authentication through JWT (JSON Web Token). Here, we will have the complete register and login functionality also.

For global state management, we will be using the latest Redux toolkit in the project. Coming to the backend, we will use ExpressJS and NodeJS. MongoDB cloud database is used to store our data.

Besides this, we are also going to Unit test our frontend using Jest and React Testing library and the backend using Jest and Supertest.

Lastly, we are going to deploy the frontend using Netlify and backend using the Heroku alternative of back4app.

Setting up a NodeJS Application

We are going to start with the backend first. So, we will create a NodeJS app.

As we are not creating the front end first, so we need Postman to test our API endpoints.

We are going to learn about it later. And we are going to use the MongoDB cloud database to store our data. The MongoDB installation can be done locally as well, but then it's become difficult to deploy it.

Project Folder Structure

While working with the backend, knowledge of the terminal is required. MacOS and Linux come in-built with the terminal, but now Windows also comes with a superior terminal app.

So, open up any terminal in any operating system. In Windows, the old `Command Prompt` will also work, but it's better to use the new terminal. We will be using a Windows terminal in this book.

So, open the Windows terminal app. We have opened it on the desktop. After that, create a new folder with the `mkdir` command. We have named the folder **Task-MERN**.

Next, change to the folder using the `cd` command. Now, we will be inside this folder and create another folder called `backend` with `mkdir` command here.

***Figure 1.3**: Project structure*

Now, we will change to the **backend** folder first with the `cd` command. Now, since the backend in NodeJS and frontend in ReactJS require node and npm to be installed on the system.

We are checking the same with `node -v` and `npm -v` commands.

Figure 1.4: *Node version*

If NodeJS is not installed on the system, then head over to https://nodejs.org to install the same. Just download the LTS version on your system and double click the package, which will be downloaded.

The installation for Mac and Windows is almost the same, just some screens and location for installation will change.

Note that when we install NodeJS on our operating system, then npm (Node Package Manager) also gets installed on the system automatically.

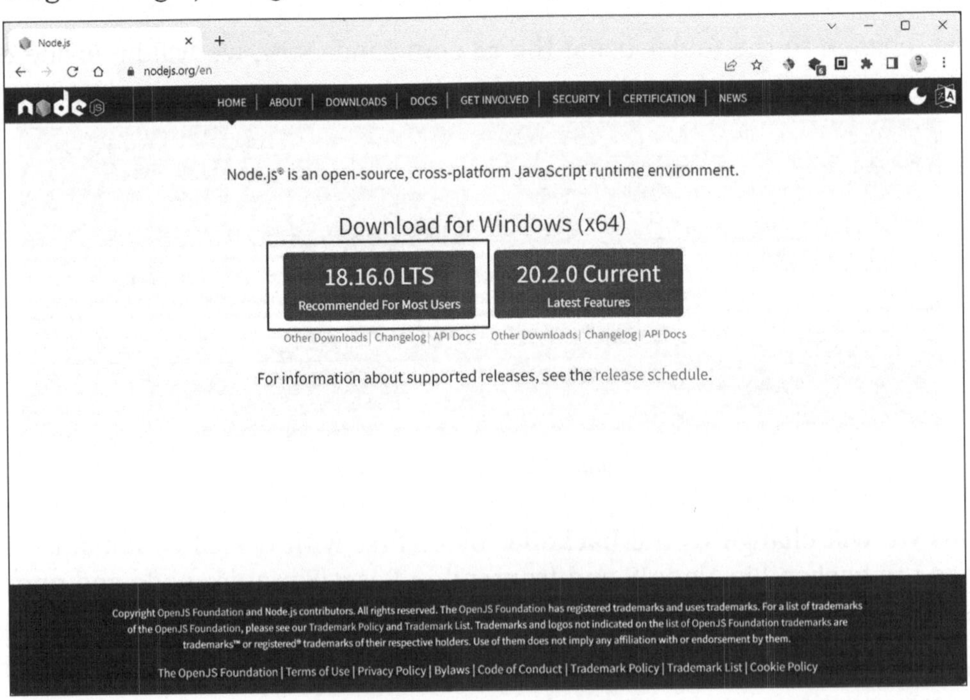

Figure 1.5: *NodeJS installation*

Now in the backend folder give the command **`npm init -y`** to create an empty **package.json** file with default options. The package.json file is a must for any modern frontend or backend project, because it is used to install node packages in the project.

Next, we will give the command **`code`** to open the project in **VS Code**. This is the default code editor recommended for this book. You can download it for free from https://code.visualstudio.com/.

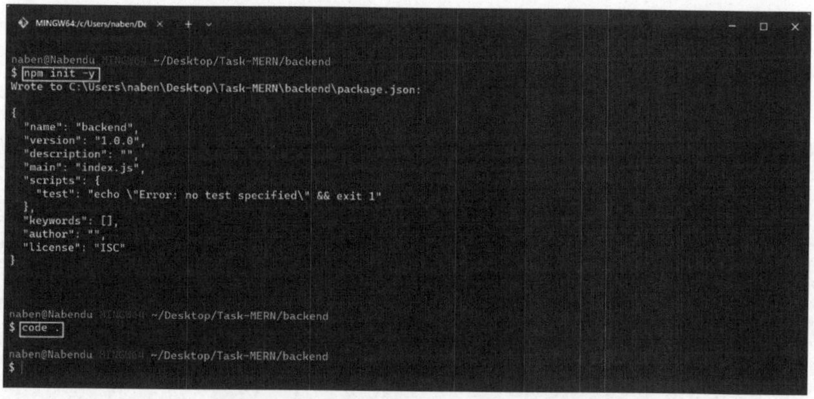

Figure 1.6: *Creating package.json*

Package installation

Once VS Code is opened, first create a **.gitignore** file. Now, whatever we put in this file will not go to the GitHub repository.

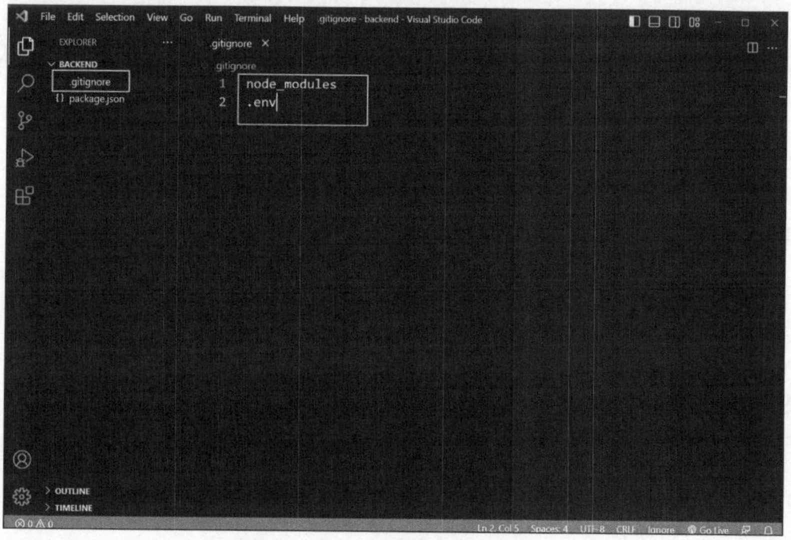

Figure 1.7: *Creating .gitignore*

Now, we will start installing the packages required in our project. Here, we have opened the Integrated terminal in VS Code, by pressing *Ctrl* + J. Next, we have installed the package of express, dotenv and mongoose by giving the following command in the terminal:

```
npm i express dotenv mongoose
```

Here, express is the NodeJS framework which we are going to use to create API endpoints. The package of mongoose will be used to connect to the MongoDB database. And the dotenv package uses an .env file to save secrets in a project.

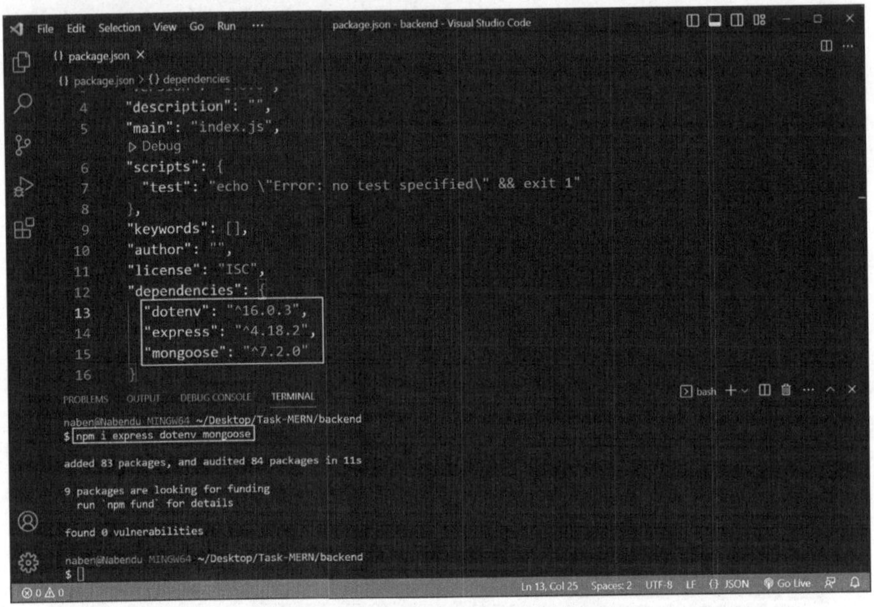

Figure 1.8: *Installing dependencies*

Now, we will also install dev dependencies. These types of packages are not used in production, so they are installed through dev dependencies.

Here, we are going to install the package of **`nodemon`**. This package will restart our backend server the moment we make any change in the code. If we run the server code using node command, it needs to be restarted every time manually for changes to appear.

So, give the following command in the terminal. Note that we need to use the **`- -save-dev`** flag to install a package as dev dependency:

```
npm i --save-dev nodemon
```

Notice that in package.json the **nodemon** package is installed as dev dependency.

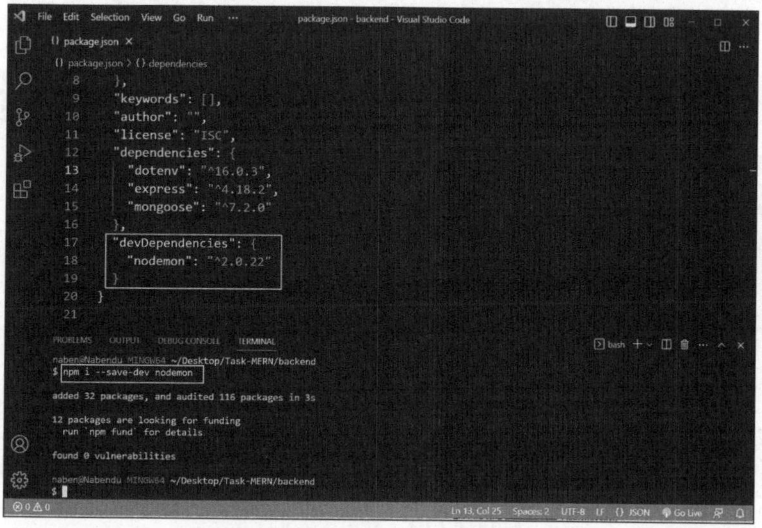

***Figure 1.9**: Installing dev dependencies*

Running the project

To run the project, we need to make some modifications in the **package.json** file. First, create a **server.js** file. And then in the package.json file change the main to **server.js**.

Next, create two scripts for production and development. Give the following lines inside scripts, as shown in *Figure 1.10*:

```
"start": "node server.js",
"dev": "nodemon server.js"
```

Now, the production code will run on deployment server back4app(heroku alternative) and it will run the node command.

But while doing development, we will run the **nodemon** command.

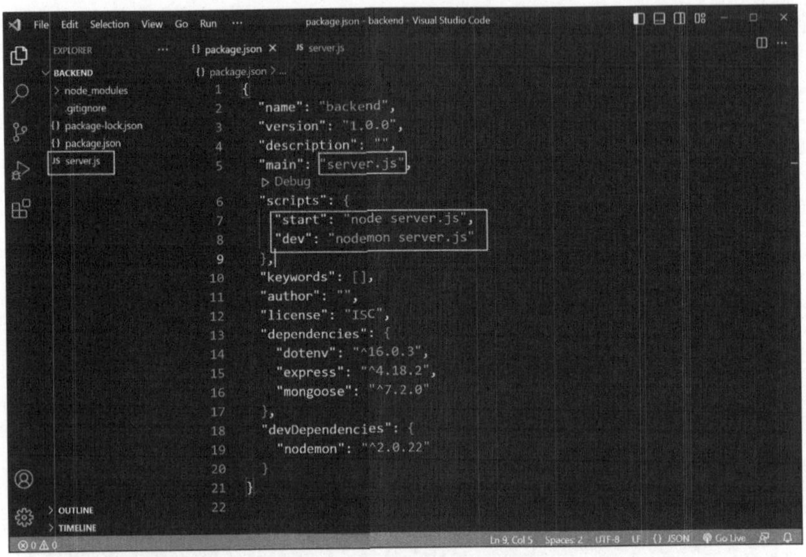

Figure 1.10: *Creating Scripts*

Now, open the server.js file and put a simple console log in this file.

```
console.log("Welcome to server");
```

After that, open the Integrated Terminal and run the command **`npm run dev`**, to run the **`nodemon`** command from **package.json** file.

Here, if everything is ok, we will see the console log of **Welcome to server**.

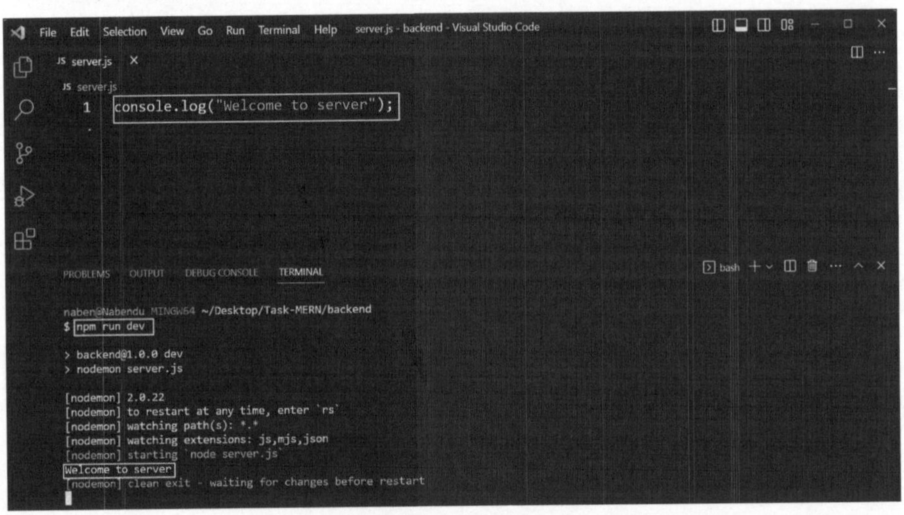

Figure 1.11: *Starting Backend*

Conclusion

In this chapter, we learned about MERN in detail. First, we learned about all four technologies: MongoDB, Express, ReactJS, and NodeJS. Beside this, we also learned about other popular stacks beyond MERN.

Next, we covered the REST API in detail. We learned about POST, GET, PUT, and DELETE in detail which are used to implement the CRUD operations. We also learned about two alternatives to REST API, namely, Firebase and GraphQL.

Next, we learned about the project we are going to create in this book. We ended this chapter with setting up the basic NodeJS app.

In the next chapter, we will learn about creating the Express server, then creating routes, controllers, and also error handling.

CHAPTER 2
Starting a NodeJS App

Introduction

This chapter talks about the Express server. Here, we will learn to use Express in our backend app. Next, we will be creating routes with Express. We are also going to add controllers to those routes. Lastly, we will learn to do error handling in our Express app.

Structure

In this chapter, we are going to discuss the following topics:

- Using Express
- Creating routes
- Creating Controllers
- Error Handling

Using Express

Back in the **server.js** file, we will first import **`Express`** which we installed in the previous chapter. After that, we will import the **`dotenv`** package. Then we created a variable port and gave it a value 8000.

Now, we will create an app variable and use Express in it. Next, we will use the listen function of NodeJS, which will be used next on the passed port.

Lastly, we have opened the integrated terminal and given the command npm run dev to run the **server.js** file. If everything is okay, we will get the message **`Server listening on 8000`**.

```
const express = require(‘express’);
const dotenv = require(‘dotenv’).config();
const port = 8000;

const app = express();

app.listen(port, () => console.log(`Server listening on ${port}`));
```

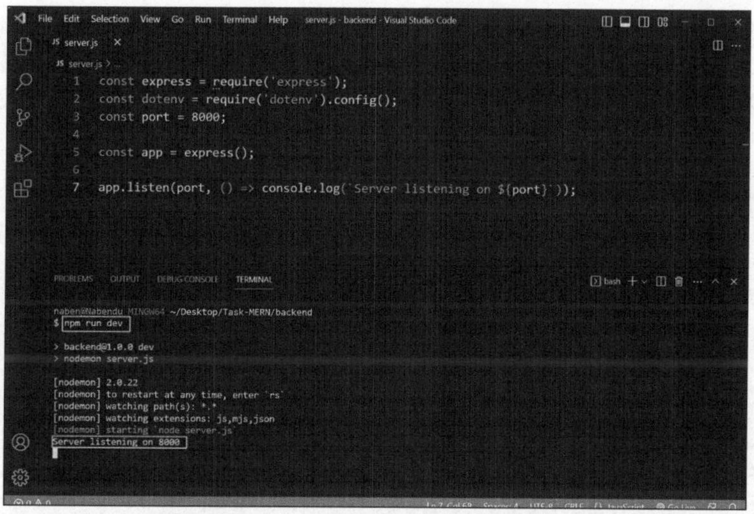

Figure 2.1: *Starting with express*

Next, we will create a **.env** file. Now, this file is used to keep all the secrets that we don't want to put in GitHub or any public view.

Here, we have created two variables **`NODE_ENV`** and **`PORT`** and given them **`development`** and **`8000`** values, respectively.

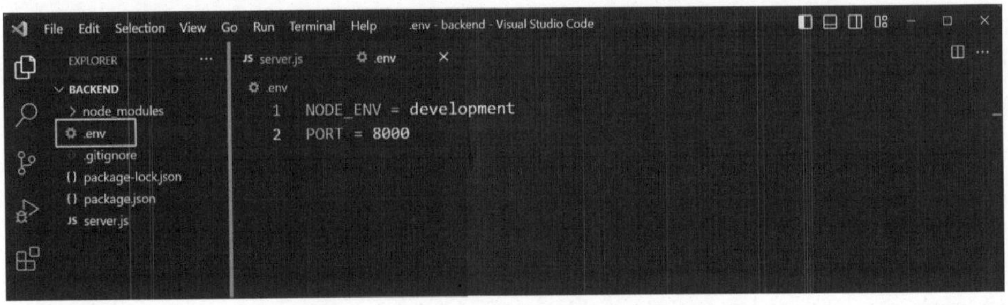

Figure 2.2: *Adding environment file*

Back in the **server.js** file, we have updated the port variable to use the value from the **.env** file first. Here, we have given **process.env.PORT** and also given 5000 with OR(||) operator.

And restarted the server by giving the **npm run dev** command. Notice that the port 8000 is taken from the **.env** file.

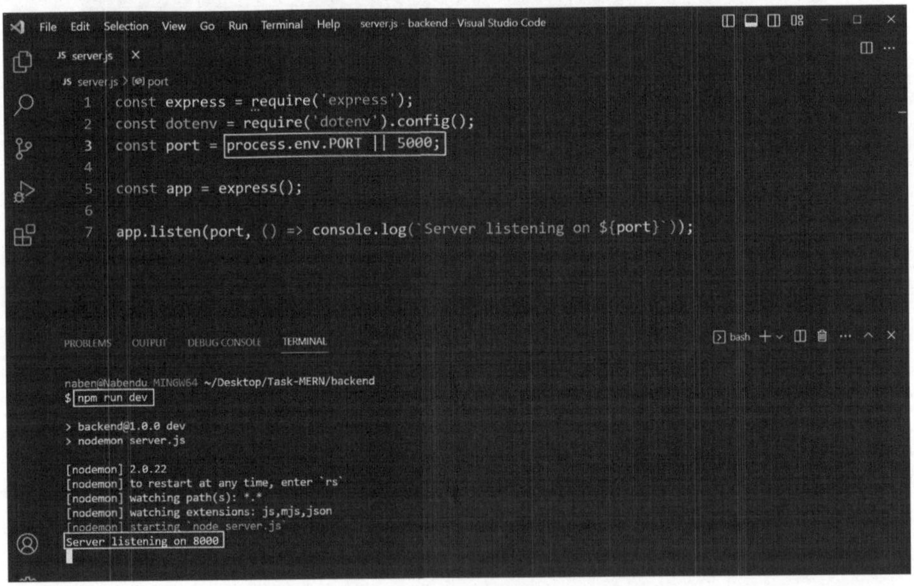

Figure 2.3: *Using environment variable*

Creating Routes

Now, we will create our routes. Routes are endpoints that are used by the frontend to perform the CRUD operations. This is achieved through the REST APIs of GET, POST, PUT, and DELETE.

Initial Routes

Back in our **server.js** file we will first add the following code to create a simple GET route:

```
app.get('/api/tasks', (req, res) => {
        res.send('Get All Tasks');
})
```

Here, we are using the get method from Express. The first parameter is the route path and it can be anything. We have given it /api/tasks.

The second parameter is a function call with req and res. In this arrow function, we are using **`res.send()`** to send back **`Get All Tasks`** text. Later on, we are going to modify this route to get all tasks.

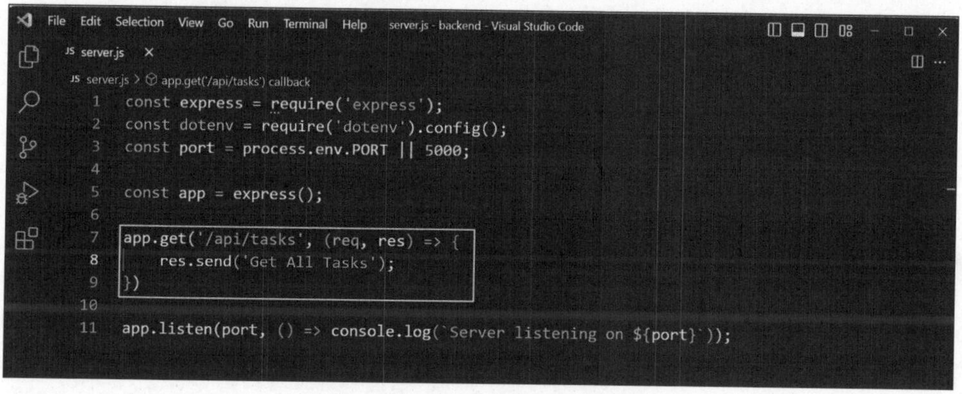

Figure 2.4: *Creating GET route*

Now, head over to a browser and go to http://localhost:8000/api/tasks and the **`Get All Tasks`** will be displayed.

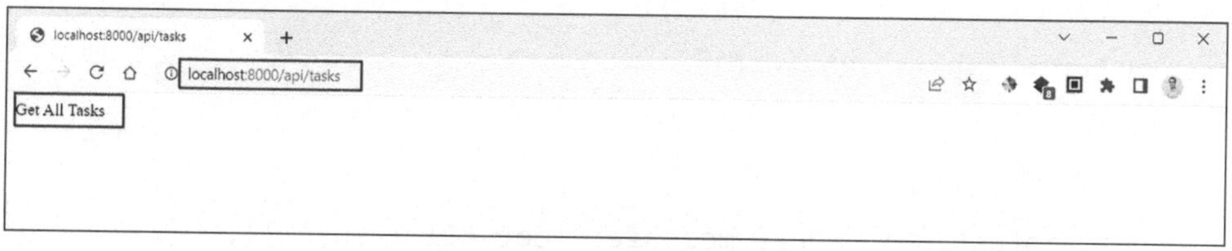

Figure 2.5: *Getting back data*

Now, in all cases we receive data from the server in JSON format. So, we will update the code in server.js file to send back a json.

Also, note that we are sending back a status code of 200.

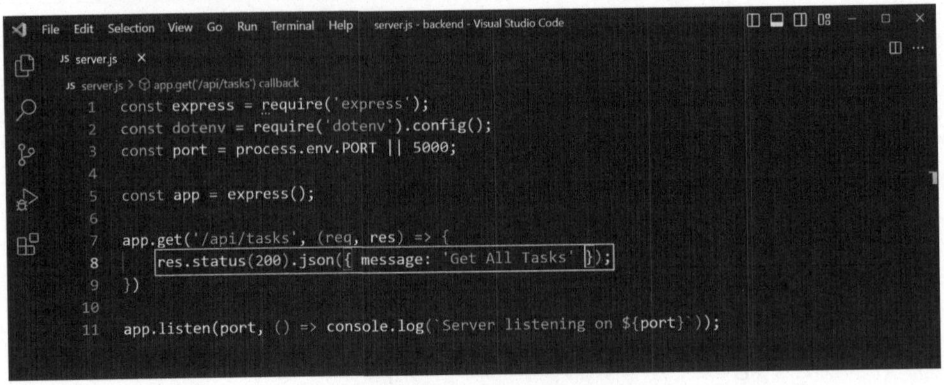

Figure 2.6: *Returning JSON data*

Now, again in the browser go to http://localhost:8000/api/tasks and we will get the JSON back.

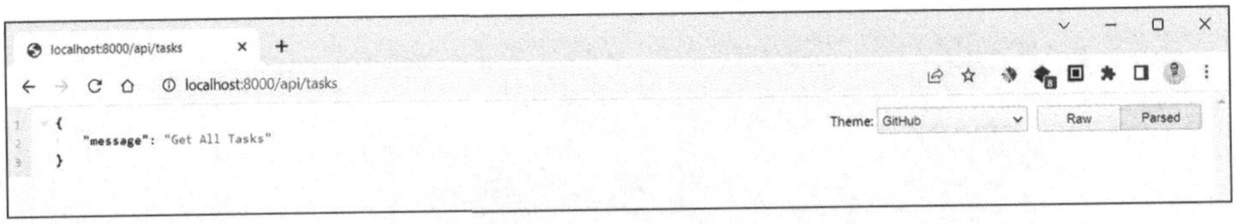

Figure 2.7: *Getting JSON data*

All Routes

Now, we will add more routes in our project. But first, we will separate the route logic to a different file.

So, create a **routes** folder and inside it, create a **taskRoutes.js** file. Put the following content in it:

```
const express = require('express');
const router = express.Router();

router.get('/', (req, res) => {
       res.status(200).json({ message: 'Get All Tasks' });
})

module.exports = router;
```

Here, we have first imported the express package. And we have also imported the router from Express. Next, we have moved the get route created in the server.js file here.

But notice that we are using a router instead of an app. And we are exporting the router at the end.

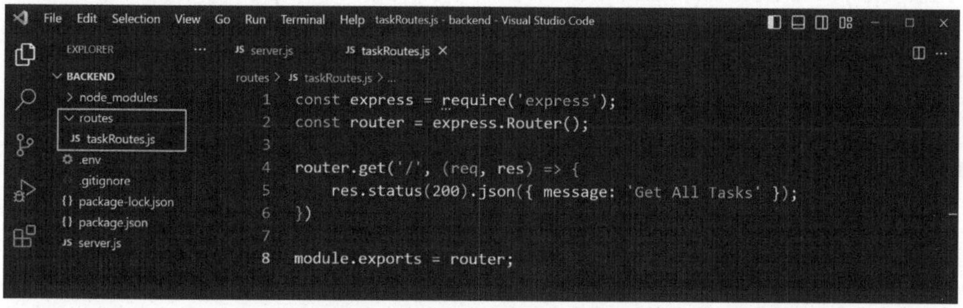

Figure 2.8: *Separating Routes*

Back in the server.js file, we have removed the get method. Also, we are using the app.use() to hit the /api/tasks route. Here, the second parameter is the taskRoutes file.

```
app.use('/api/tasks', require('./routes/taskRoutes'));
```

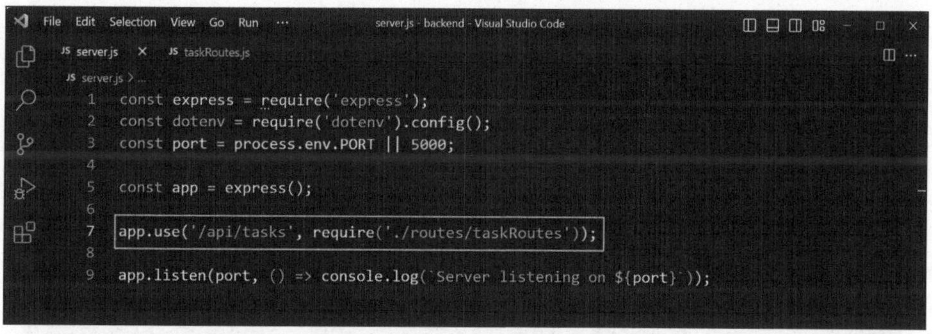

Figure 2.9: *Adding route path*

Now again, in the browser, go to http://localhost:8000/api/tasks, and we will get the JSON back. This means our new changes are working fine.

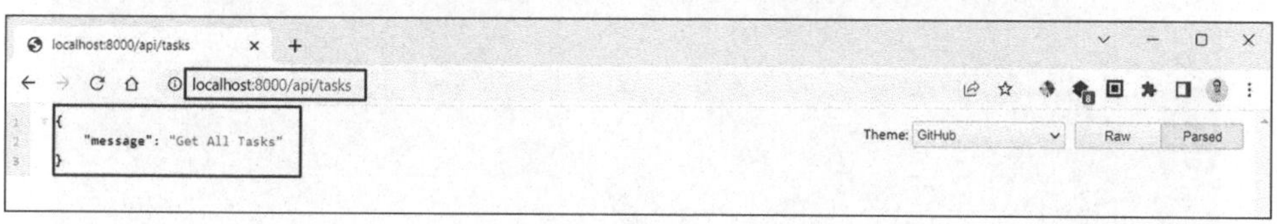

Figure 2.10: *Getting all routes*

Back in the **taskRoutes.js** file, we will add a POST, PUT, and DELETE route. Here, we are just using the respective methods.

All these methods, for now, will return simple json. The real logic will be added later on. The **`post()`** is similar to **`get()`** as of now.

But the put() and delete() take a will route of /:id. This special route can take any provided item. This id will be sent through the browser address bar. We can get access to it with the req.params.id variable.

```
router.post(‘/’, (req, res) => {
	res.status(200).json({ message: ‘Create Task’ });
})

router.put(‘/:id’, (req, res) => {
	res.status(200).json({ message: `Task ${req.params.id} updated.`
});
})

router.delete(‘/:id’, (req, res) => {
	res.status(200).json({ message: `Task ${req.params.id} deleted.`
});
})
```

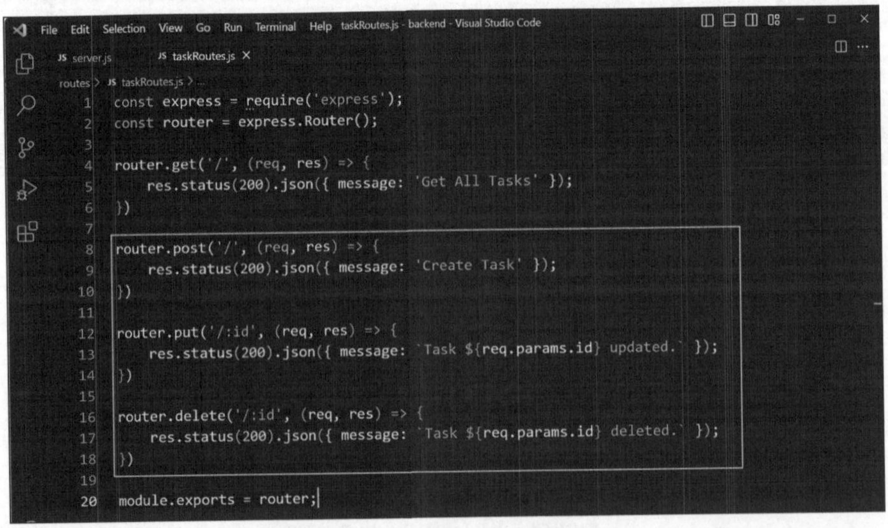

Figure 2.11: *Adding more routes*

Testing through Postman

The GET route can be seen in the browser, but to check the other routes, we need the frontend. Now, since the front end has not even started, we will use the POSTMAN tool.

This tool is always used by backend engineers because they don't wait for the frontend to be completed. This tool mimics the way the request will be sent from a frontend app through the browser.

The free tool Postman can be installed from https://www.postman.com/ . After this, once it is opened, we will make the method as **POST** and in the address bar, give http://localhost:8000/api/tasks .

After that, hit the **Send** button. We will receive back the correct json and also the Status of 200.

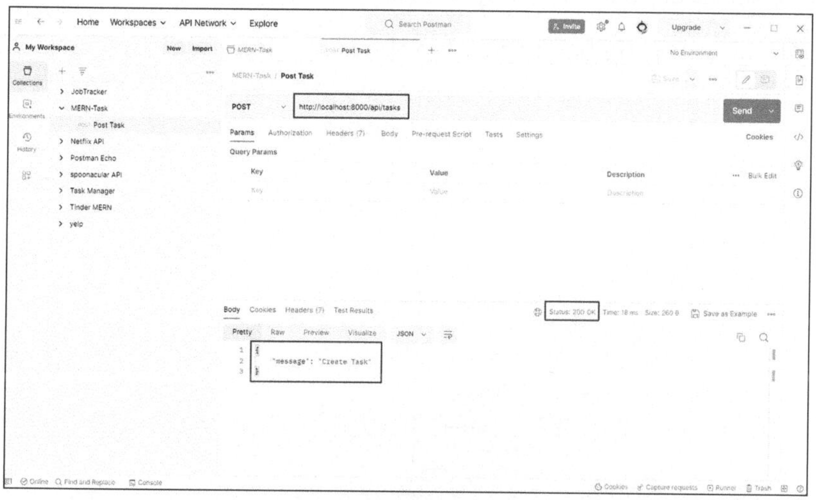

***Figure 2.12**: POST request*

Now, for the PUT method, we also have to provide any id. So, we are visiting the endpoint http://localhost:8000/api/tasks/23 .

Here, we are also getting back this id in the json, along with the status of 200.

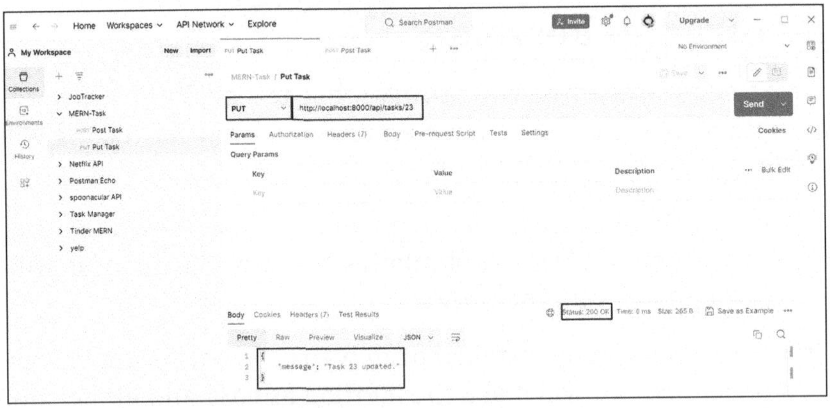

***Figure 2.13**: PUT request*

For the **DELETE** method also, we have to provide any id. Again, we are visiting the endpoint http://localhost:8000/api/tasks/23 .

Here, we are also getting back this id in the json, along with status of 200.

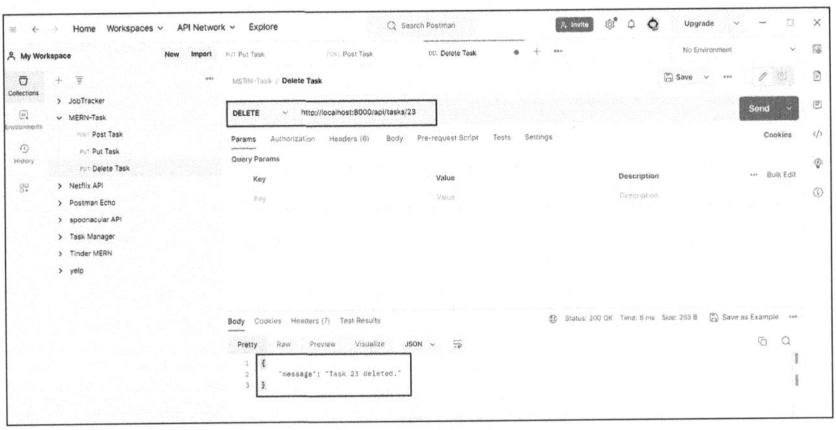

***Figure 2.14**: DELETE request*

Creating Controllers

Now, we will separate the controller part. For this create a **controllers** folder. Inside it create a **taskController.js** file and add the following content:

```
const getTasks = (req, res) => {
        res.status(200).json({ message: 'Get All Tasks' });
}
```

```
module.exports = { getTasks }
```

Here, the **getTasks** function will contain the main functionality. Right now, it is sending the response json back.

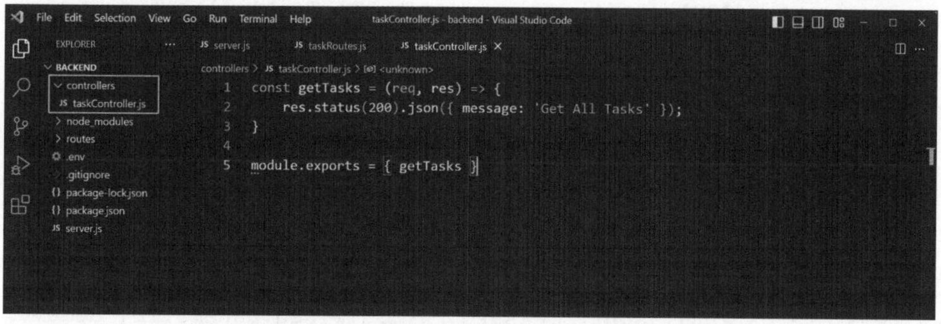

Figure 2.15: *Creating controllers*

Back, in **taskRoutes.js** file we will remove the code for the controller. And add the function of **getTasks** in it. We have also imported the **getTasks** file.

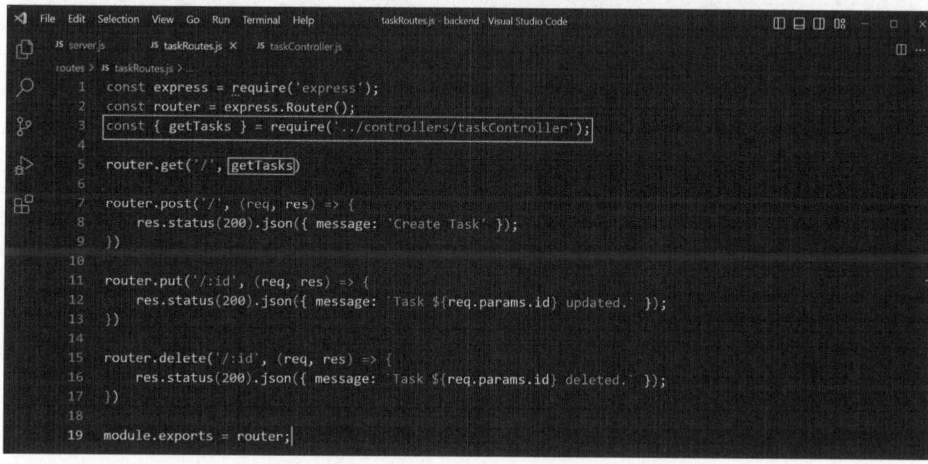

Figure 2.16: *Adding Controller in Routes*

Now, again in the browser, go to http://localhost:8000/api/tasks and we will get the JSON back. This means our new changes are working fine.

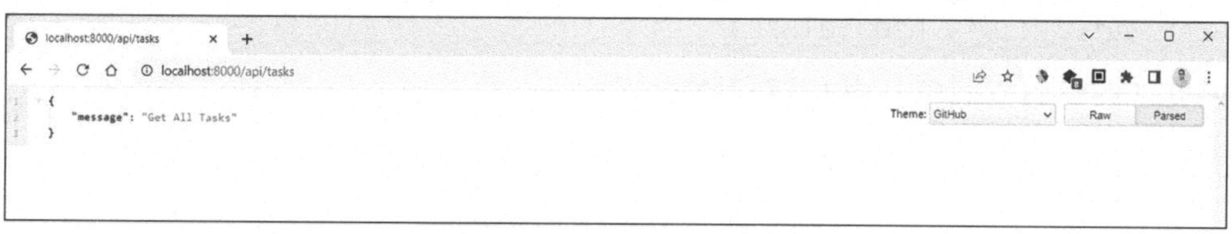

Figure 2.17: *Getting JSON back*

Now, in the `taskController.js` file, we will add the rest of the controllers for `setTask`, `updateTask` and `deleteTask`. We have also added the exports for the same.

```
const setTask = (req, res) => {
        res.status(200).json({ message: ‘Create Task’ });
}
const updateTask = (req, res) => {
        res.status(200).json({ message: `Task ${req.params.id} updated.`
});
}
const deleteTask = (req, res) => {
        res.status(200).json({ message: `Task ${req.params.id} deleted.`
});
}
```

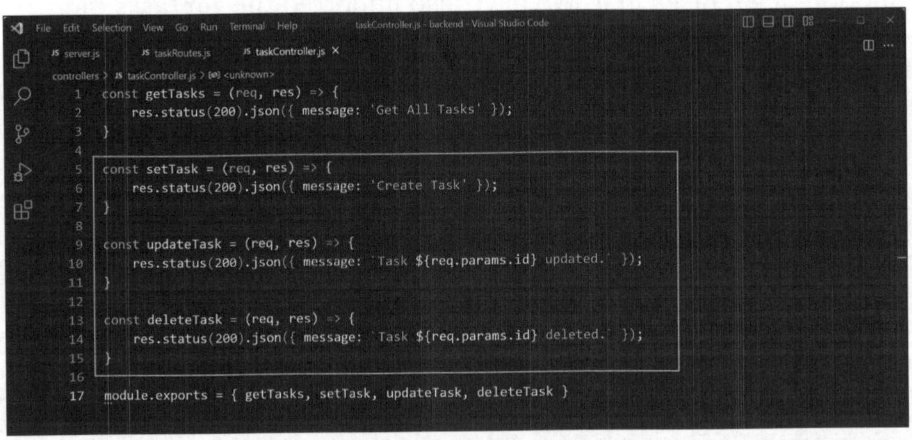

Figure 2.18: *Adding more controllers*

Back in the **taskRoutes.js** file, we will add these function calls. Now, our taskRoutes file has become small and manageable.

```
router.post(‘/’, setTask)
router.put(‘/:id’, updateTask)
router.delete(‘/:id’, deleteTask)
```

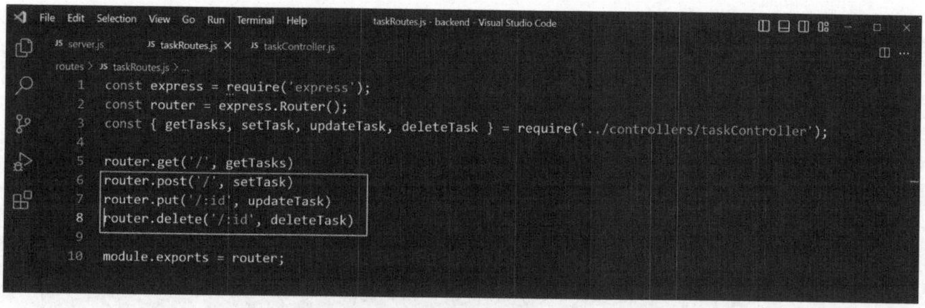

Figure 2.19: *Updating task routes*

We are also checking the **`PUT`** route through Postman, to check if everything is working fine.

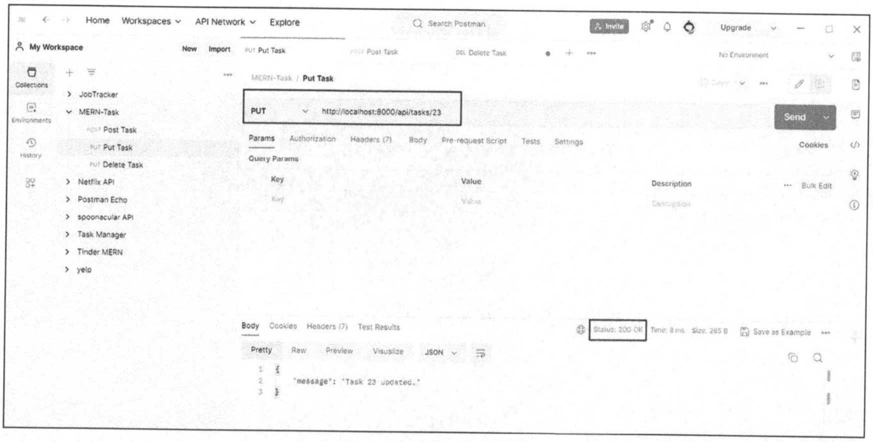

Figure 2.20: *PUT route*

Using JSON

We will add the logic to use JSON in our project. Here in the **server.js** file, we will add the following code:

```
app.use(express.json());
app.use(express.urlencoded({ extended: false }));
```

Here, through **`app.use()`** we have added the functions to use json and urlencoded bodies.

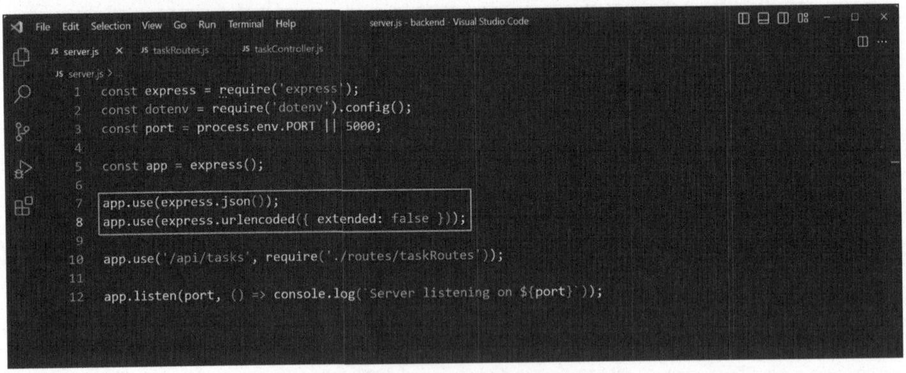

Figure 2.21: *Using JSON*

Back in the **taskController.js** file, in the **`setTask`** function, we are console logging the req.body.

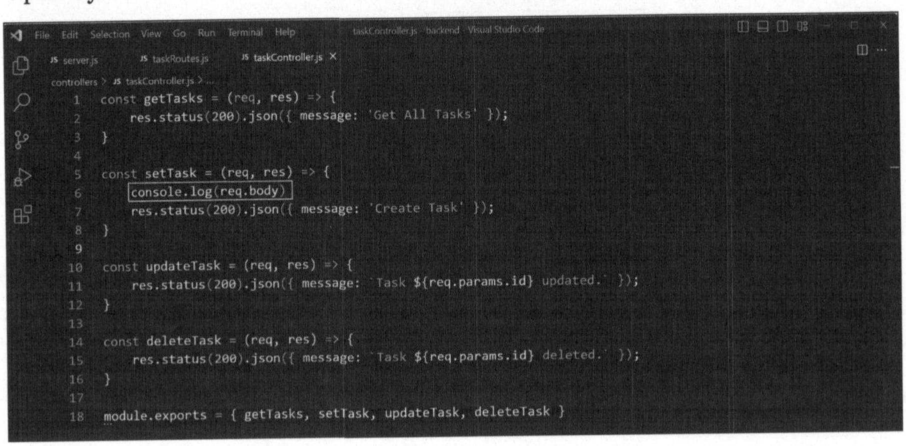

Figure 2.22: *Console log in controller*

Now, in Postman we will update our POST request. Here, first go to Body and then select **x-www-form-urlencoded**. After that, make a key as **text**. Also, give any value and we are giving Learn Flutter.

Also, make sure the checkbox is selected and then click the **`Send`** button.

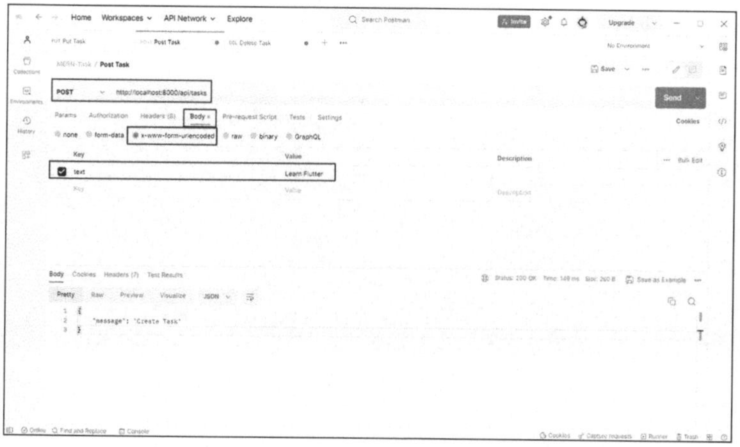

Figure 2.23: *JSON message in POST*

Now, in the terminal where the server is running, we will get **`{ text: 'Learn Flutter' }`** as shown in *Figure 2.24*:

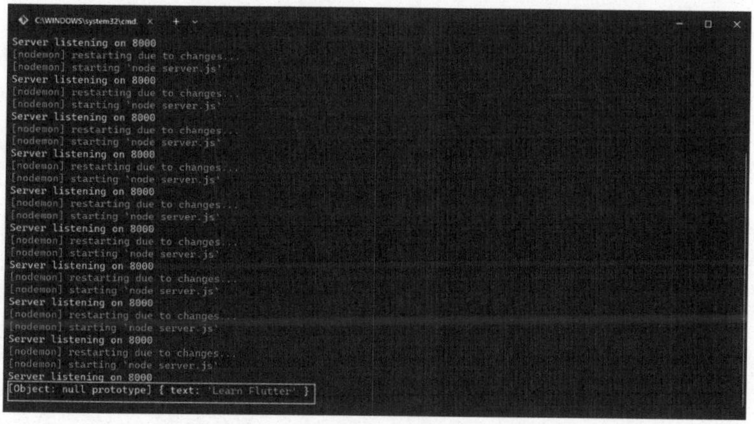

Figure 2.24: *JSON message console log*

Error Handler

Lastly, in this chapter we will add error handling in our project. So, in the setTask.js in **taskController.js** file we will add the following code:

```
if(!req.body.text){
  res.status(400).json({ message: 'Please enter a task' })
}
```

Here we are checking if **req.body.text** doesn't exist, then we are sending back the error message:

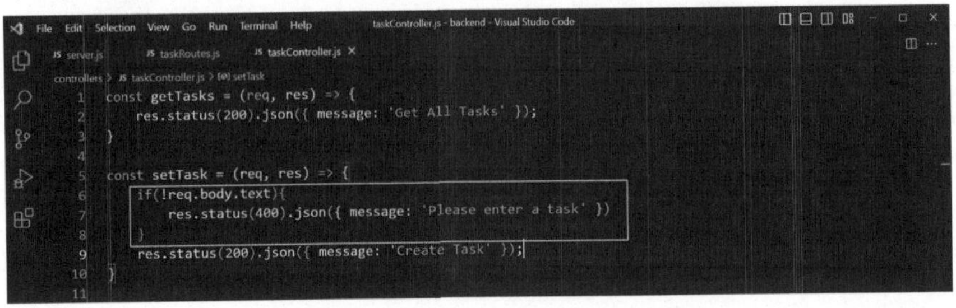

Figure 2.25: *Error handling in controller*

Now, back in Postman, remove the checkbox beside the text. Then click the `Send` button. We will get the **400 Bad Request** and the following JSON.

```
{ "message": "Please enter a task" }
```

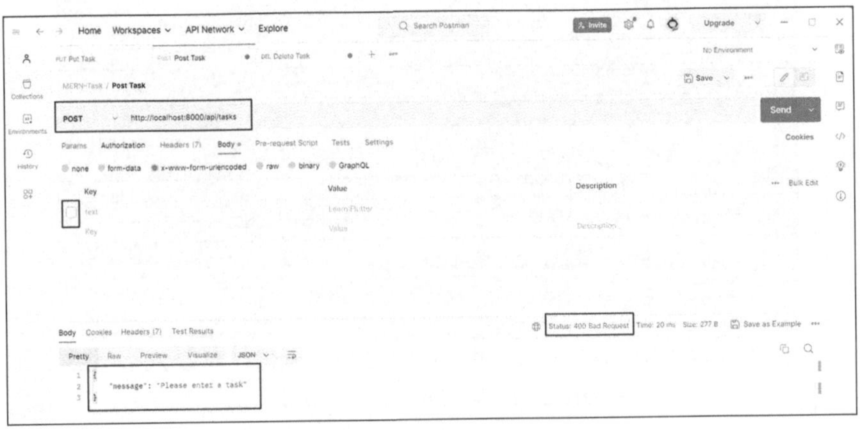

Figure 2.26: *Error in Postman*

Now, we have updated the code in **taskController.js** file. Here, we will be using the in-built error handler in NodeJS. In the following code, we are throwing the error from the if statement:

```
res.status(400)
throw new Error('Please enter a task')
```

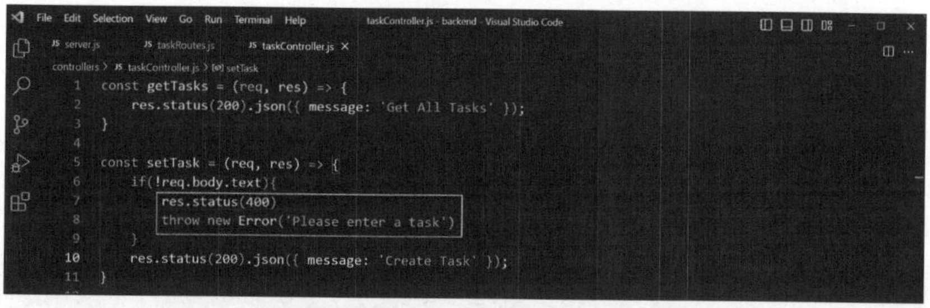

Figure 2.27: *Throwing error from controller*

But in Postman, we are not getting the correct error result after hitting the **Send** button.

We are getting a big HTML back. Next, we will update the code to fix this issue.

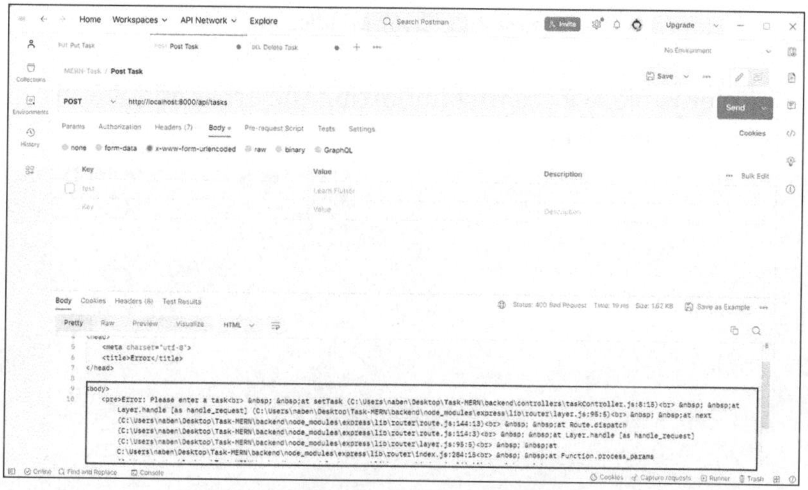

Figure 2.28: *Wrong data in Postman*

To fix the same we need to have middleware in our NodeJS code. So, create a **middleware** folder and inside it a file **errorMiddleware.js** file, add the following code:

```
const errorHandler = (err, req, res, next) => {
      const statusCode = res.statusCode ? res.statusCode : 500
      res.status(statusCode)
      res.json({ message: err.message })
  }
```

```
module.exports = { errorHandler }
```

Here, we have an errorHandler function, which we are exporting also. Inside the function, we will take the passed status code or by default 500. We are also setting the error to the json object.

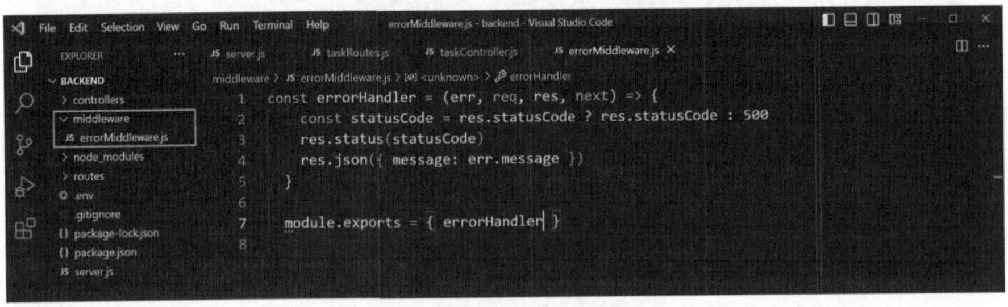

***Figure 2.29**: Error Middleware*

Back in the **server.js** file, we are first importing the error middleware. After that, we are using it with **`app.use()`**:

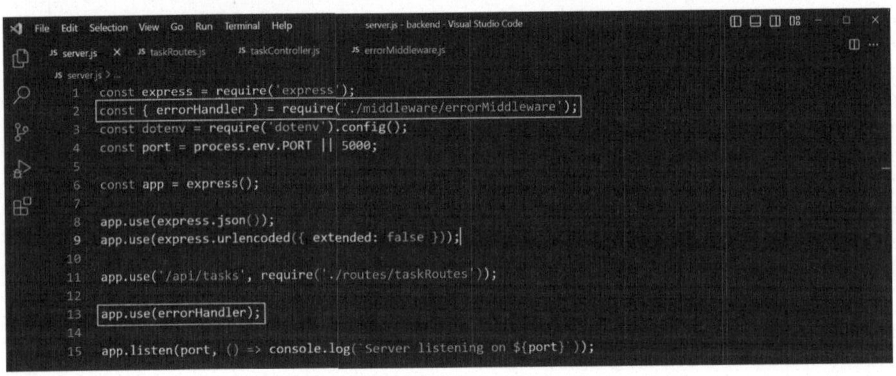

***Figure 2.30**: Using error handler*

Back to Postman, we will again send the **`Post`** request. This time we will get the correct error response back.

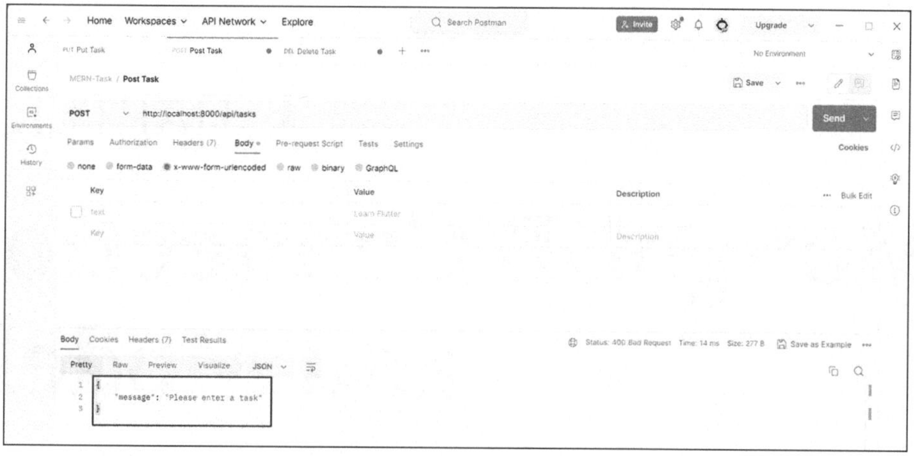

Figure 2.31: *Perfect Error message*

Conclusion

In this chapter, we have learned about using Express in our app. After that, we created routes in our project, which included the GET, POST, PUT, and DELETE routes. Next, we learned to test routes through Postman.

Next, we separated the controller part and created a controller for getting the tasks, creating the tasks, updating the tasks, and deleting the tasks. Then, we learned to use JSON in our project. Finally, we learned to use the in-built NodeJS error handler in our project.

In the next chapter, we will learn about the MongoDB database, and how to connect our server to MongoDB using Mongoose. We will also learn about Model creation and more routes.

CHAPTER 3

MongoDB Connection and Models

Introduction

This chapter talks about the MongoDB database. Here, we will first learn to use the MongoDB database in our backend app. Next, we will be connecting MongoDB to the backend NodeJS code through the package of mongoose. Lastly, we will learn to create routes in our Express app.

Structure

In this chapter, we are going to discuss the following topics:

- MongoDB database
- Connecting through Mongoose
- Model creation
- Creating routes

MongoDB Database

Before creating the MongoDB database, we have a small task remaining. We will add the package of express-async-handler. Now this package helps us to get rid of `try..catch` block, which is common express code.

```
npm i express-async-handler
```

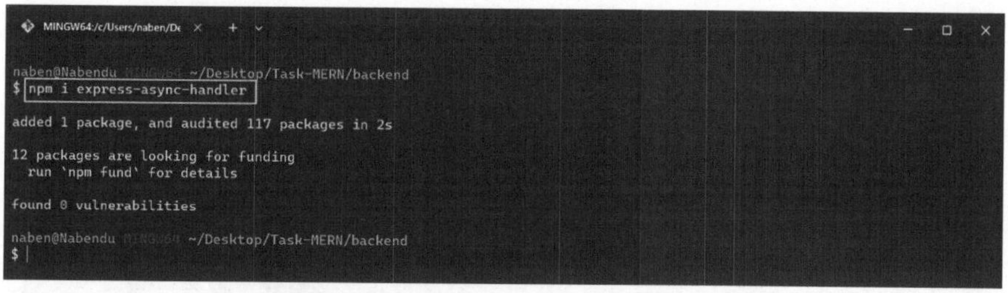

Figure 3.1: *Installing express async handler*

Now, we will first import the express-async-handler in our project. After that, we will wrap all functions in **taskController.js** file with asyncHandler.

```
const asyncHandler = require('express-async-handler')
```

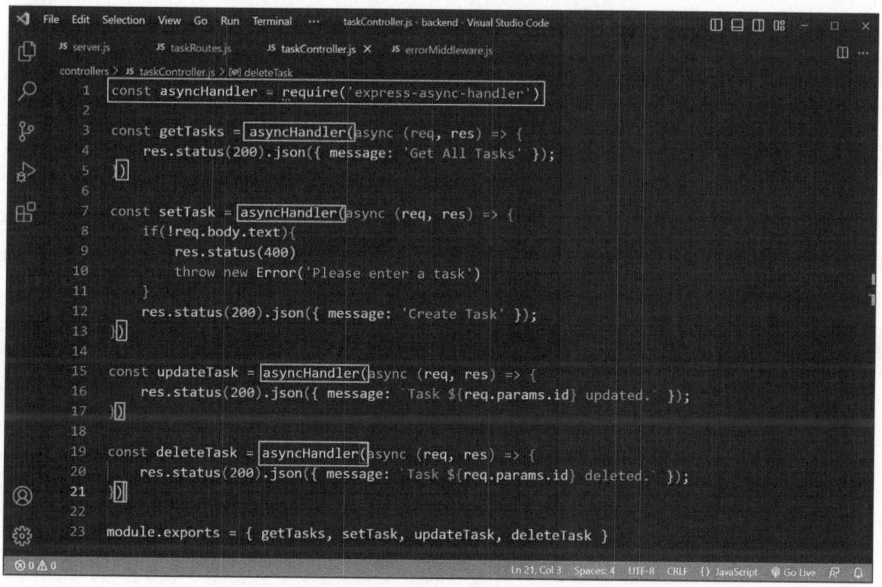

Figure 3.2: *Adding express async handler*

Now, we will use MongoDB on the cloud. So, go to https://cloud.mongodb.com/, and click Google and sign in or sign up with your Gmail account.

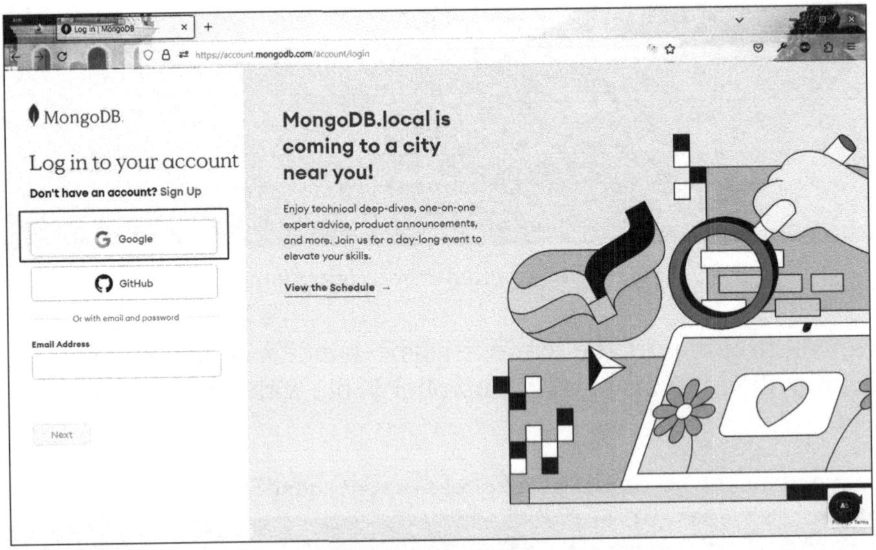

Figure 3.3: *MongoDB Cloud*

Basic Setup

If you have a lot of projects, then it will open a screen as follows. Here, click the **`New Project`** button. Even if you are logging into the MongoDB cloud for the first time, then also find the **`New Project`** button and click it.

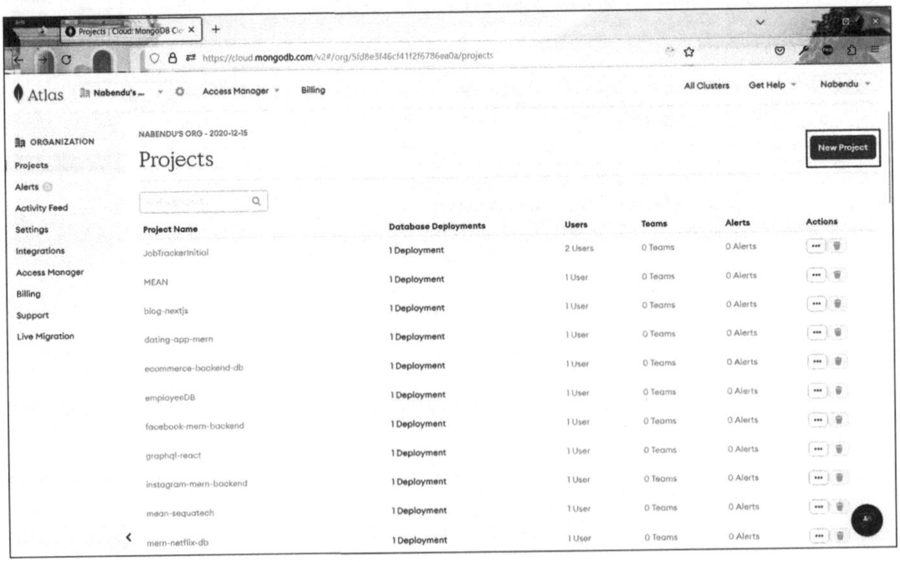

Figure 3.4: *New Project*

On the next screen, we need to give the project a name, which is **`MERN-Task-App`** in our case. After that, click the **`Next`** button.

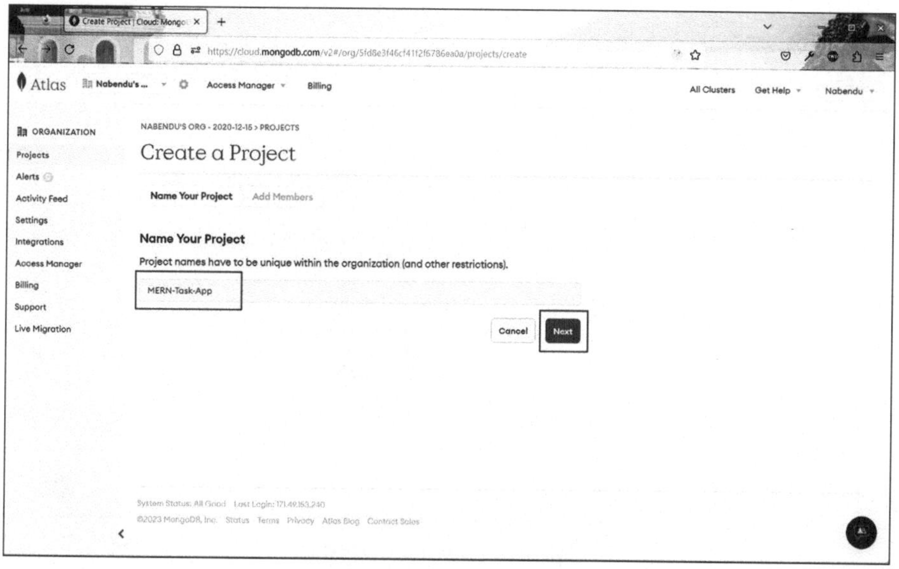

***Figure 3.5**: Project Name*

On the next screen, it will confirm your email id. Here, just click the **`Create Project`** button.

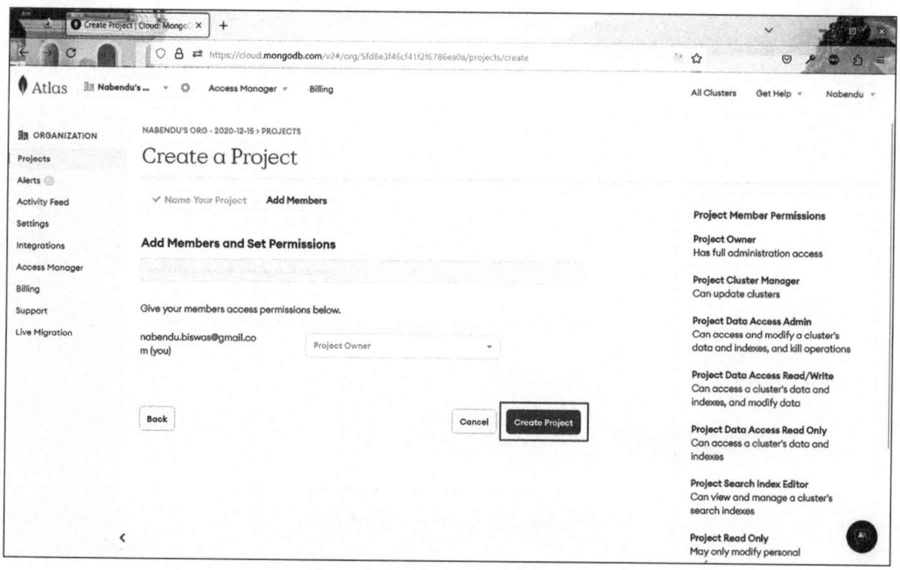

***Figure 3.6**: Project Permissions*

The next screen will allow us to create a database. Here, click the **`Build a Database`** button.

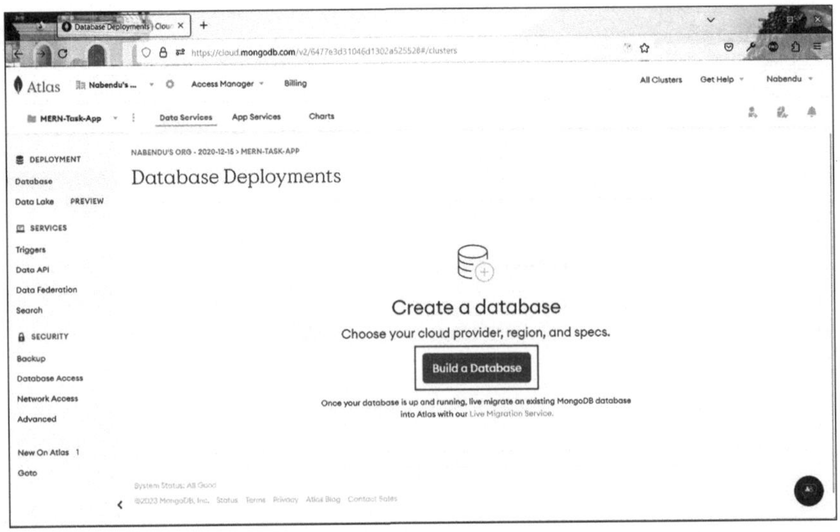

Figure 3.7: *Build a Database*

On the next screen, click the **`M0`** tier which is free. Also, keep the provider as **`AWS`**.

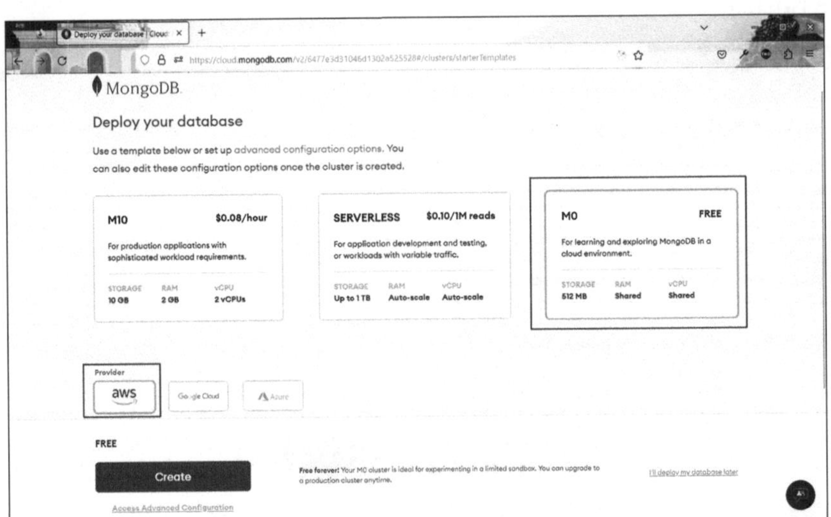

Figure 3.8: *Deploy a Database*

Scroll a bit down and choose the Region in your country. We have chosen Mumbai as we are located in India. We have also changed the Name to **`NabenduCluster`**. After that, click the **`Create`** button.

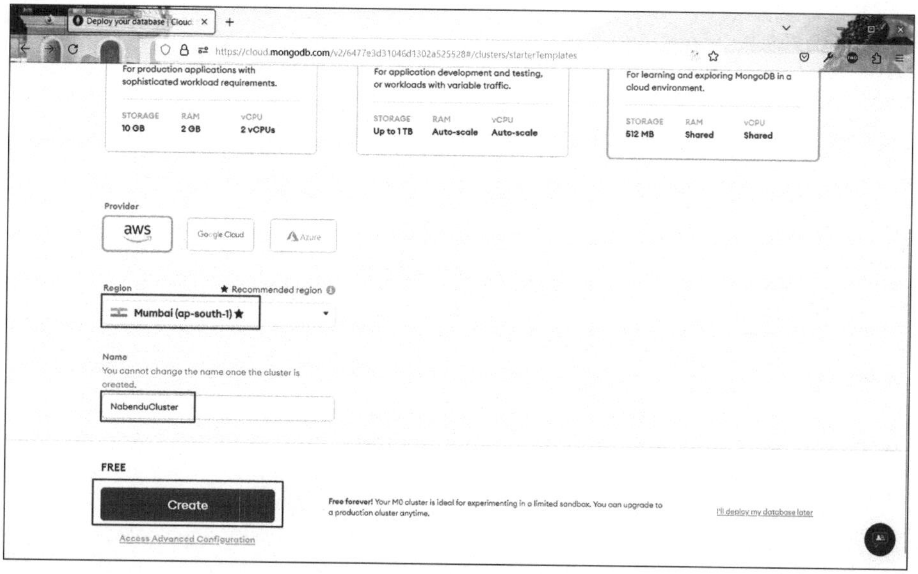

Figure 3.9: *Region of Database*

On the next screen, it will ask for username and password. To keep it simple for the tutorial we have given it as admin. After that, click the **`Create User`** button.

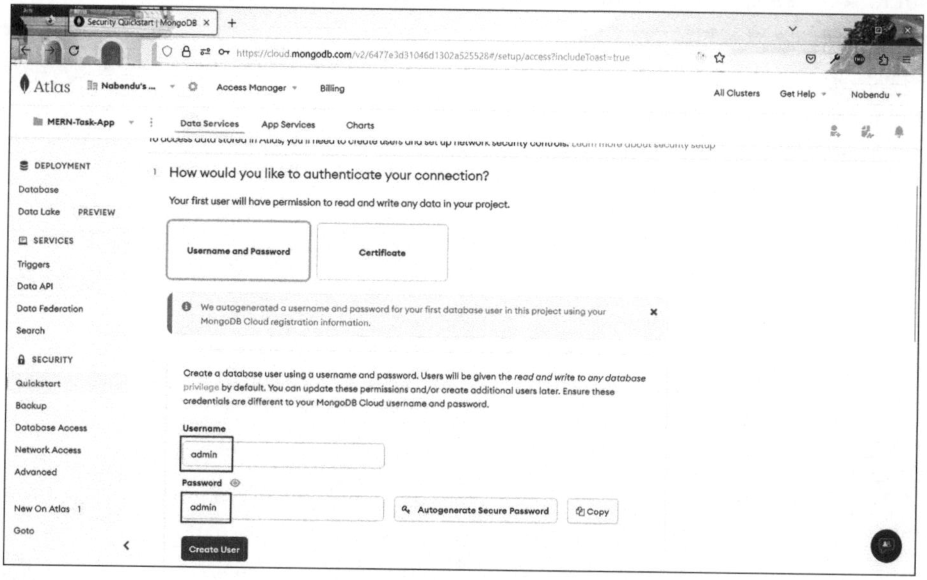

Figure 3.10: *Create User*

Creating the user, will automatically add your current IP address. If you try to click Add Entry, it will give an error that **`This IP address has already been added`**. Lastly, click the **`Finish and Close`** button.

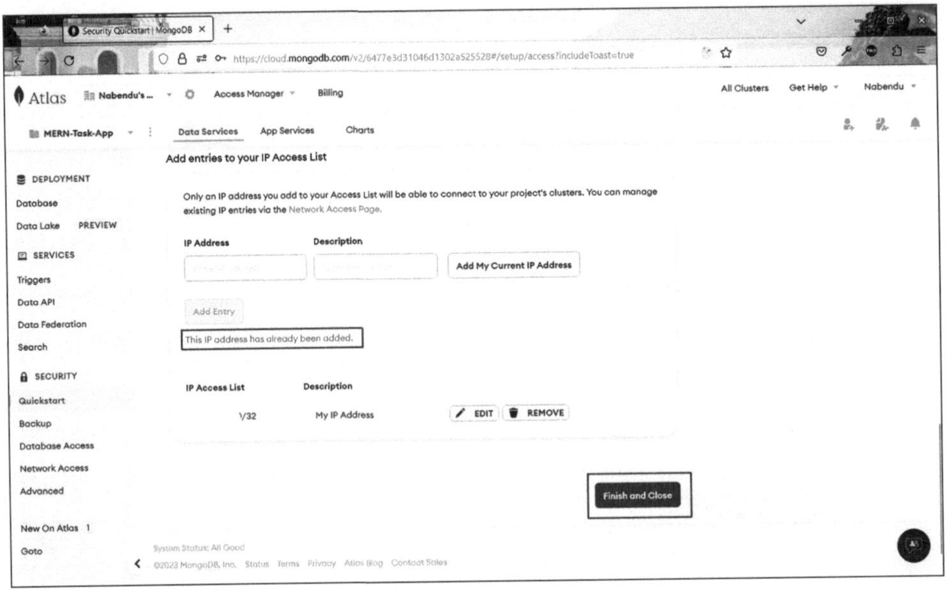

Figure 3.11: IP Address

Now, we need to do one more setup for our application to run properly. Click the **`Network Access`** tab. After that click the **`+ADD IP ADDRESS`** button.

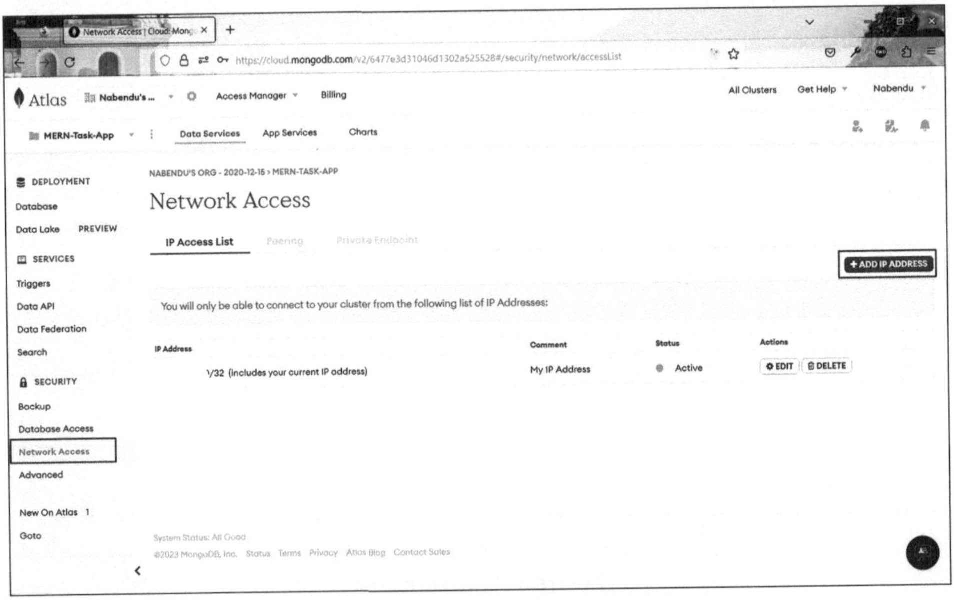

Figure 3.12: Network Address Configuration

In the pop-up, click on **`ALLOW ACCESS FROM ANYWHERE`** button and then the **`Confirm`** button.

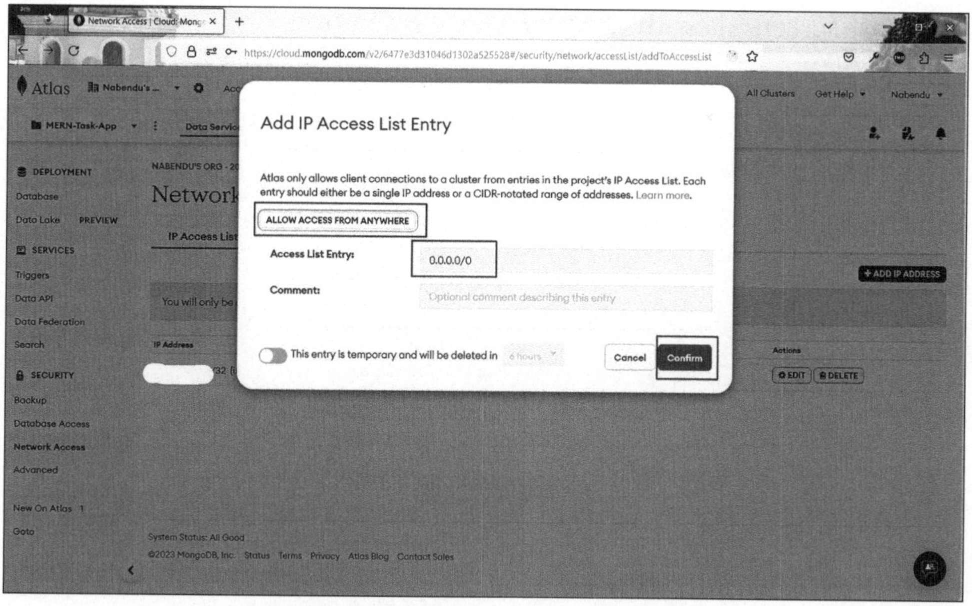

Figure 3.13: Allow access from Anywhere

Adding Collection and Connection URL

Now, we will add a Collection in our project. For this, click the `Database` tab and after that click `Browse Collections` button.

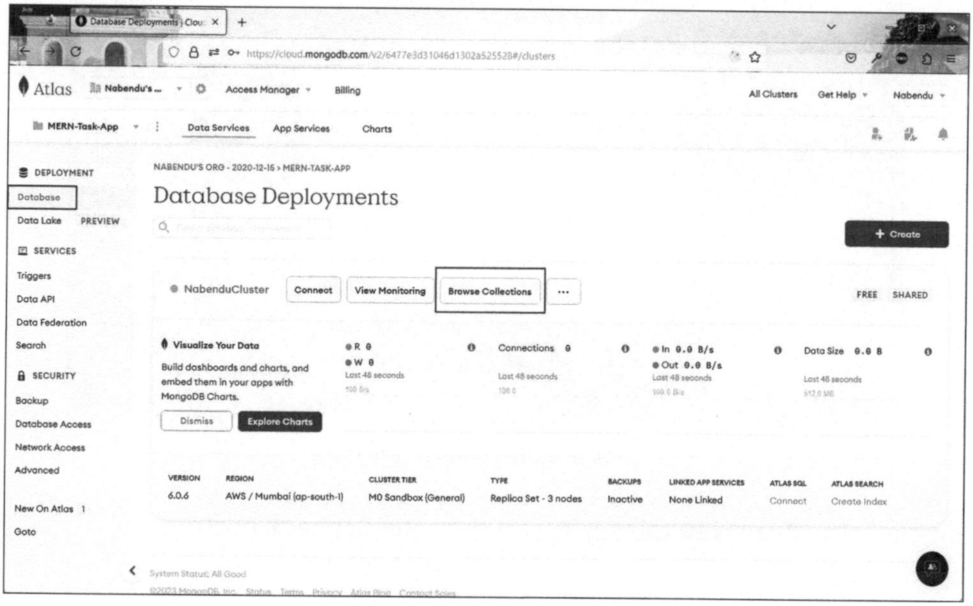

Figure 3.14: Browse Collections

On the next screen, click the **`Add My Own Data`** button.

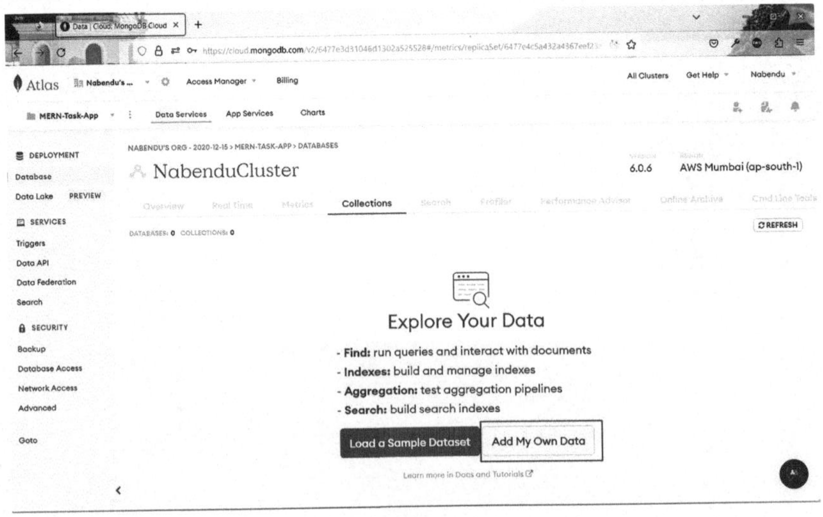

***Figure 3.15**: Add My Own Data*

In the pop-up, give the database name and collection name. We have given it **`taskApp`** and **`tasks`**, respectively.

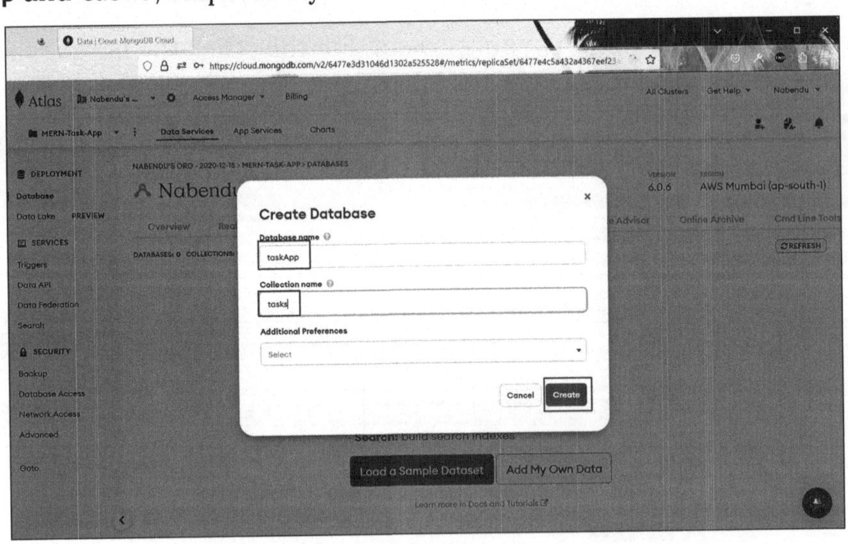

***Figure 3.16**: Create Database*

Now, click the **`Overview`** tab again and then the **`Connect`** button.

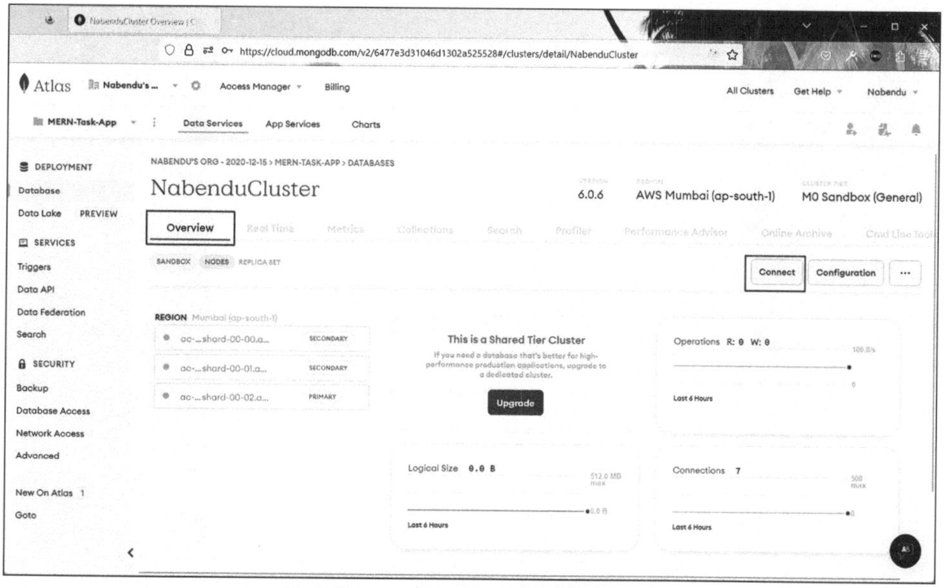

***Figure 3.17**: Connect to cluster*

Now, in the pop-up click the **`MongoDB for VS Code`** button.

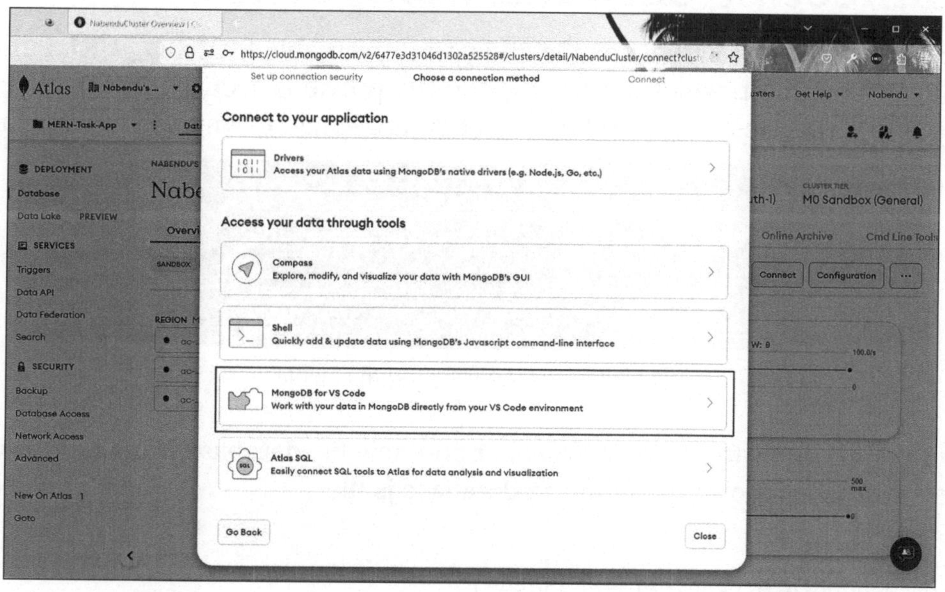

***Figure 3.18**: MongoDB for VS Code*

In the next screen, we will get the Connection String. This connection string will be used to connect to MongoDB from the backend in the next section.

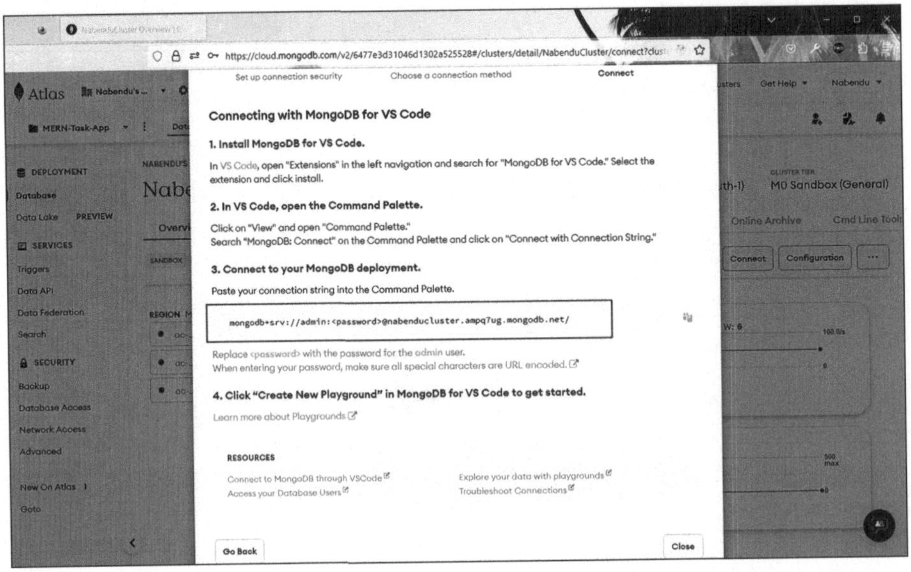

***Figure 3.19**: MongoDB Connection url*

Connecting through Mongoose

Back to VS Code, open the **.env** file and create a variable **MONGO_URI**. Put the connection url in it, which we have got in the previous section. Notice that we have added the password and the correct database name, which is **taskApp** in it.

***Figure 3.20**: MONGO_URI in env file*

Now, create a new folder called **connect** and new file **database.js** inside **connect**. Then place the following content in **database.js** file:

```
const mongoose = require('mongoose')

const connectDB = async () => {
  try {
      const connect = await mongoose.connect(process.env.MONGO_URI)
```

```
        console.log(`MongoDB Connected: ${connect.connection.host}`)
    } catch (err) {
        console.log(err)
        process.exit(1)
    }
}

module.exports = connectDB
```

Here, we are first importing mongoose. After that, we have a **connectDB** function, inside which we have a **try...catch** block. Here, in the try block we are first connecting through mongoose to our **MONGO_URI** stored in the **.env** file. We are also console logging the connected message.

In the catch block, we are just showing the error and exit the process.

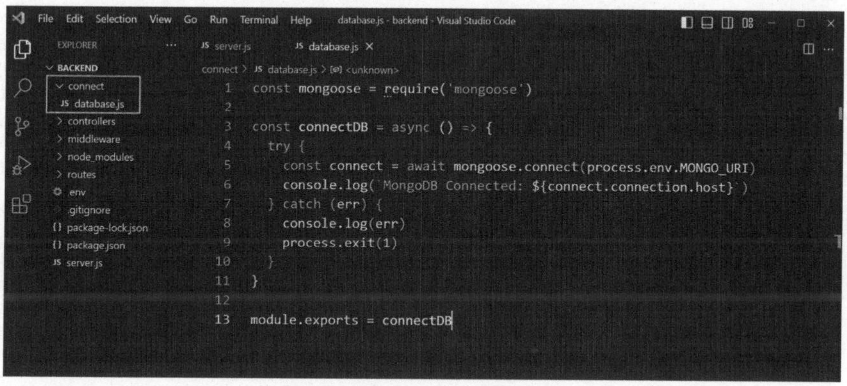

Figure 3.21: *database.js file*

Next, go to **server.js** file and first import the connectDB function. Next, we are just calling it.

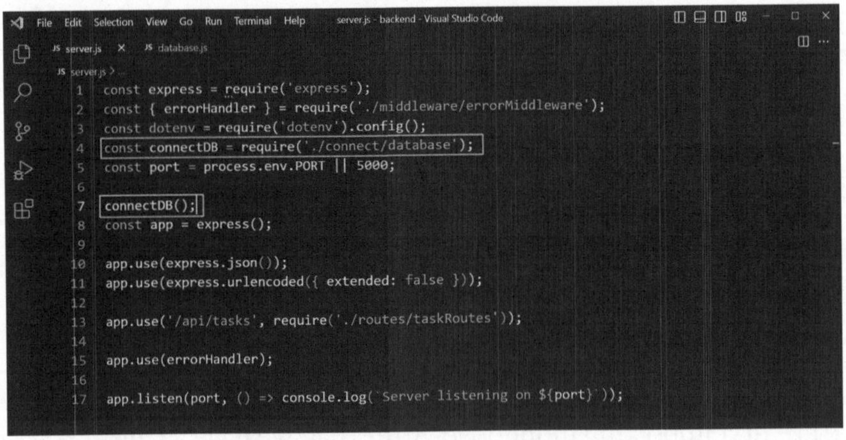

Figure 3.22: *Using database in server.js*

Back in the terminal, restart the server with the `npm run dev` command. If everything is right we will also get the MongoDB Connected with the server name log.

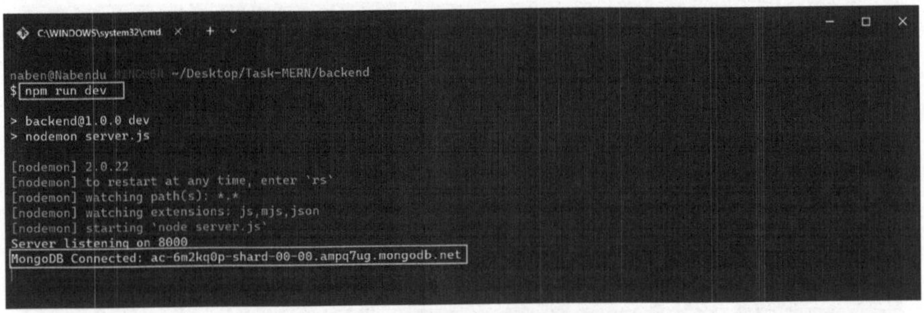

Figure 3.23: *Command line*

Model Creation

Models are required for the backend to interact with the database. They are used to do the CRUD operation in the database. The Models are the way to represent the data in the database. So, create a new folder **models** in the project and a file **taskModel.js** in **models** folder. Then, place the following content in **taskModel.js** file to create Task model:

```
const mongoose = require('mongoose')
const taskSchema = mongoose.Schema(
  {
```

```
        text: { type: String, required: [true, 'Please add a text value']
}
    },
    {
        timestamps: true
    }
)

module.exports = mongoose.model('Task', taskSchema)
```

Here, we have a **taskSchema**, where we have a field of text. This field is of type String and also required. It will give the error **Please add a text value** if we don't send it on request.

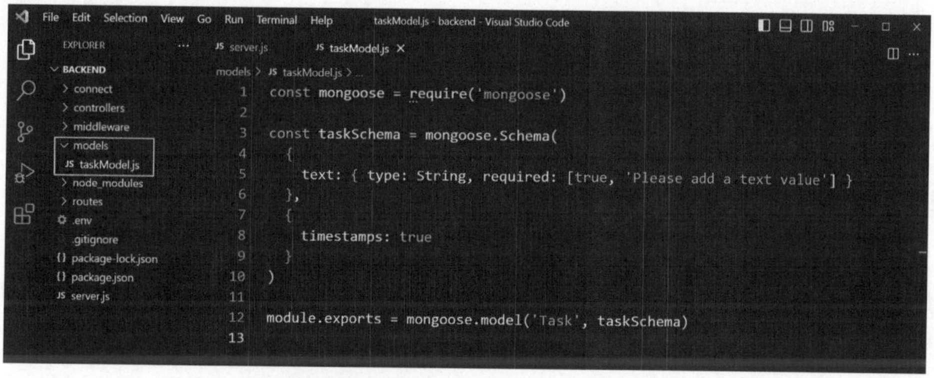

Figure 3.24: *Creating models*

Now, in the **taskController.js** file we will first import the taskModel. And after that in the **getTasks()** method, we will use the **find()** function of mongoose to get all tasks from the database. Lastly, we are sending the status 200 and the tasks back.

```
const Task = require('../models/taskModel')

const tasks = await Task.find()
res.status(200).json(tasks);
```

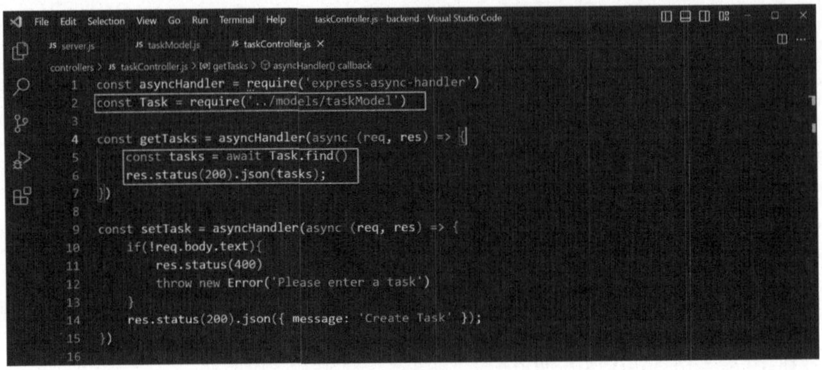

***Figure 3.25**: Updating getTasks*

Now, in any browser go to http://localhost:8000/api/tasks, and we will get an empty array, since we don't have any tasks.

***Figure 3.26**: Checking all Tasks*

Creating Routes

We have already updated the **`getTasks`** route and now we will create more routes. Now, we will update the rest of the routes, so that we get basic working routes.

POST Route

First, we will update the PUT route. So, in the **`setTask()`** function we will use the **`create()`** method from mongoose and pass the text. Notice, that we have to use the Task model to run the **`create()`** method. Lastly, we are sending the status 200 and the task back.

```
const task = await Task.create({ text: req.body.text })
res.status(200).json(task);
```

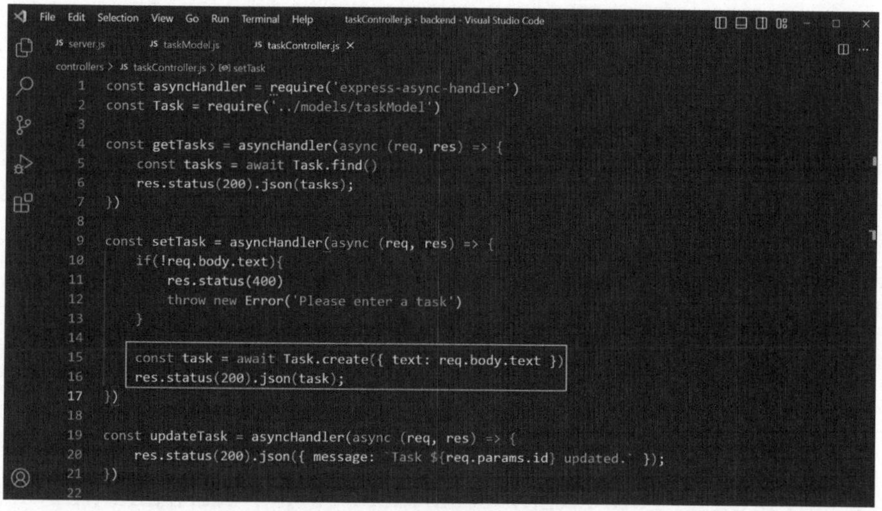

Figure 3.27: *Updating setTasks*

Back in Postman, we will send a text with value and we will get back a Status of 200. Also, the json will be returned back to us.

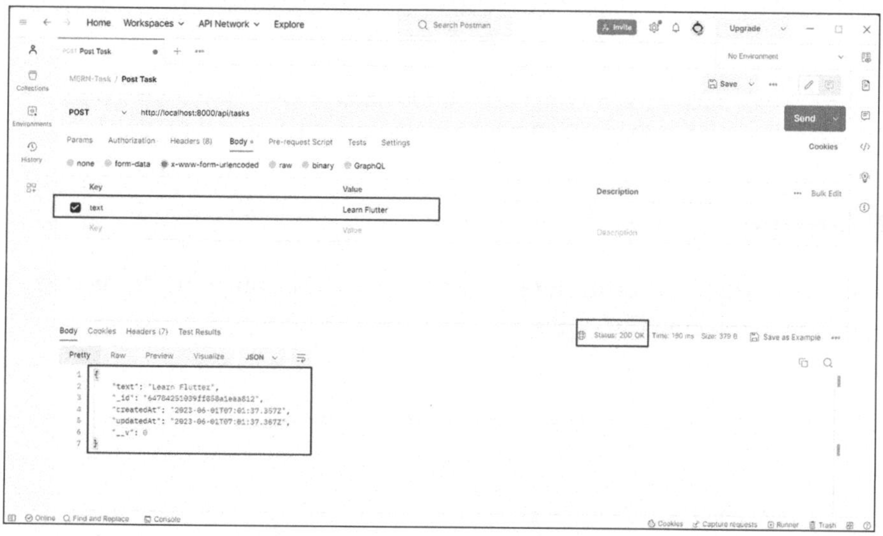

Figure 3.28: *Sending Post Request*

We have also added one more task through Postman. And after that, we checked in the MongoDB Cloud database. Here, we can find both tasks being saved in the database.

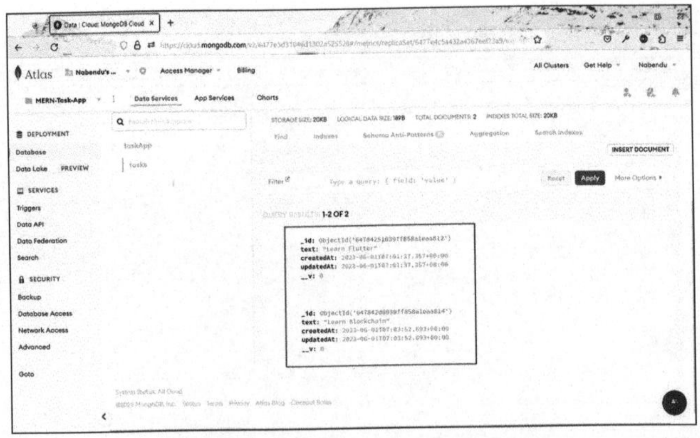

***Figure 3.29**: Checking Tasks in MongoDB*

Again, in any browser goto http://localhost:8000/api/tasks and we will get an array of objects. It contains the two tasks saved previously.

***Figure 3.30**: Checking Tasks in Browser*

PUT Route

Now, we will update the complete code for the PUT route. In the **`updateTask()`** function, add the following code:

```
const task = await Task.findById(req.params.id)

if (!task) {
res.status(400)
throw new Error('Task not found')
}
const updatedTask = await Task.findByIdAndUpdate(req.params.id,
req.body, {   new: true })
res.status(200).json(updatedTask)
```

Here, we are first using the findById method to find the task. Here, we are passing the req.params.id in it, which we get from the request header. After that, we are checking if no task is there and here we are throwing an error.

Next, we are updating the task with **findByIdAndUpdate** method. Here, we are passing the params, body and also new: true. The new: true returns us the latest updated value from the database. Lastly, we are sending the status 200 and the updatedTask back.

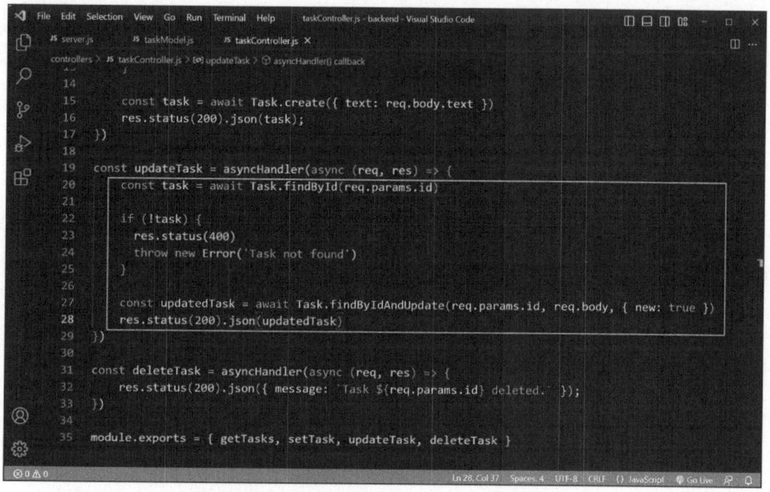

Figure 3.31: *Updating updateTask*

Back in Postman, we are sending a **PUT** request. Here, we have updated the text of a task. On sending it we are getting a Status 200 and also the updated task back.

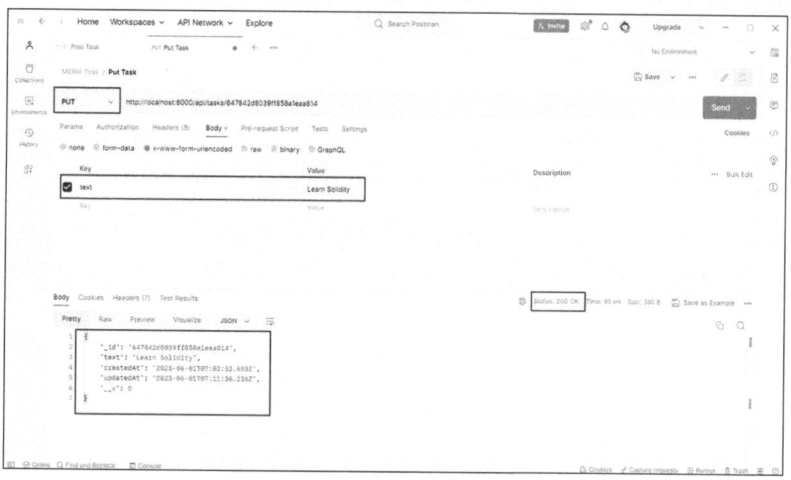

Figure 3.32: *Sending PUT Request*

We can also confirm the same by getting all tasks at http://localhost:8000/api/tasks and we are getting the updated task.

***Figure 3.33**: Checking Updated data in Browser*

DELETE Route

Now, we will update the complete code for the DELETE route. In the **`deleteTask()`** function, add the following code:

```
const task = await Task.findById(req.params.id)

if (!task) {
res.status(400)
throw new Error('Task not found')
}

await Task.findByIdAndDelete(req.params.id)
res.status(200).json({ id: req.params.id })
```

Here, we are first using the findById method to find the task. After that, we are checking if no task is there and here we are throwing an error.

Next, we are deleting the task with findByIdAndDelete method. Here, we are passing the params. Lastly, we are sending the status 200 and the delete id back.

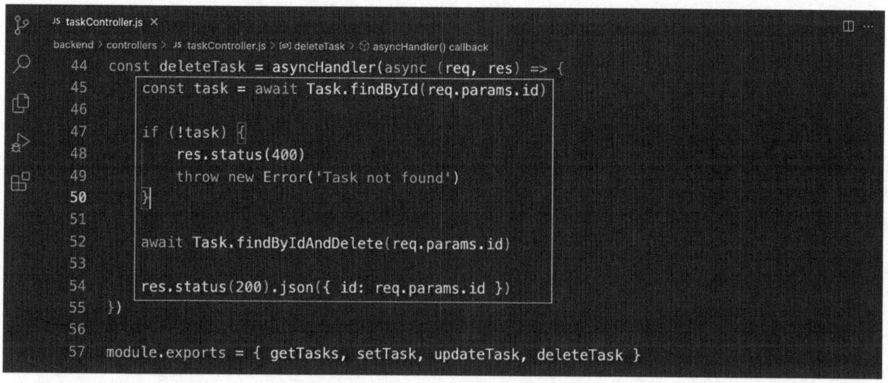

Figure 3.34: *Updating deleteTask*

Back in Postman we are sending a Delete request with a task id. The task is successfully deleted and we are getting a Status 200 and also the id back.

Figure 3.35: *Sending DELETE Request*

We can also confirm the same by getting all tasks at http://localhost:8000/api/tasks and we are getting only one task back. The deleted task is not there anymore.

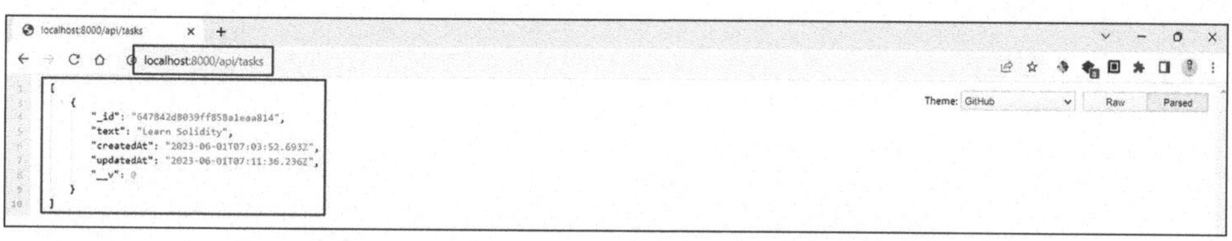

Figure 3.36: *Confirming deleted data in Browser*

Conclusion

In this chapter, we have learned about creating a MongoDB database through MongoDB Cloud. After that, we connected MongoDB to the backend code through the package of mongoose. Next, we did model creation which is required for CRUD operation in MongoDB through Mongoose.

Next, we have updated the GET, POST, PUT, and DELETE routes to work and do CRUD operations in the database.

In the next chapter, we will learn about JWT authentication. We will also create user model, routes, and controllers. Lastly, we will learn about hashing passwords.

Points to remember

- We use the folder structure consisting of connect, controllers, middleware, routes and a server.js file, when using Express.
- We are using MongoDB in the Cloud, which is easily setup using the GUI.
- Routes are created using different functions from Express, like `create()`, `findById()`, `findByIdAndUpdate()`, `findById()`, and `Delete()` in the Controller file.
- We test the different routes through the Postman app, because our frontend is not yet created.

CHAPTER 4

JWT Authentication and Hashing Password

Introduction

This chapter talks about JWT(JSON Web Token) and Hashing passwords. Here, we will first create a new user model in our backend app. We will create the routes and the controller for the same. Next, we learn to hash the password with the library of `bcrypt`. Lastly, we use the package of `jsonwebtoken` to generate JWT and add authentication to our app.

Structure

In this chapter, we are going to discuss the following topics:

- User Model and Controller
- Register User with Hashed Password
- Login User
- Understanding JWT
- Using JWT

User Model and Controller

Now, we will create the user model because we are going to store the User data also in our database. So, create a new file **userModel.js** inside the **models** folder and add the following code in **userModel.js**:

```
const mongoose = require('mongoose')

const userSchema = mongoose.Schema(
  {
      name: {
        type: String,
        required: [true, 'Name is required'],
      },
      email: {
        type: String,
        required: [true, 'Email is required'],
        unique: true,
      },
      password: {
        type: String,
        required: [true, 'Password is required'],
      },
  },
  { timestamps: true }
)

module.exports = mongoose.model('User', userSchema)
```

Here, in the **userSchema** we have three fields of name, email, and password. All of them are strings and required. The email is also unique, which means we can't have the same email twice.

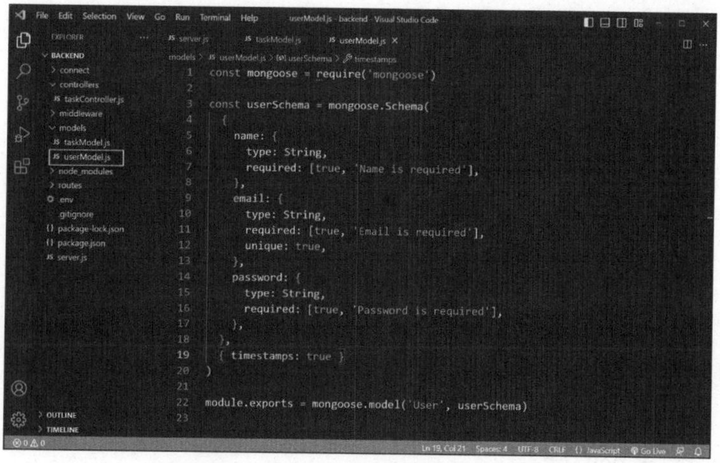

Figure 4.1: *Creating User Model*

Now, each of the tasks will also be associated with a user. So, we will update our **taskModel.js** file to have a field of the user. The type of it will be the **`ObjectId`** and it will refer to the User.

```
user: { type: mongoose.Schema.Types.ObjectId, required: true, ref:
'User' }
```

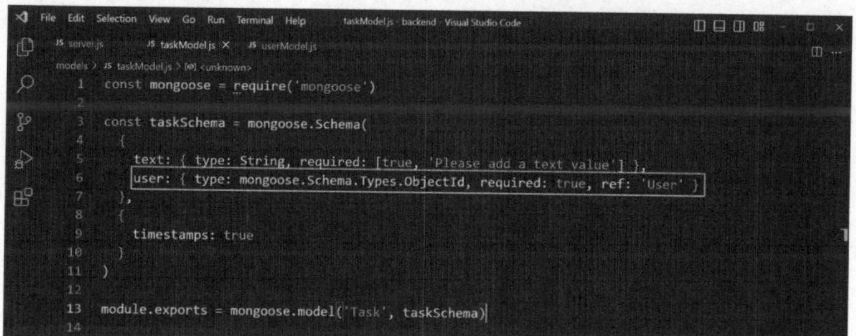

Figure 4.2: *Updating Task Model*

Next, we will create the new **userRoutes.js** file in the **routes** folder. In it, we are first importing express and router.

After that, we are also importing some functions from the **userController** file, which we are going to create next. Using the router, we have created two POST routes and one GET route.

```
const express = require('express')
const router = express.Router()
const { registerUser, loginUser, getCurrentUser } =
require('../controllers/userController')

router.post('/', registerUser)
router.post('/login', loginUser)
router.get('/current', getCurrentUser)

module.exports = router
```

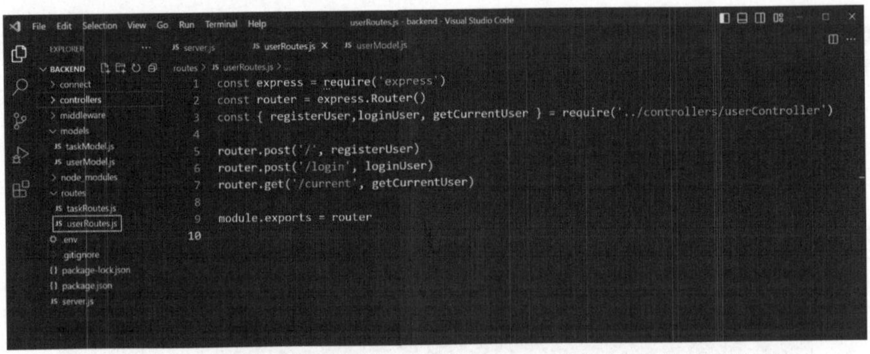

Figure 4.3: *Creating User Routes*

Now, in the **controllers** folder, we will create a file **userController.js** file. Here, we are right now creating the three functions of **registerUser**, **loginUser**, and **getCurrentUser** and returning simple json messages.

```
const asyncHandler = require('express-async-handler')

const registerUser = asyncHandler(async (req, res) => {
      res.json({ message: 'Register User successful' })
})

const loginUser = asyncHandler(async (req, res) => {
      res.json({ message: 'Login User successful' })
```

```
})

const getCurrentUser = asyncHandler(async (req, res) => {
      res.json({ message: 'Current user data' })
})

module.exports = { registerUser, loginUser, getCurrentUser }
```

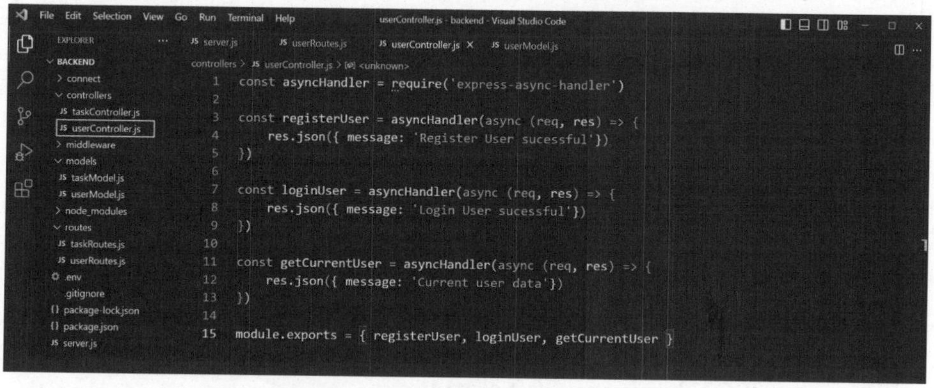

Figure 4.4: *Creating User Controllers*

Finally, we are going to create a new **/api/users** route in the **server.js** file.

```
app.use('/api/users', require('./routes/userRoutes'));
```

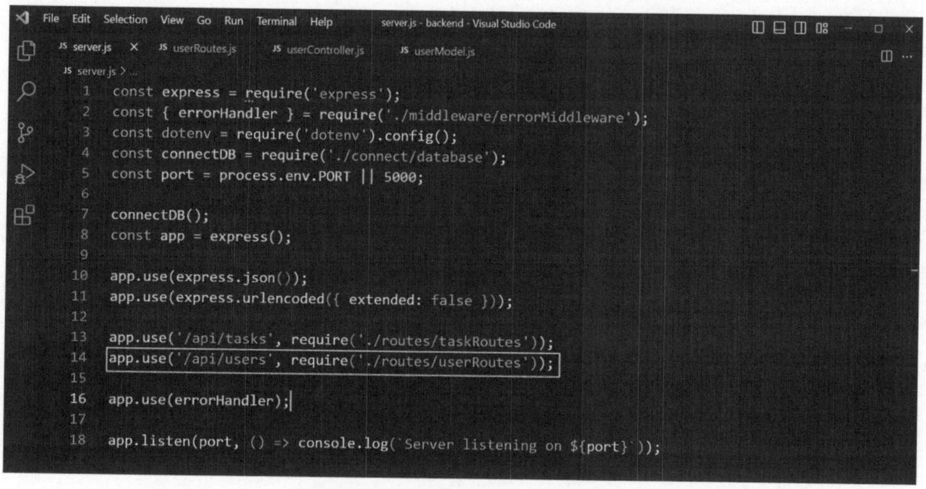

Figure 4.5: *Updating server.js*

In Postman do a **POST** request to http://localhost:8000/api/users and we will get back the correct JSON back and 200 status.

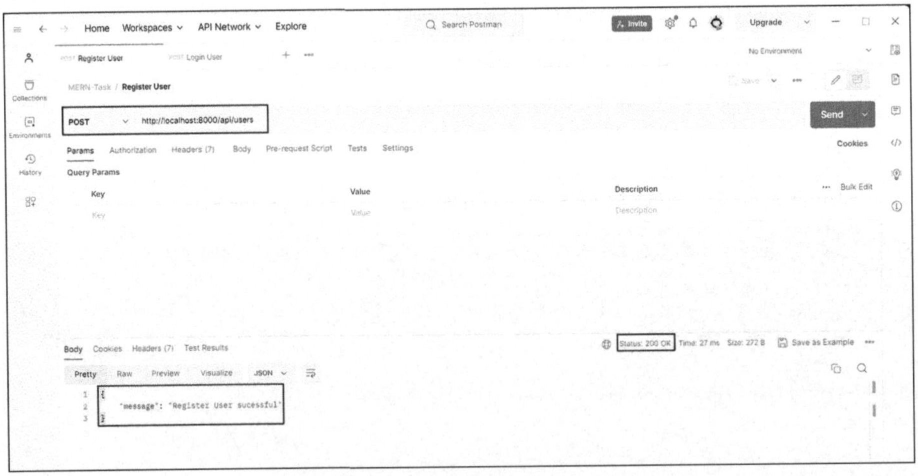

Figure 4.6: *Register route in Postman*

Similarly, a **POST** request to http://localhost:8000/api/users/login will give back the correct JSON back and 200 status.

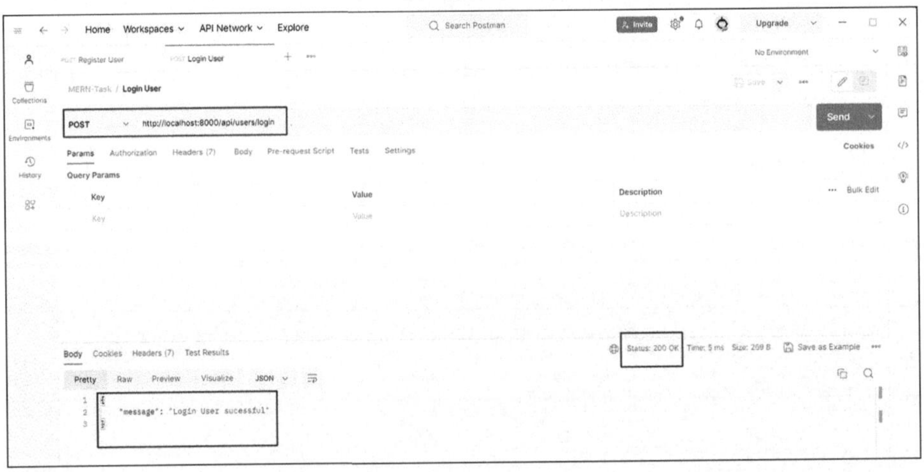

Figure 4.7: *Login route in Postman*

To check the **GET** request, we can use a browser. So, in a browser go to http://localhost:8000/api/users/current, and we will get the correct JSON data.

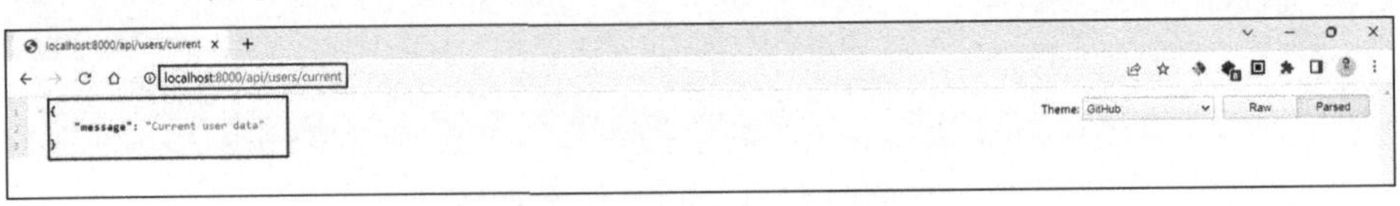

Figure 4.8: *Get users in browser*

Register User with Hashed Password

Before updating the register user function, we will install the package of **`bcryptjs`** and **`jsonwebtoken`**. These packages are used for password hashing and creating JWT respectively.

```
npm i bcryptjs jsonwebtoken
```

We are also importing **`jwt`**, **`bcrypt`**, and **`userModel`** in our **userController.js** file.

```
const jwt = require(‘jsonwebtoken’)
const bcrypt = require(‘bcryptjs’)
const User = require(‘../models/userModel’)
```

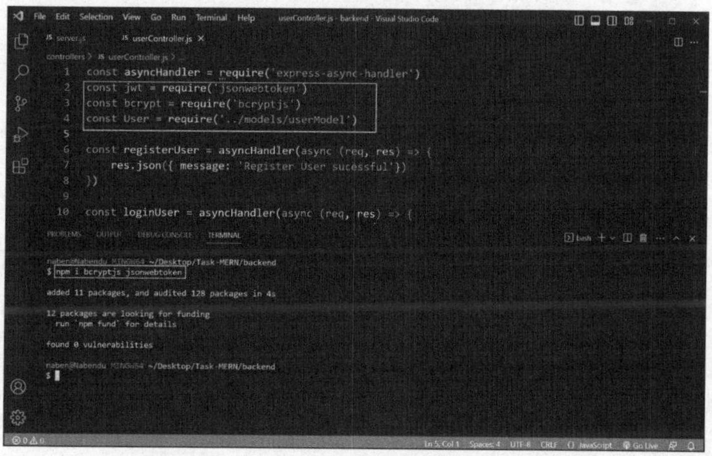

***Figure 4.9**: Adding bcryptjs and jsonwebtoken*

Now, in the **userController.js** file, we will update the **`registerUser()`**. Add the following code in the function:

```
const { name, email, password } = req.body

if (!name || !email || !password) {
  res.status(400)
  throw new Error(‘All fields are mandatory’)
```

```
}

const userExists = await User.findOne({ email })
if (userExists) {
  res.status(400)
  throw new Error(‘User Exists’)
}
```

Here, we are first destructuring the name, email, and password from the req. body. After that, we are checking if any field is missing and throwing an error, if that is the case.

We are using the **findOne()** on the User model to get the user data. Here, we are giving the email. Now, if the user already exists, we are throwing an error.

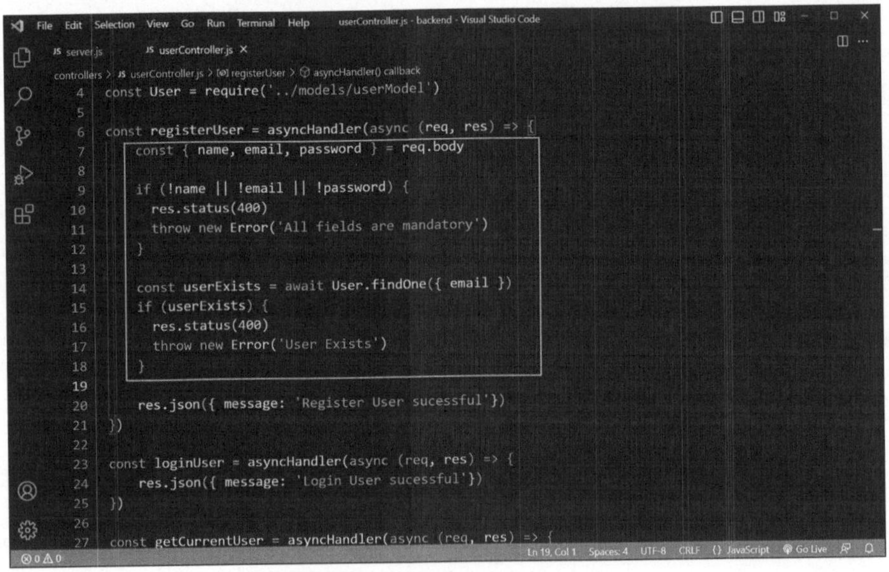

Figure 4.10: *Updating Register User*

In Postman, if we pass the **name**, **email**, and **password** fields, we will get back **Status 200** and the correct JSON back.

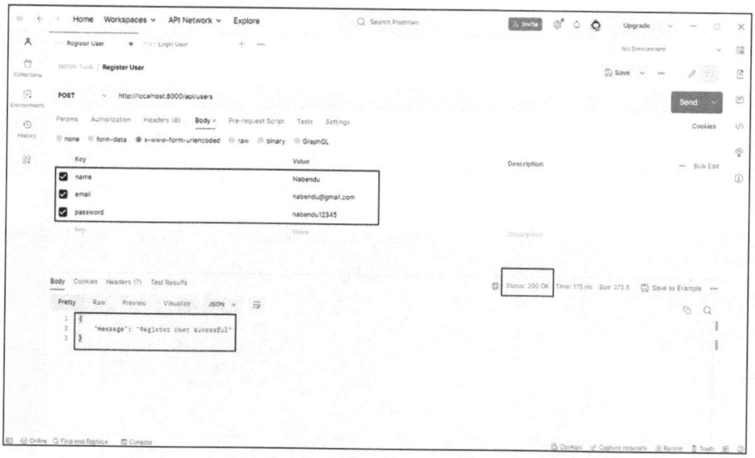

***Figure 4.11**: Checking Register User in Postman*

Now, we don't want to save a plain password in our database for the user. Because if someone hacks the database, they get all username and passwords. So, we are going to use bcrypt now in **`registerUser()`** in the **userController.js** file. Update the file with the following code:

```
        const salt = await bcrypt.genSalt(10)
        const hashedPassword = await bcrypt.hash(password, salt)

        const user = await User.create({ name, email, password: hashed-
Password })

        if (user) {
         res.status(201).json({ _id: user.id, name: user.name, email:
user.email })
        } else {
         res.status(400)
         throw new Error('Invalid user data')
}
```

Here, we are first creating a random variable with the **`genSalt()`** method. After that, we are using the **`hash()`** method to generate a hash password. Here, we are passing the password and the salt value.

Now, we are using the mongoose create method on the User model to add the name, email, and **hashedPassword** of the user in the database.

If the user was saved successfully, we are sending back the **id**, **name**, and **email**. And if there is some error, we are throwing it back with an **Invalid user data** message.

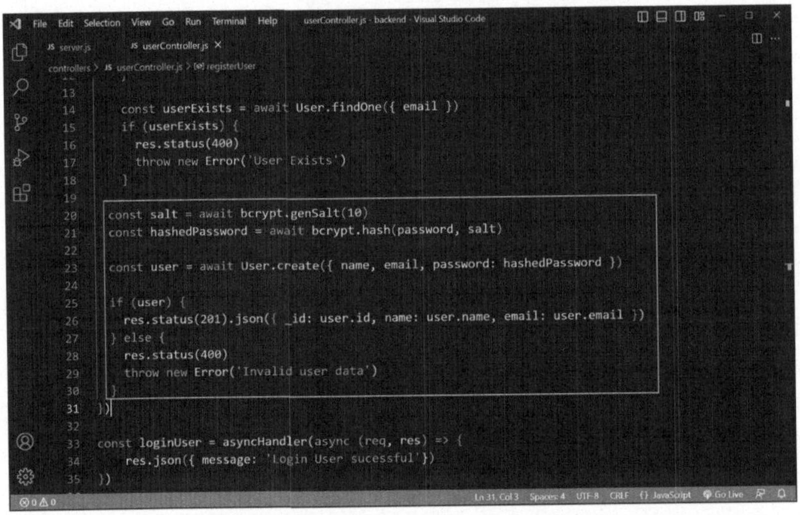

Figure 4.12: *Adding hashed password*

Back in Postman if we give all data again and hit the **Send** button, we will get a **Status 201**. And the correct JSON will also be returned back.

Figure 4.13: *Registering user with Postman*

We can also confirm the same in the MongoDB cloud database. Here, in the users the new user with the hashed password will be saved.

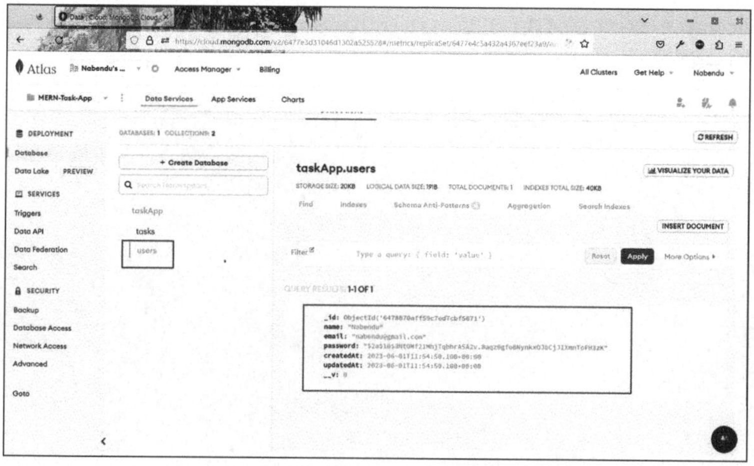

Figure 4.14: *Saved user in database*

Login User

Now, we will update the Login user functionality. So, in the **loginUser** function of the **userController.js** file, add the following code:

```
const { email, password } = req.body
const user = await User.findOne({ email })

if (user && (await bcrypt.compare(password, user.password))) {
 res.json({ _id: user.id, name: user.name, email: user.email })
} else {
 res.status(400)
 throw new Error('Invalid data')
}
```

Here, we are first destructuring the email and password from the req.body. We are using the **findOne()** on the User model to get the user data. Here, we are giving the email.

Now, if the user exists and password matched, we are sending back the id, name, and email. Notice that since the password is hashed in the database, we are using **bcrypt.compare()** to compare the passwords.

If the user doesn't exist or the password doesn't match, we are throwing an error with '**Invalid data**' message.

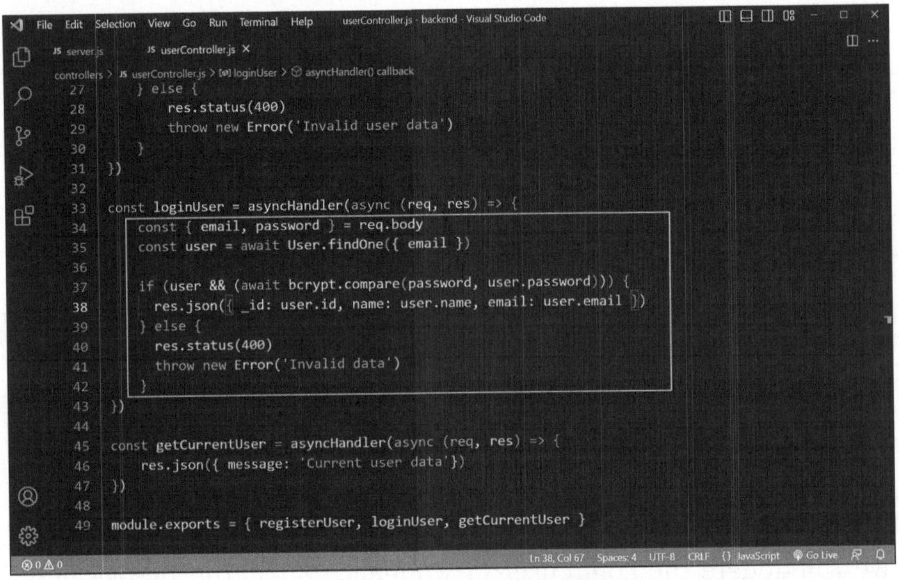

Figure 4.15: *Updating Login User*

Back in Postman, a POST request to http://localhost:8000/api/users/login with no data, will give us an error JSON back.

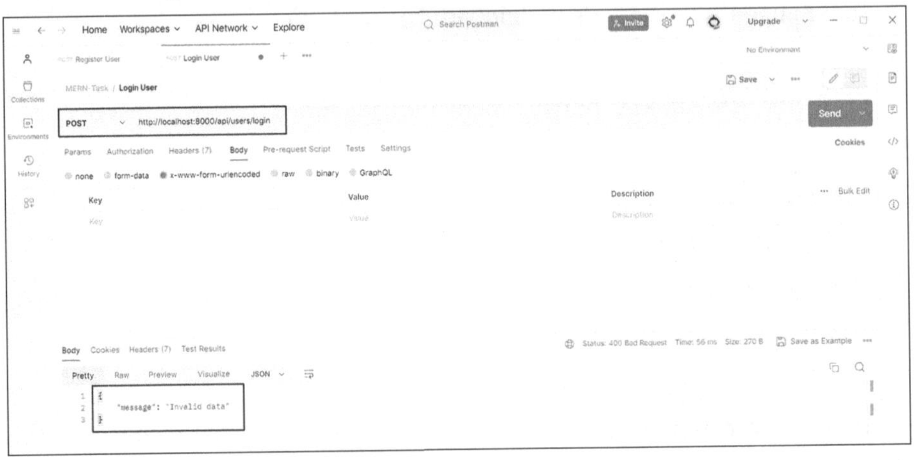

Figure 4.16: *Login User with no data*

Even a **POST** request to http://localhost:8000/api/users/login with the wrong password, will give us an error JSON back.

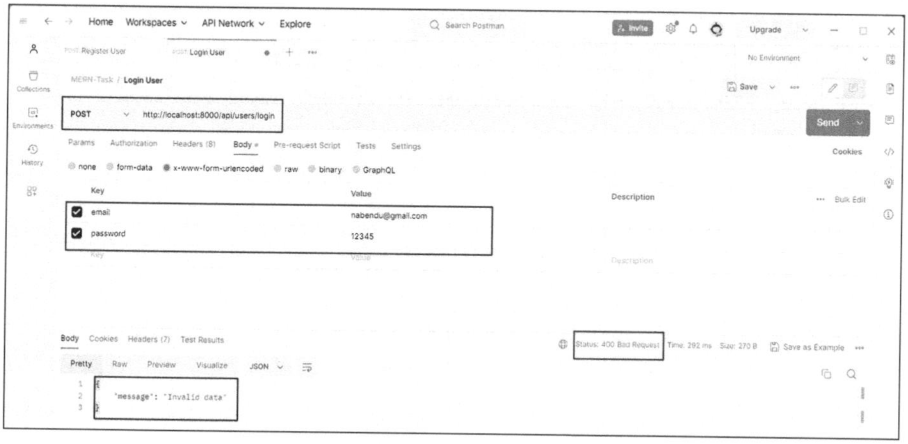

Figure 4.17: *Login User with wrong password*

Only a POST request to http://localhost:8000/api/users/login with all correct data, will give us Status 200 and id, **`name`** and **`email`** back.

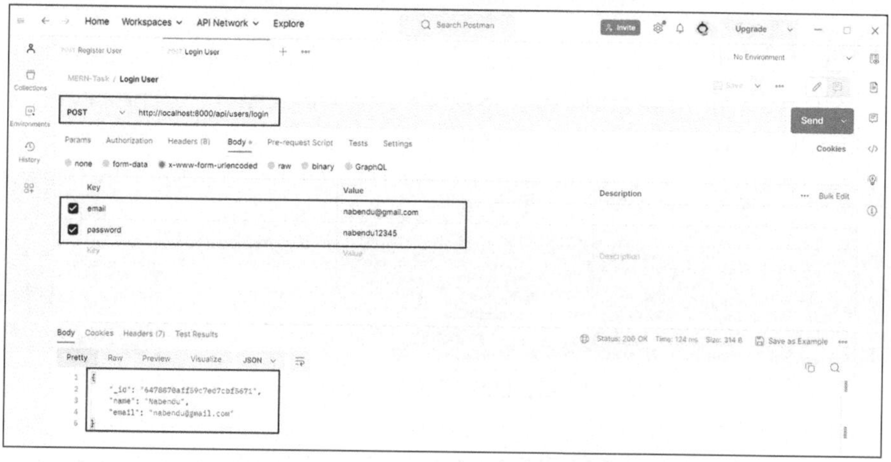

Figure 4.18: *Login User successfully*

Understanding JWT

JWT(JSON Web Token) is often used to add authentication in web apps. The official site for JWT is https://jwt.io/ and as per it, the JWT token consists of three parts. The first part is the Header, the second is the Payload, and the third is the Verify Signature.

Out of these, the second is the most important, because it contains the details of the payload. But the third one also contains the signature without which the token cannot be verified.

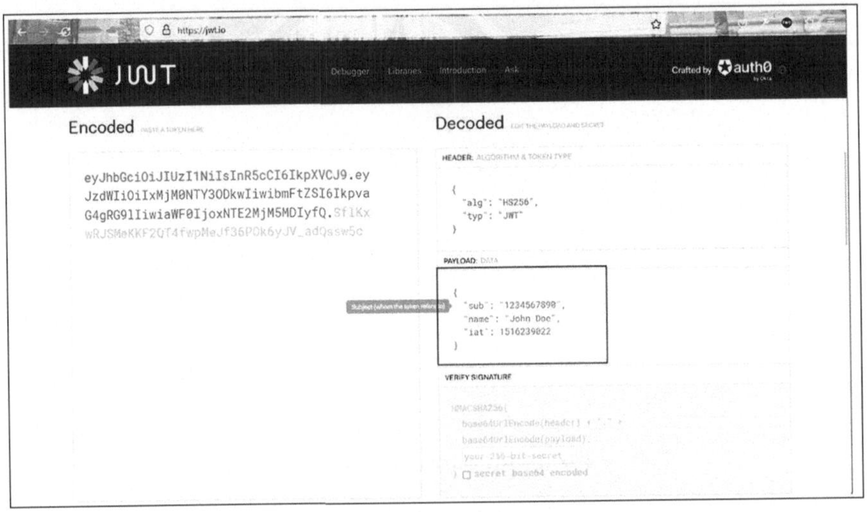

Figure 4.19: The JWT Token

Using JWT

To use JWT, we will first add **JWT_SECRET** in the **.env** file. The secret can be anything and we have kept it **thewebdev**.

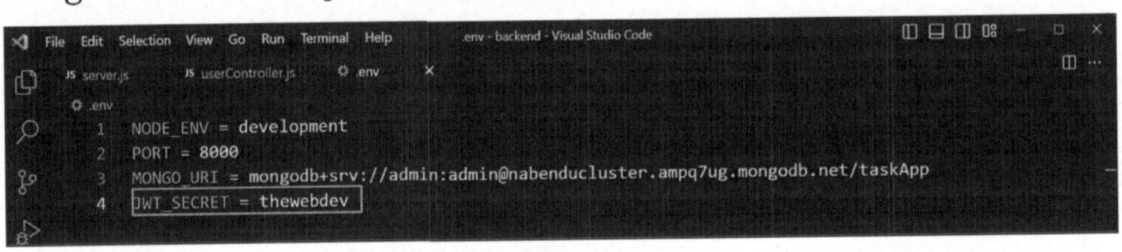

Figure 4.20: The JWT Secret

Then, in the **userController.js** file, we will add the following function:

```
const generateJWTtoken = id => jwt.sign({ id }, process.env.JWT_SECRET,
{ expiresIn: '5d' })
```

Now, the function **generateJWTtoken** is taking an id. And it is using the **jwt.sign()** method. Here, it is taking the id and secret from the environment file as the first two parameters.

In the third parameter, we are giving the expiresIn parameter. Here, we can specify after how much time our JWT will expire, and we need to generate a new one. We have kept it for five days.

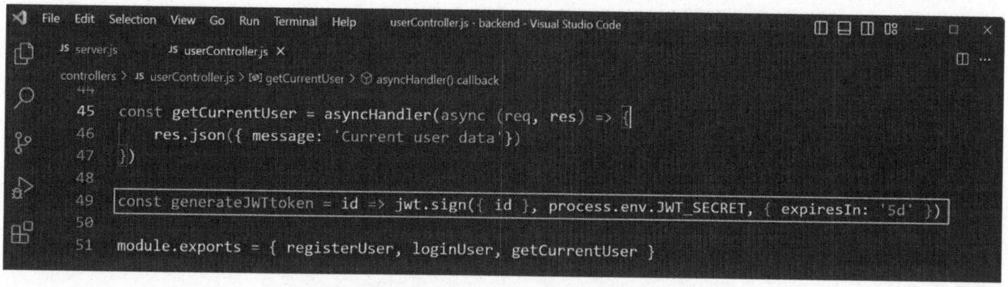

Figure 4.21: *The generate token method*

Then, in the **registerUser** and **loginUser** function in the **userController.js** file, we are also passing back the token when the request is successful. The token is generated by passing the id in the **`generateToken()`** function.

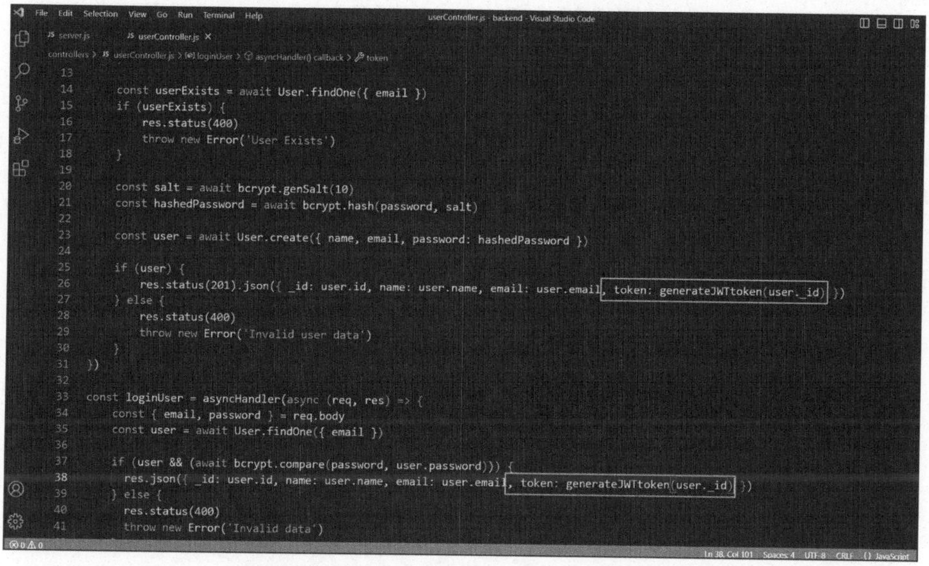

Figure 4.22: *Using generate token method*

Now, in Postman the login route http://localhost:8000/api/users/login with all correct data, will give us Status 200. It will also return back id, name, email, and JWT token.

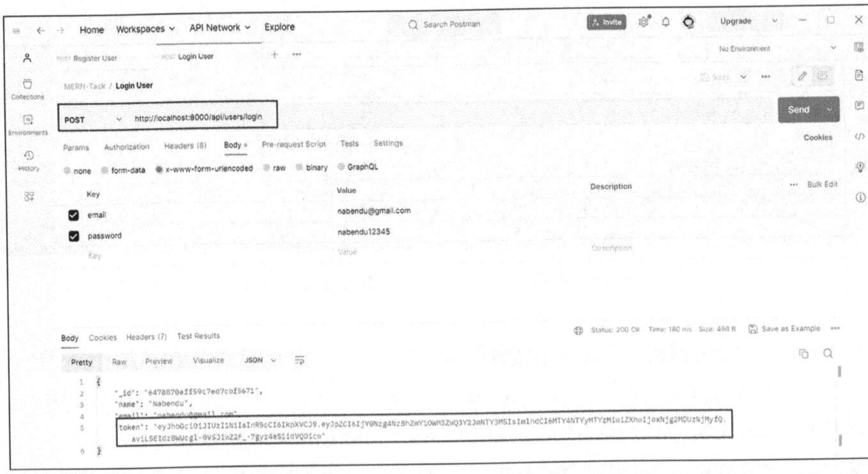

Figure 4.23: Login route getting JWT Token

Similarly, the register route http://localhost:8000/api/users with all correct data, will give us `Status 200`. It will also return back **`id`**, **`name`**, **`email`**, and JWT **`token`**.

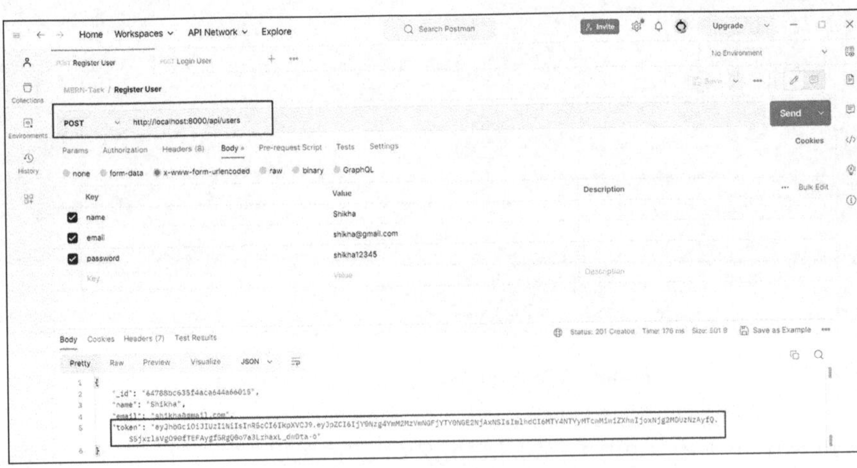

Figure 4.24: Register route getting JWT Token

But, if we try to Register with the same details, we will get back the error of `User Exists` in the Register route:

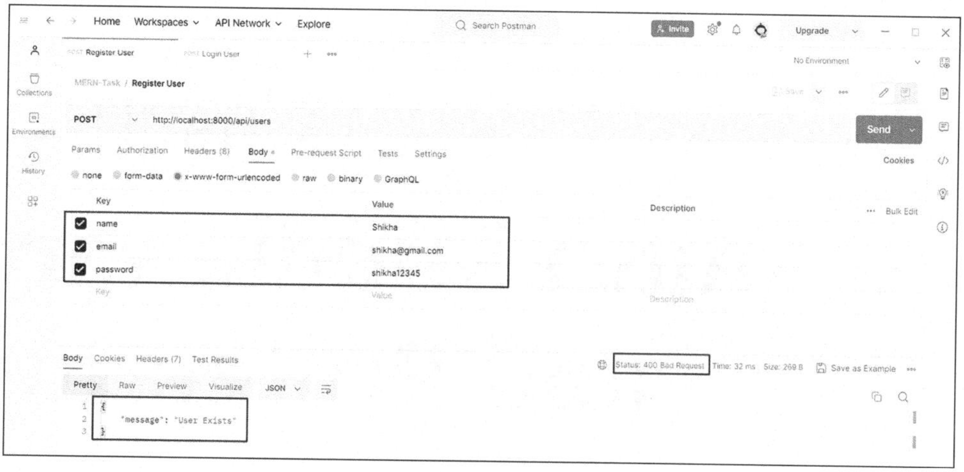

***Figure 4.25**: Register route getting error*

Conclusion

In this chapter, we have learned about JWT tokens and hashing passwords. Here, we have first created a user model and controller. Next, we have created the register user functionality. Here, while saving the password, we used the **`bcrypt`** package to hash it.

Next, we created the login functionality. Here, to compare the passed password to the saved password, we had to use **`bcrypt`** again. Then, we learned about JWT tokens and implemented them in our project.

In the next chapter, we will use JWT to protect routes.

Points to Remember

- We have created the user model with name, email, and password as String. We have also added basic validation in it.
- We have used the library of bcryptjs to hash the password, before saving it to the database. JWT(JSON Web Token) is used to authenticate web-apps. We are using the library of **`jsonwebtoken`** in our project.
- We have generated a JWT token using the method of **`jwt.sign()`** in which we can also give the days after which this token will expire.

CHAPTER 5

Auth Middleware and Protecting Routes

Introduction

This chapter talks about Auth middleware and Protecting routes. Here, we will first create an Auth middleware using the JWT created in the last chapter. After that, we will protect some of the routes using this Auth middleware, which require the JWT token to be verified.

Structure

In this chapter, we are going to discuss the following topics:

- Creating Auth middleware
- Understanding Protect Routes
- Protecting Task Routes

Creating Auth middleware

We will create a file **authMiddleware.js** in the middleware folder and add the following content in **authMiddleware.js** file:

```
const jwt = require('jsonwebtoken')
const asyncHandler = require('express-async-handler')
```

```
const User = require('../models/userModel')


const protect = asyncHandler(async (req, res, next) => {
  let token;


  if (req.headers.authorization && req.headers.authorization.
startsWith('Bearer')) {
      try {
       token = req.headers.authorization.split(' ')[1]
       const decoded = jwt.verify(token, process.env.JWT_SECRET)
       req.user = await User.findById(decoded.id).select('-password')
       next()
      } catch (error) {
       console.log(error)
       res.status(401)
       throw new Error('You are not authorized')
      }
  }
})


module.exports = { protect }
```

Here, we are importing the required imports of **`jwt`**, **`asyncHandler`**, and **`User`** model. After that, we wrote a function called protect. Inside the function, we are checking if the authorization header is present with an `if` statement.

Inside the `if` statement, we have a try..catch block. In the try, we are first splitting the token with the split command because it will be like "Bearer XXXXYYYMM". Next, we are using the verify method from jwt and passing the token and Secret. After that, we are getting the user details back with **`findById()`**. Notice that we are omitting the password here. After that, the required **`next()`** of the middleware is there.

In the catch part, we are returning a 401 and also throwing an error **`You are not authorized`**.

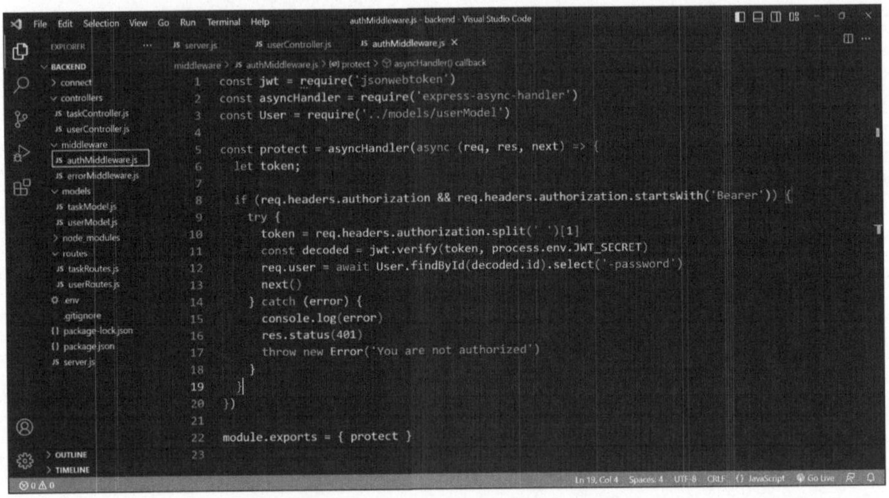

Figure 5.1: *Creating authMiddleware.js file*

Next, we will also add the following code in **authMiddleware.js** file:

```
if (!token) {
    res.status(401)
    throw new Error('Not authorized, no token')
}
```

Here, we are checking if the token is not available. Then we are sending a **`401`** and also an error **`Not authorized, no token`**.

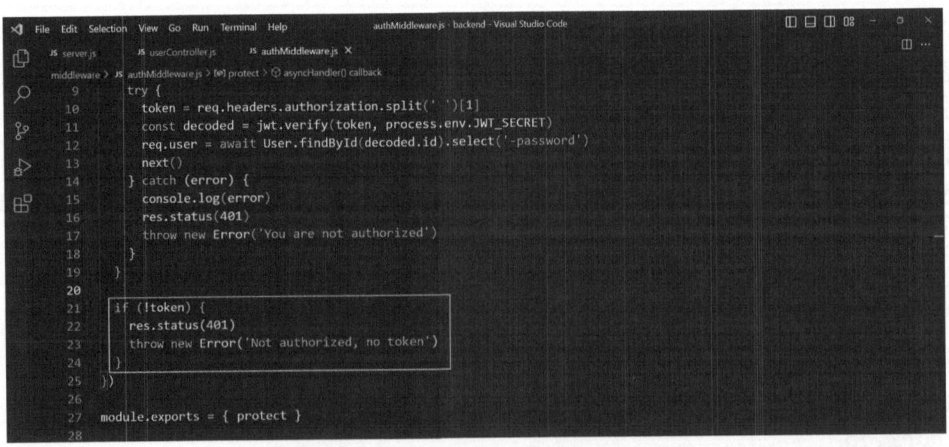

Figure 5.2: *Updating authMiddleware.js file*

Understanding Protect Routes

To protect a route, we need to add the protect function in the route. So, we will go to the **userRoutes.js** file and import the protect function. After that, in the get route for /current, we will add the **`protect`** function.

```
const { protect } = require('../middleware/authMiddleware')
```

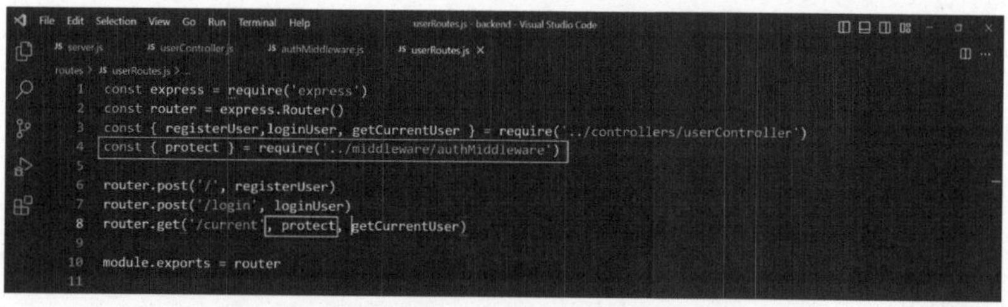

***Figure 5.3**: Adding protect in userRoutes.js*

Now, in Postman go to http://localhost:8000/api/users/current and we will get the **`Not authorized, no token`** message. This message is from the authMiddleware.js file because we didn't provide a token that was required.

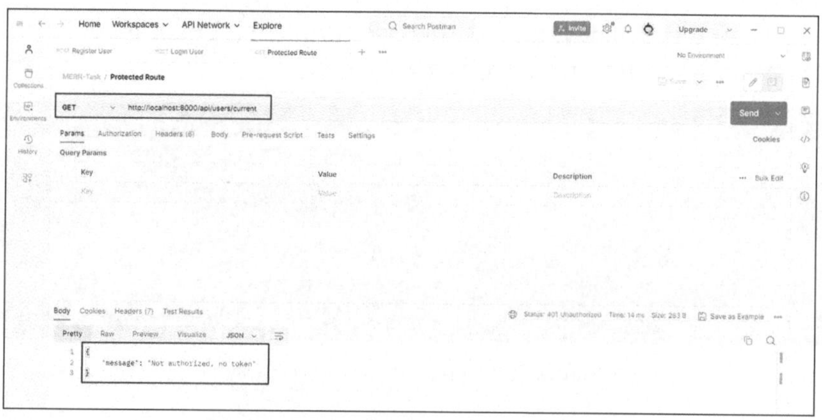

***Figure 5.4**: Current user route with error*

Now, in Postman to add a token, we will first go to the **`Authorization`** tab. Here, in the Type select **`Bearer Token`**. And after that, in the Token field add the token, which we have got from the Login User POST request in the previous chapter.

After that click the `Send` button and we will get a status 200 with successful message of **Current user data**.

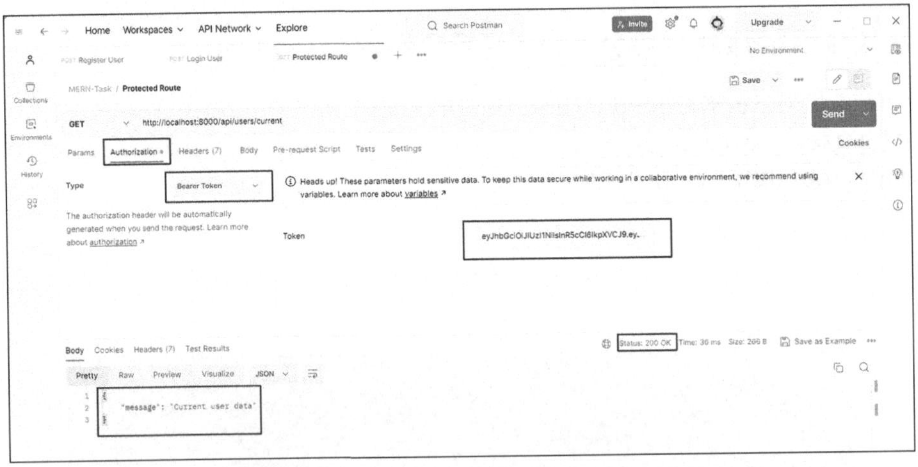

Figure 5.5: *Current user route with token*

Now, in the **userController.js** file and inside the **`getCurrentUser()`** add the following code:

```
const { _id, name, email } = await User.findById(req.user.id)
res.status(200).json({ id: _id, name, email })
```

Here, we are using the **`findById()`** on the User and then getting back the **`id`**, **`name`**, and **`email`**. We are sending this back as a success.

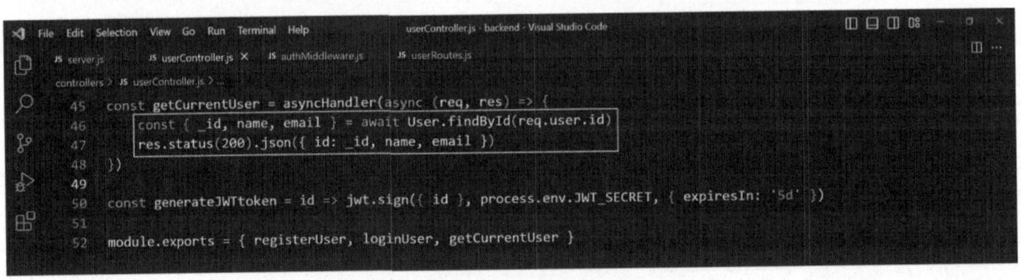

Figure 5.6: *Updating getCurrentUser*

Again, in Postman go to http://localhost:8000/api/users/current,and we get the current user data back.

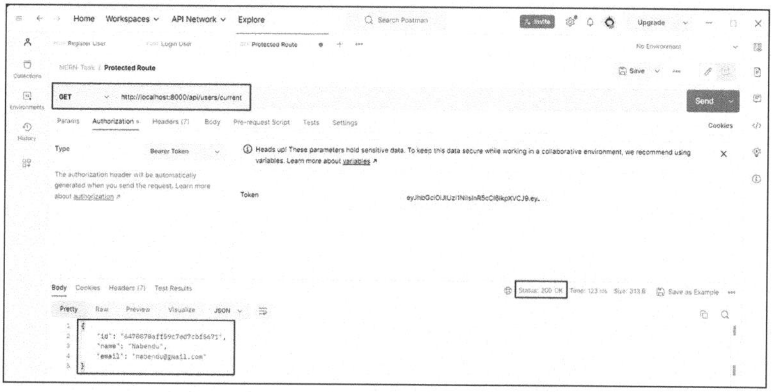

***Figure* 5.7**: *Getting User data back*

Protecting Task Routes

Now, we will protect all of our task routes that we created earlier. Here, again we will follow the same process as in the earlier section.

GET and POST Route

We will first protect the GET and POST route in Task. First, in the **taskRoutes.js** file, we will protect the **GET** route. Here, again we are importing the protect function and adding it to the get route.

```
const { protect } = require(‘../middleware/authMiddleware’)
```

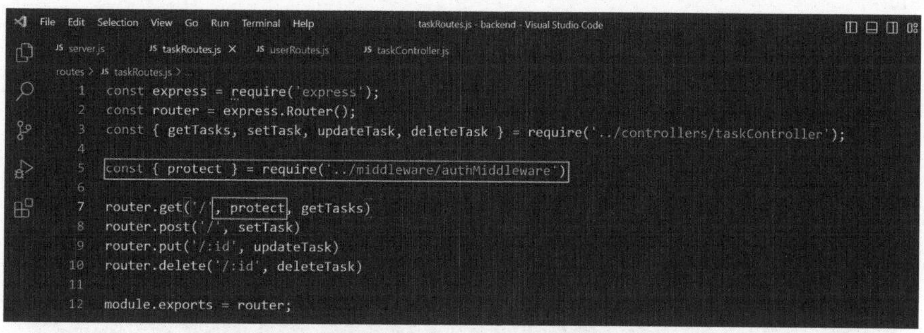

***Figure* 5.8**: *Protecting GET route for task*

Now, in Postman we will go to the GET route http://localhost:8000/api/tasks, and hit the **Send** button. We will get an error since we have not given any token.

Figure 5.9: *GET route for task error in Postman*

Now, we will also add the **protect** function to all the routes in **taskRoutes.js** file.

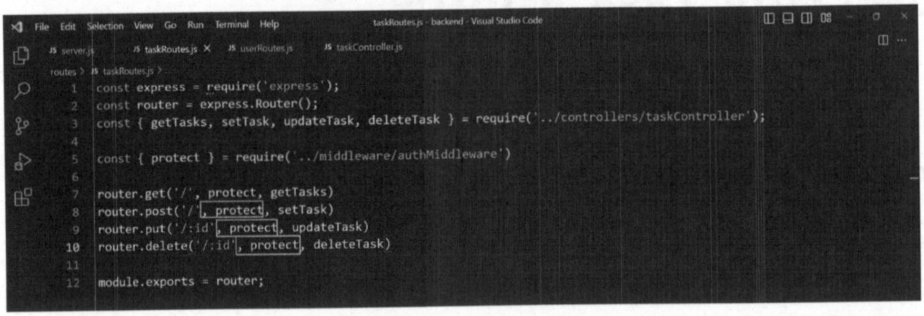

Figure 5.10: *Protecting all Task routes*

We will modify the **`getTask`** and **`setTask`** functions in **taskController.js** file. Here, we are finding by the user's id and also saving the user's id in through the POST request.

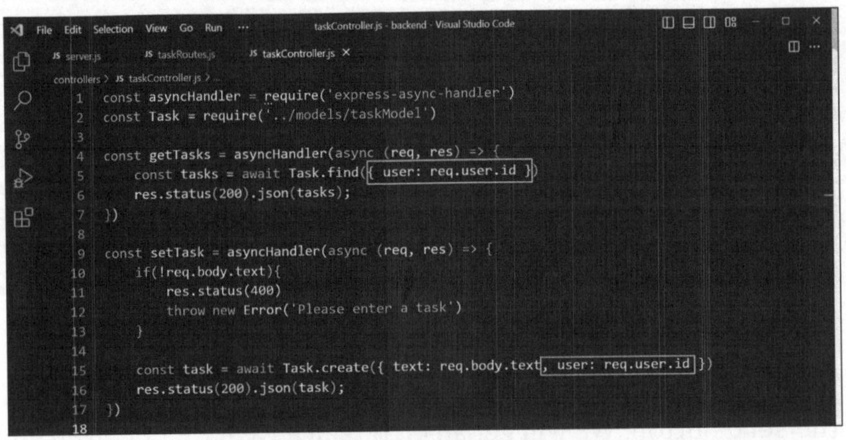

Figure 5.11: *Updating getTasks function*

Back, in Postman we will go to the POST route http://localhost:8000/api/tasks, add a task and hit the `Send` button. We will get an error since we have not given any token.

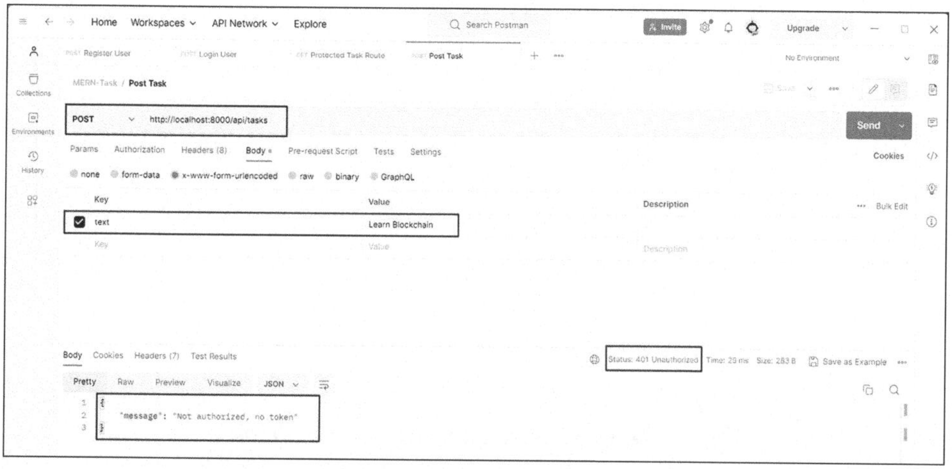

***Figure 5.12**: POSTMAN with POST route without token*

Now in the **`Authorization`** tab, we will add a Bearer token and we will be able to successfully add the task.

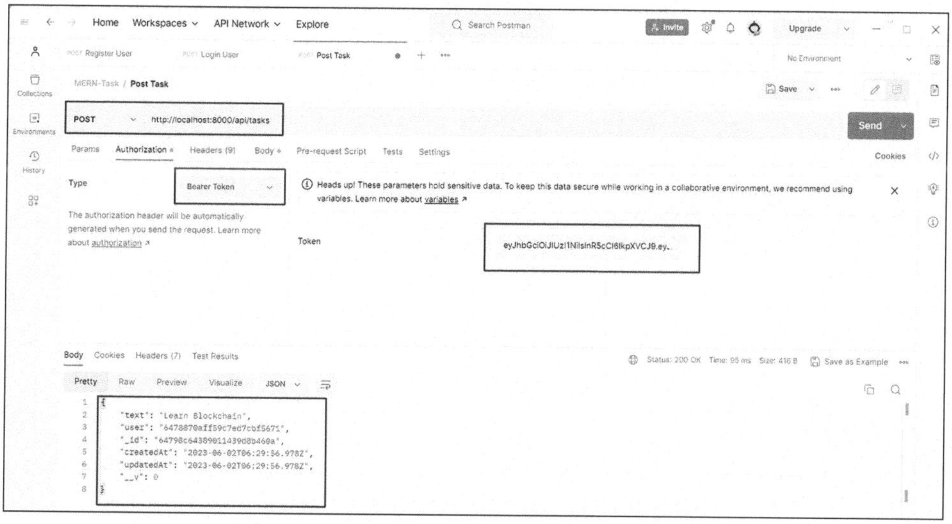

***Figure 5.13**: POSTMAN with POST route with token*

We have added one more task for the same user. Now, in Postman, go to the GET route http://localhost:8000/api/tasks, and add the token of the user in the **`Authorization`** tab. Now, on clicking the **`Send`** button, we will get the tasks of this user.

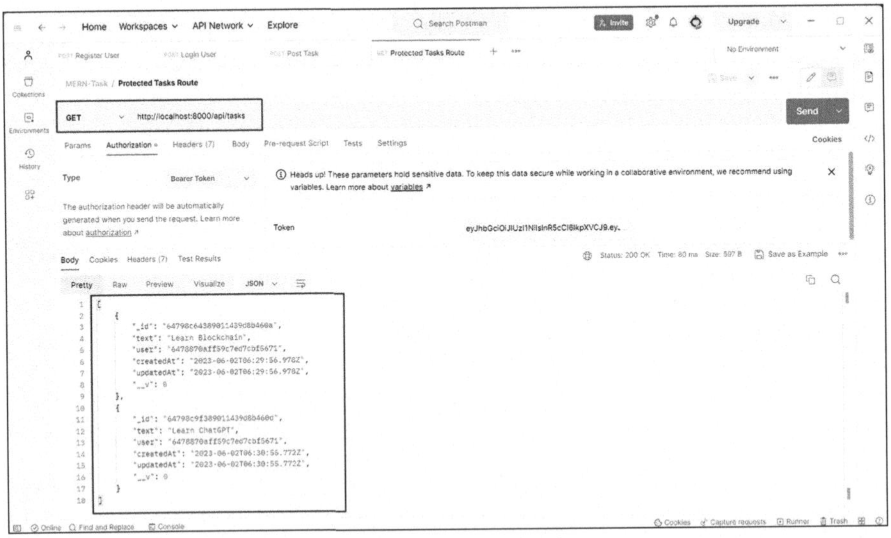

Figure 5.14: POSTMAN *with GET route with token*

We have added two more tasks for a different user through the **POST** route. Now in the **GET**, when we use this user's token, we will get back this user's tasks.

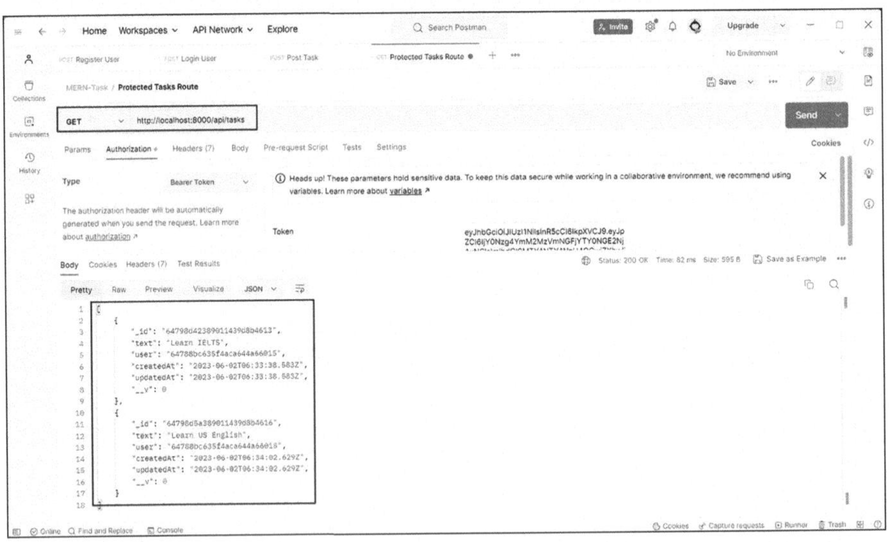

Figure 5.15: *Added more tasks for Users*

PUT and DELETE Route

First, we are going to update the PUT route. This is done in the updateTask function in the **taskController.js** file. Here, we are first finding the user with **findById()** method, by passing the user id.

Next, if we do not find any user, we are throwing an error. We are also throwing an error if a wrong token is used to update the task.

```
const user = await User.findById(req.user.id)

if(!user){
  res.status(401)
  throw new Error('No such user found')
}

if (task.user.toString() !== user.id) {
  res.status(401)
  throw new Error('User is not authorized to update')
}
```

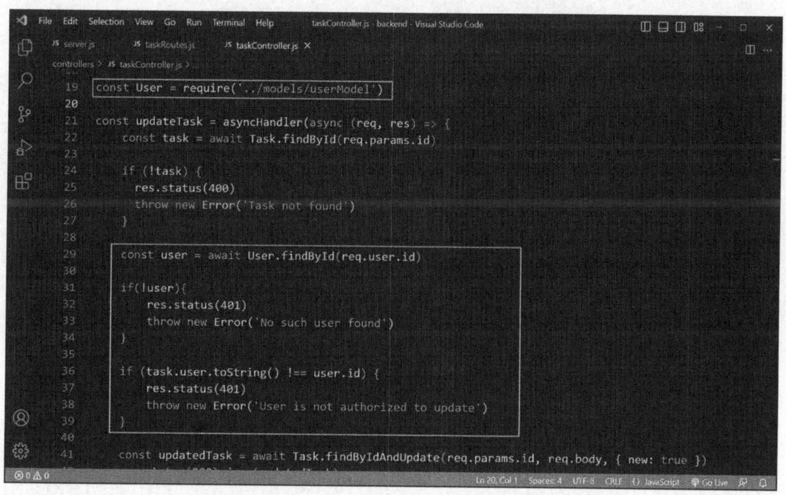

***Figure 5.16**: Updating updateTask function*

Now we are going to update the DELETE route. This is done in the **`deleteTask`** function in the **taskController.js** file. Here, we are again using the same logic as the **`updateTask`** function.

```
const user = await User.findById(req.user.id)
```

```
if(!user){
  res.status(401)
  throw new Error('No such user found')
}

if (task.user.toString() !== user.id) {
  res.status(401)
  throw new Error('User is not authorized to update')
}
```

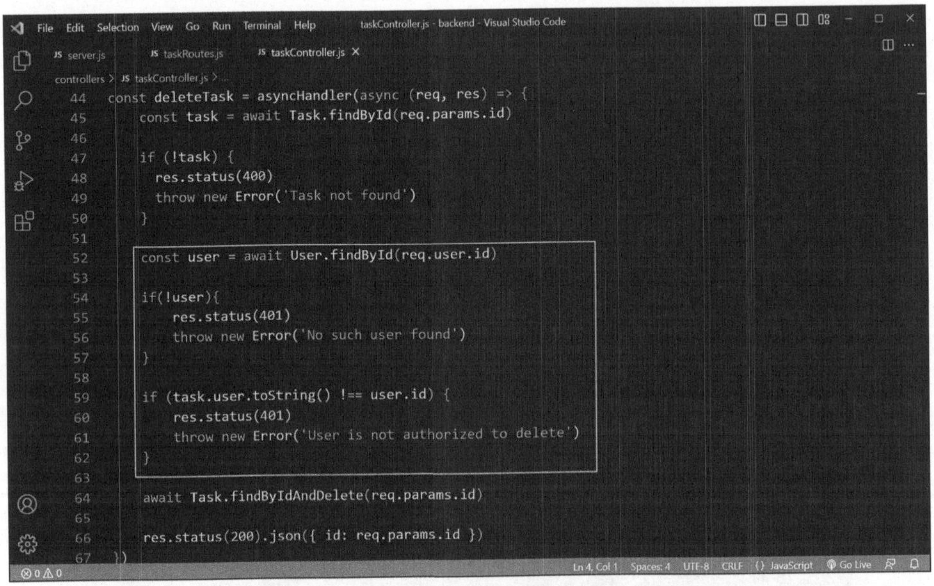

Figure 5.17: *Updating deleteTask function*

Now, in Postman, we will put a DELETE request with a url like http://localhost:8000/api/tasks/64798d42389011439d8b4613. Here, take any task id of a user. Now, when we hit the **Send** button, we will get an error, since we have not provided any token.

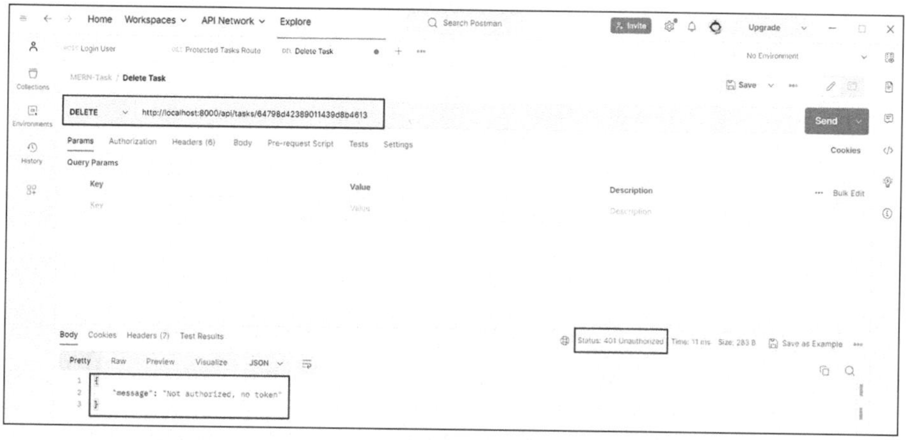

***Figure 5.18**: POSTMAN with DELETE route without token*

Now, we will add a token in the Authorization tab. But this token will be of a different user. Now, when we hit **Send**, we will get the **`User is not authorized to delete`** error.

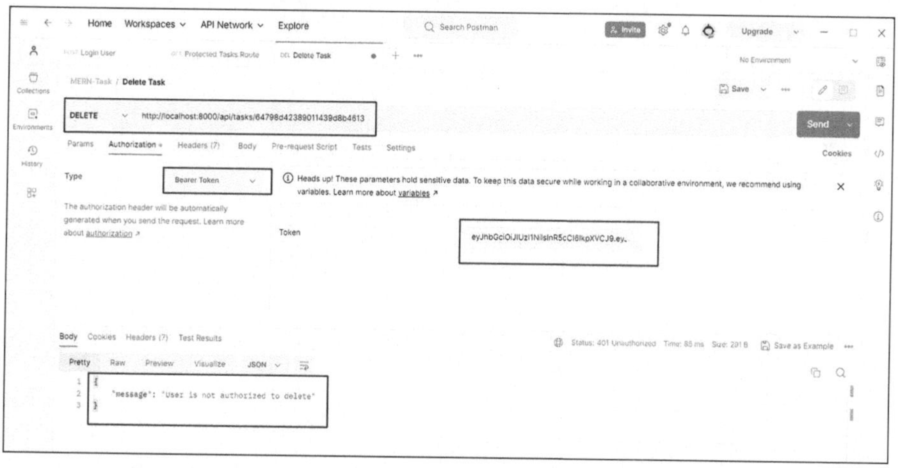

***Figure 5.19**: POSTMAN with DELETE route with wrong token*

We will give the correct token of the user, who has this task. Now, we are able to delete the task and get the correct message back with **`Status 200`**.

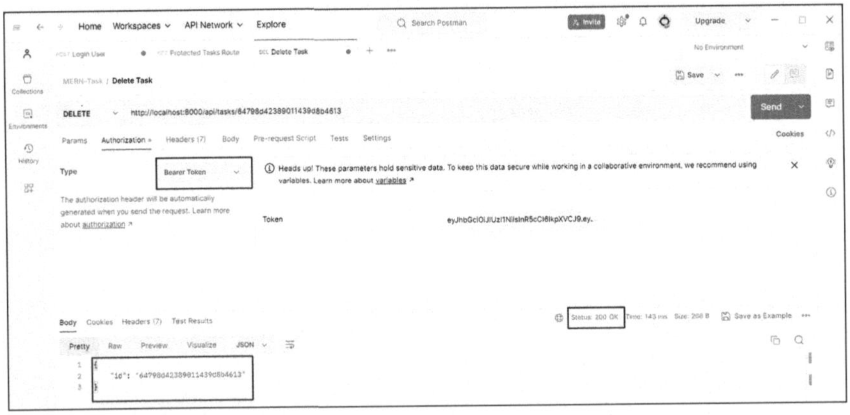

Figure 5.20: POSTMAN *with DELETE route with right token*

Also, we are confirming the same by going to http://localhost:8000/api/tasks and giving this user's token. Here, we can see only one task, with the other being deleted.

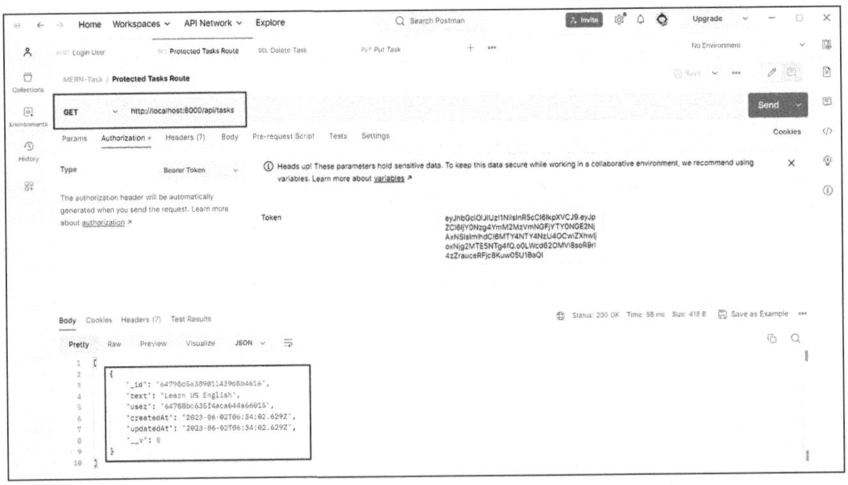

Figure 5.21: POSTMAN *with GET route with right token*

Now, in Postman we will do a PUT request with a url like http://localhost:8000/api/tasks/64798d5a389011439d8b4616. Here, take any task id of a user. Now, when we hit the **Send** button, we will get an error, since we have not provided any token.

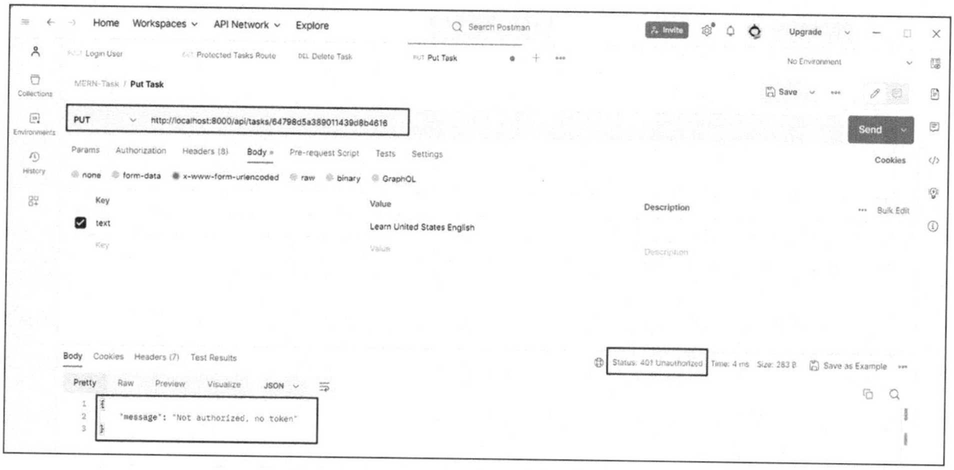

Figure 5.22: POSTMAN *with PUT route with wrong token*

This time we will give the correct token for the user and the task will be updated.

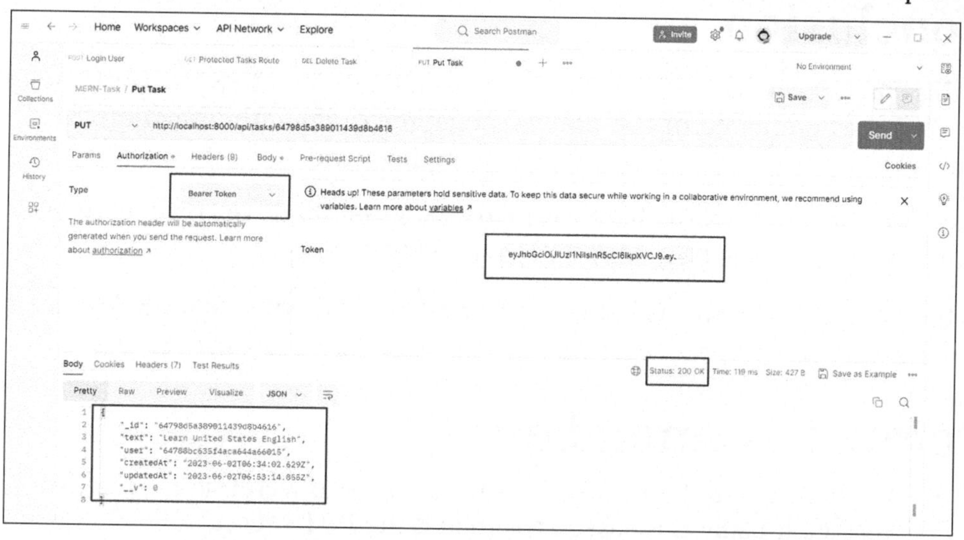

Figure 5.23: POSTMAN *with PUT route with right token*

Also, we are confirming the same by going to http://localhost:8000/api/tasks and giving this user's token. Here, we can see that the task has been updated.

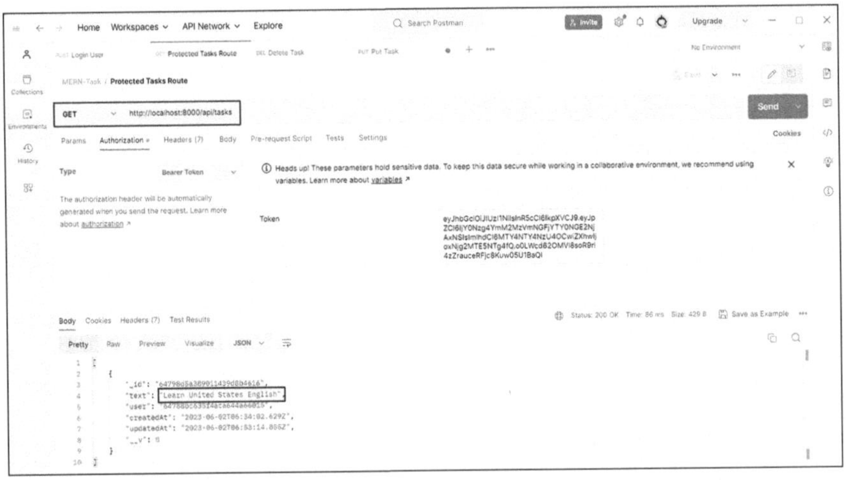

***Figure 5.24**: POSTMAN with GET route with right token*

Conclusion

In this chapter, we have learned about creating Auth middleware. Here, we used the JWT token created in the previous chapter to do authentication. Next, we learned to protect routes using this Auth middleware.

Here, we first protected the current route. After that, we protected all Task routes, which include **`GET`**, **`POST`**, **`PUT`**, and **`DELETE`** routes.

In the next chapter, we will start with the frontend with ReactJS. We are also going to do React Router setup and create **`Register`** and **`Login`** pages.

Points to remember

- We have created auth middleware using json web token. Here, we have verified it using the passed token and the JWT secret.
- We have protected various routes using the auth middleware. Now, routes can be accessed only after providing a valid token.
- We generated the token in Postman and used the token through Postman in protected routes.

Multiple Choice Questions

1. Authorization tokens start with the Keyword.
    a. Header
    b. Creator
    c. Bearer
    d. Berer
2. To protect routes we add ______ to it.
    a. Middle Layer
    b. Middleware
    c. Tailware
    d. Headware
3. In Postman, we add Token in which tab?
    a. Params
    b. Headers
    c. Authorization
    d. Test
4. In PUT route, we add both ____ and ____ in Postman.
    a. body, params
    b. headers, tests
    c. params, Authorization
    d. body, tests
5. In DELETE route, we add only ____ in Postman.
    a. body
    b. headers
    c. params
    d. tests

Answers

1. c
2. b
3. c
4. a
5. c

CHAPTER 6
Creating Frontend and React Router

Introduction

This chapter talks about the creation of frontend using ReactJS. We will also cover the setup for React Router version 6 in the project, which is used for navigation in React. We will also create the Header, Register, and Login components in the frontend.

Structure

In this chapter, we are going to discuss the following topics:

- Creating Frontend with ReactJS
- Basic Project setup
- React Router setup
- Creating Components and Pages

Creating Frontend with ReactJS

The browser that shows the HTML, CSS, and JavaScript site doesn't understand ReactJS. So, we installed React with the famous create-react-app from Facebook. Here, we are also adding the template to add the basic structure of Redux in our application.

Note that we have to run the following command inside the app:

```
npx create-react-app frontend --template redux
```

Figure 6.1: *Creating React app*

If everything is perfect, we will get the message, **`Happy hacking!`**. After that, we also opened the whole app in VS Code by giving the command **`code.`**

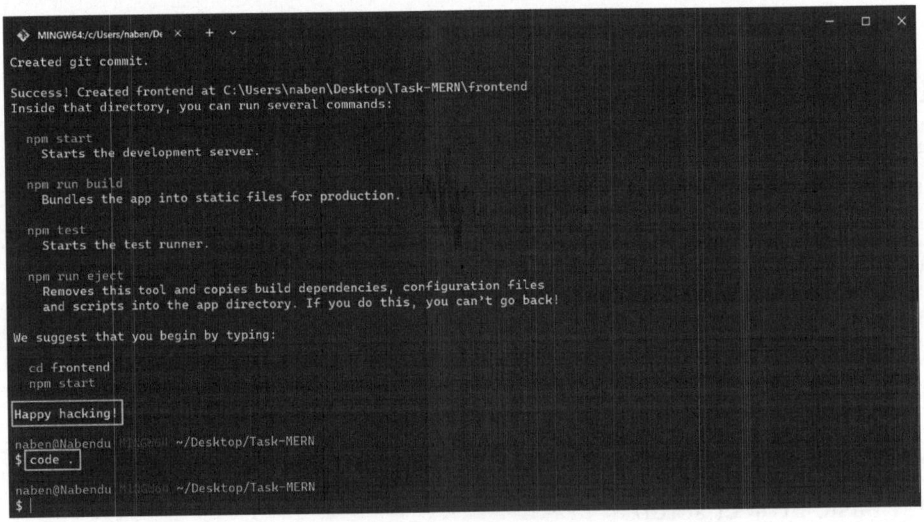

Figure 6.2: *Successful React app*

Now, as per the instructions, we will change to the new folder of frontend with the cd command. Also, run **`npm start`** to start our frontend app.

Figure 6.3: *Starting React app*

After some statements, we will get a message of frontend been started on http://localhost:3000/.

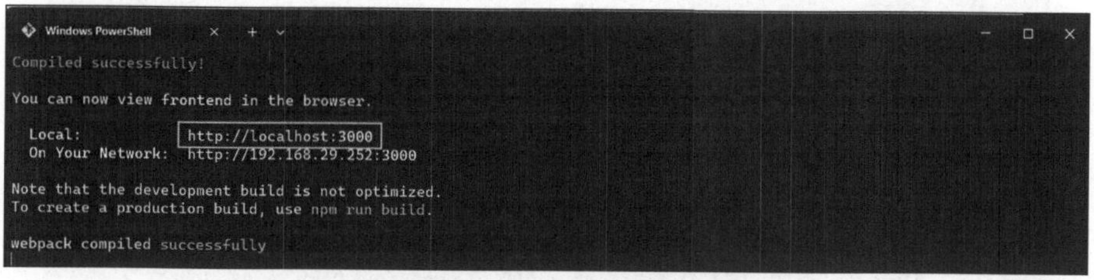

Figure 6.4: *React App started*

Open any browser and go to http://localhost:3000/ url and we will see the default content for a React app with Redux template.

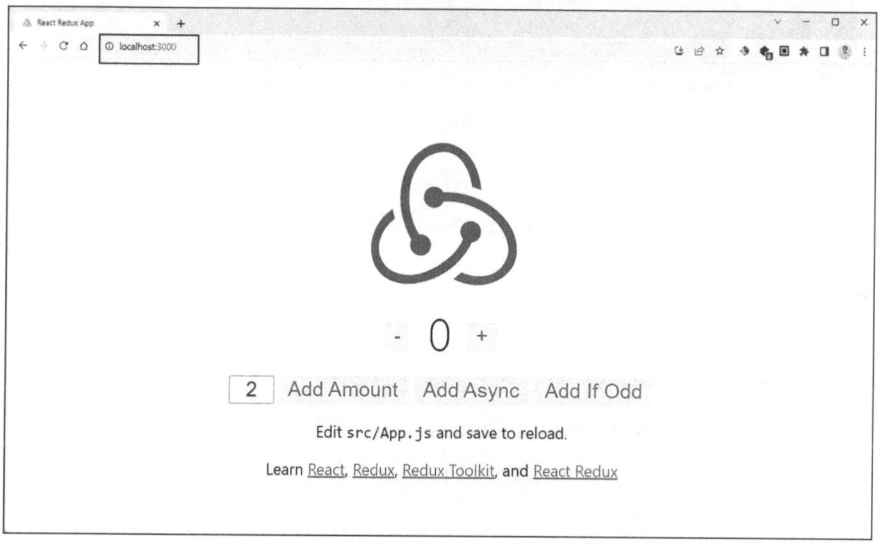

Figure 6.5: *React Redux app on browser*

Basic Project Setup

First, we will remove this basic boilerplate code to start with our project setup. So, in VS Code delete the following files in the screenshot.

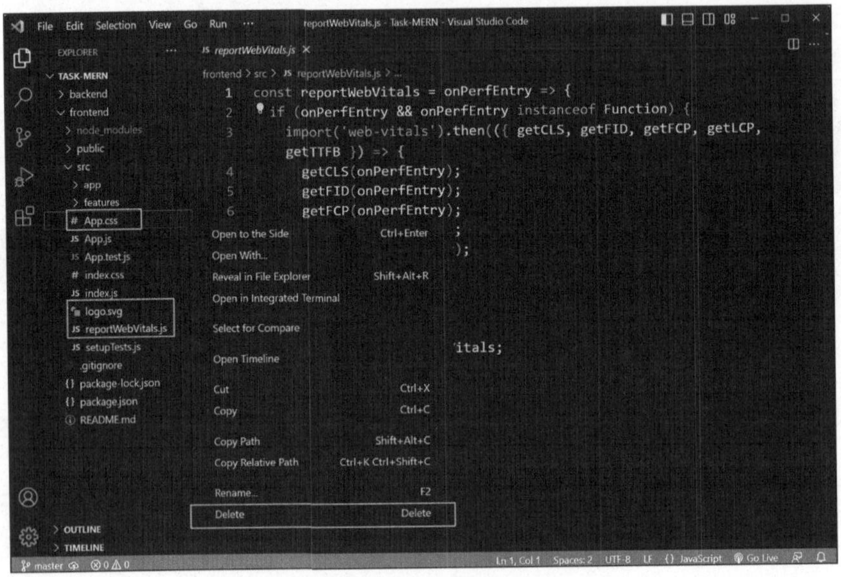

Figure 6.6: *Removing boilerplate files*

Next, we will remove some code referring to the preceding deleted items and update our **index.js** file as follows:

```
import React from ‘react’;
import { createRoot } from ‘react-dom/client’;
import { Provider } from ‘react-redux’;
import { store } from ‘./app/store’;
import App from ‘./App’;
import ‘./index.css’;

const container = document.getElementById(‘root’);
const root = createRoot(container);

root.render(
  <>
    <Provider store={store}>
      <App />
    </Provider>
```

```
  </>
);
```

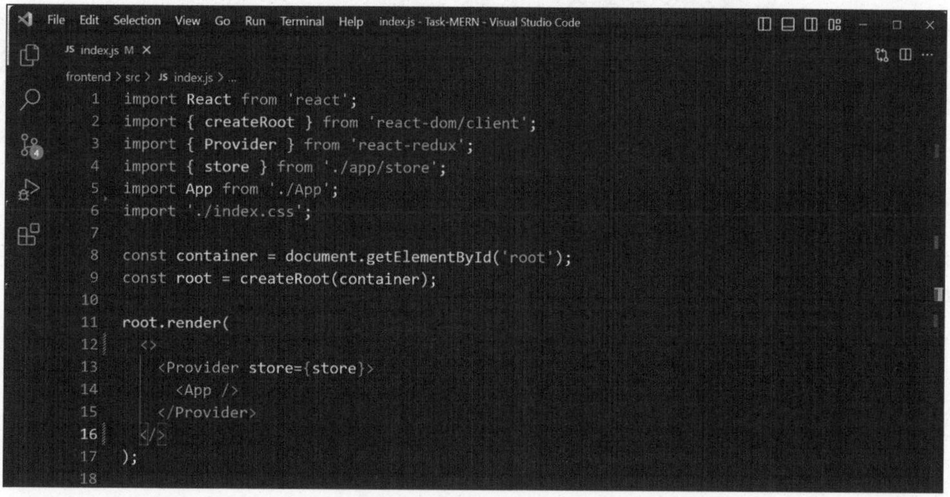

Figure 6.7: *Basic index.js file*

We will also delete all code from the **App.js** file and only keep the following code. It will update our app running in the browser on http://localhost:3000/ as shown in the screenshot.

```
function App() {
 return (
  <div>
      <h1>React App</h1>
  </div>
 );
}

export default App;
```

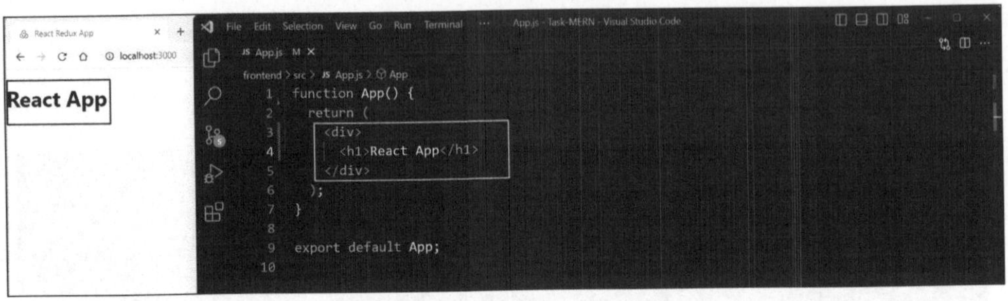

***Figure 6.8**: Basic App.js file*

We will also remove the earlier content from the **store.js** file inside the **app** folder and add the following content. This is the basic code for **`store`** of reducer in our app.

```
import { configureStore } from '@reduxjs/toolkit';

export const store = configureStore({
 reducer: {
 },
});
```

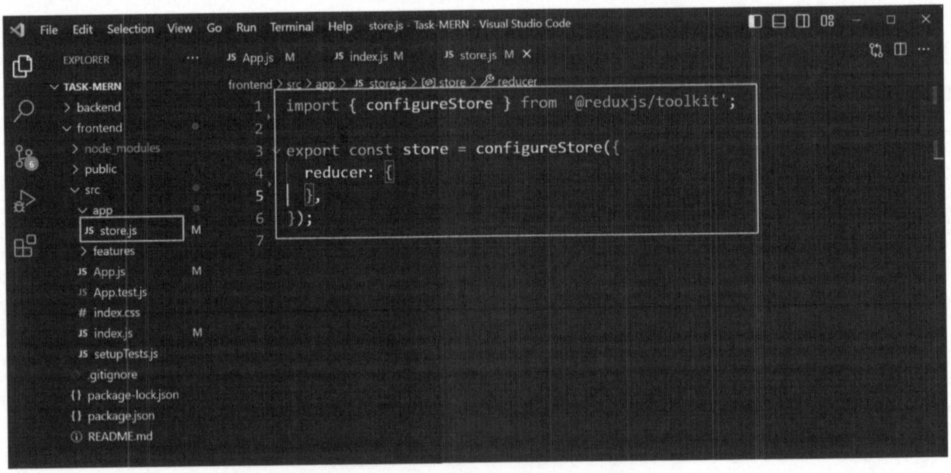

***Figure 6.9**: Basic store.js file*

Also, delete the whole content of the **index.css** file and add the following content to it. This will contain all of our styles for the project.

```
@import url('https://fonts.googleapis.com/css2?family=Karla:w-
ght@300;400;600;700&display=swap');

* {
  margin: 0;
  padding: 0;
  box-sizing: border-box;
}

body {
  font-family: ‹Karla›, sans-serif;
  height: 100vh;
}

a {
  text-decoration: none;
  color: #000;
}

p {
  line-height: 1.7;
}

ul {
  list-style: none;
}

li {
  line-height: 2.2;
}

h1,
h2,
```

```
h3 {
  font-weight: 600;
  margin-bottom: 10px;
}

.container {
  width: 100%;
  max-width: 960px;
  margin: 0 auto;
  padding: 0 20px;
  text-align: center;
}

.header {
  display: flex;
  justify-content: space-between;
  align-items: center;
  padding: 20px 0;
  border-bottom: 1px solid #e6e6e6;
  margin-bottom: 60px;
}

.header ul {
  display: flex;
  align-items: center;
  justify-content: space-between;
}

.header ul li {
  margin-left: 20px;
}

.header ul li a {
```

```
  display: flex;
  align-items: center;
}

.header ul li a:hover {
  color: #777;
}

.header ul li a svg {
  margin-right: 5px;
}

.heading {
  font-size: 2rem;
  font-weight: 700;
  margin-bottom: 50px;
  padding: 0 20px;
}

.heading p {
  color: #828282;
}

.goals {
  display: grid;
  grid-template-columns: repeat(2, 1fr);
  gap: 10px;
}

.goal {
  background-color: #f4f4f4;
  margin: 10px 0;
  padding: 20px 0 10px;
```

```
  position: relative;
}

.goal .close {
  position: absolute;
  top: 10px;
  right: 15px;
  cursor: pointer;
  border: none;
  background: none;
}

.form,
.content {
  width: 70%;
  margin: 0 auto;
}

.form-group {
  margin-bottom: 10px;
}

.form-group input,
.form-group textarea,
.form-group select {
  width: 100%;
  padding: 10px;
  border: 1px solid #e6e6e6;
  border-radius: 5px;
  margin-bottom: 10px;
  font-family: inherit;
}
```

```
.form-group label {
  text-align: left;
  display: block;
  margin: 0 0 5px 3px;
}

.btn {
  padding: 10px 20px;
  border: 1px solid #000;
  border-radius: 5px;
  background: #000;
  color: #fff;
  font-size: 16px;
  font-weight: 700;
  cursor: pointer;
  text-align: center;
  appearance: button;
  display: flex;
  align-items: center;
  justify-content: center;
}

.btn svg {
  margin-right: 8px;
}

.btn-reverse {
  background: #fff;
  color: #000;
}

.btn-block {
  width: 100%;
```

```
  margin-bottom: 20px;
}

.btn:hover {
  transform: scale(0.98);
}

.loadingSpinnerContainer {
  position: fixed;
  top: 0;
  right: 0;
  bottom: 0;
  left: 0;
  background-color: rgba(0, 0, 0, 0.5);
  z-index: 5000;
  display: flex;
  justify-content: center;
  align-items: center;
}

.loadingSpinner {
  width: 64px;
  height: 64px;
  border: 8px solid;
  border-color: #000 transparent #555 transparent;
  border-radius: 50%;
  animation: spin 1.2s linear infinite;
}

@keyframes spin {
  0% {
    transform: rotate(0deg);
  }
```

```
  100% {
    transform: rotate(360deg);
  }
}

@media (max-width: 600px) {
  .form {
    width: 90%;
  }

  .heading h1 {
    font-size: 2rem;
  }

  .heading p {
    font-size: 1.5rem;
  }
}
```

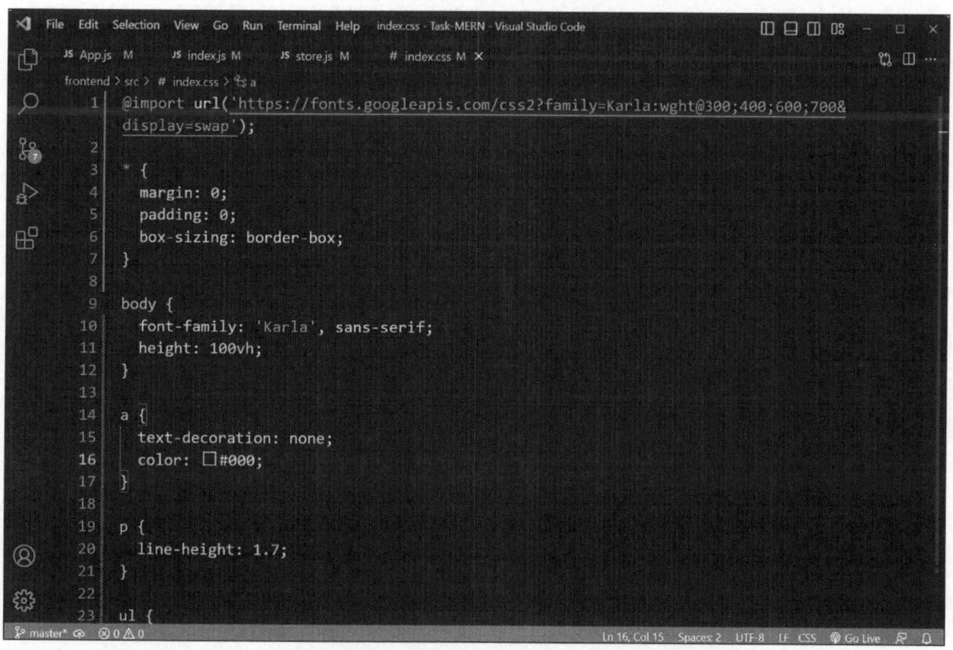

Figure 6.10: *Styles in index.css file*

We will also delete the counter folder, which contains most of our default Redux code.

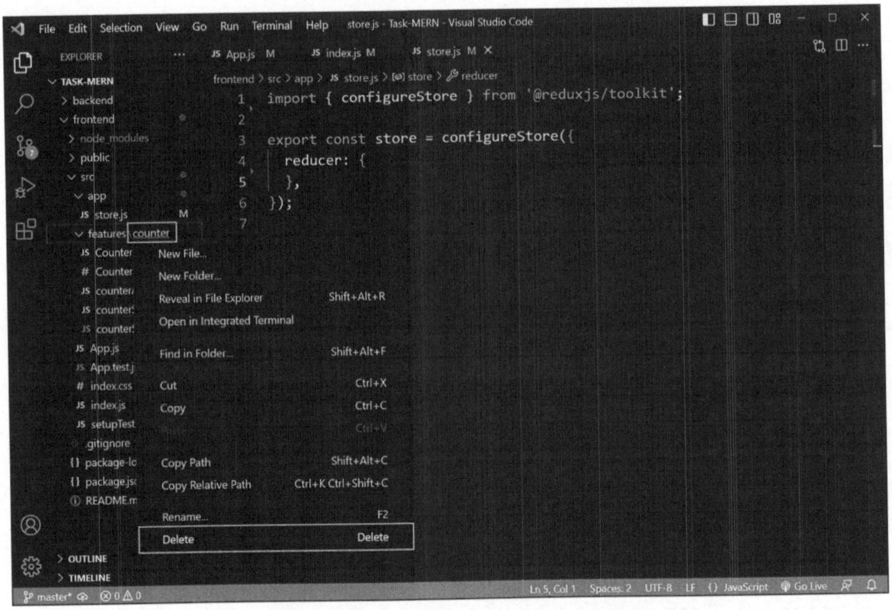

***Figure 6.11**: Removing counter folder*

Now, we will create some of the components which we will use in our project. So, first create a **components** folder inside **src** and add a **Dashboard.js** file in it. Add the following basic content to it:

```
import React from ‘react’



const Dashboard = () => {
  return (
    <div>Dashboard</div>
  )
}



export default Dashboard
```

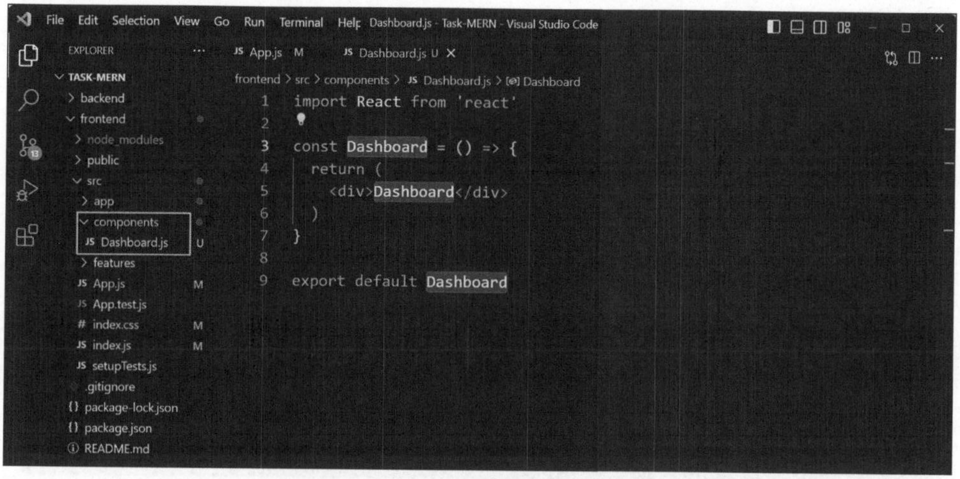

Figure 6.12: *Creating Dashboard.js file*

Next, create a **Login.js** file inside the **components** folder and add the basic code to it.

```
import React from ‘react’



const Login = () => {
 return (
  <div>Login</div>
 )
}



export default Login
```

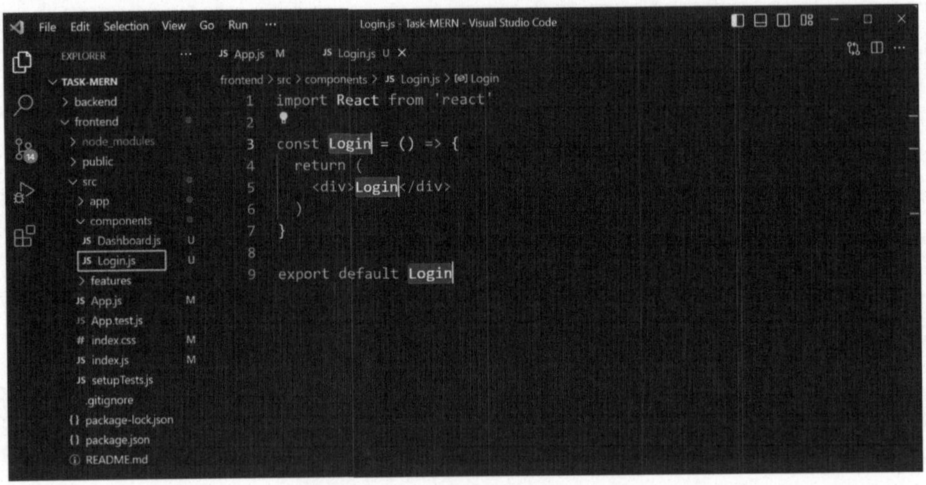

Figure 6.13: *Creating Login.js file*

Lastly, create a **Register.js** file inside the **components** folder and add the basic code to it.

```
import React from 'react'

const Register = () => {
  return (
    <div>Register</div>
  )
}

export default Register
```

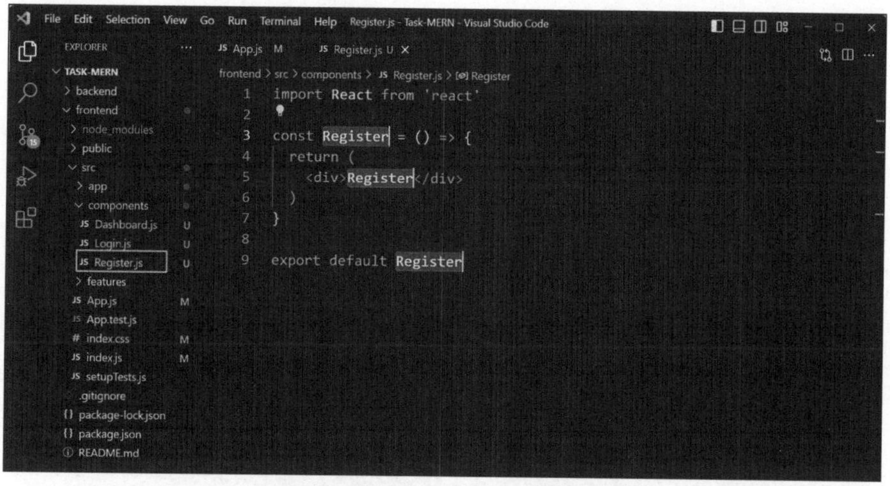

Figure 6.14: *Creating Register.js file*

React Router Setup

Now, we will set up a react router in our project. React router is an external package that needs to be installed in the project, because react doesn't come in-built with routing functionalities.

So, in the frontend folder in the terminal install react router using the following command:

```
npm i react-router-dom
```

Also, we will update our App.js file as follows. Here, we are first importing BrowserRouter, Routes and Route from **react-router-com**. After that, we are using it inside the return statement as shown here:

```
import { BrowserRouter as Router, Routes, Route } from 'react-router-dom'

function App() {
  return (
    <Router>
      <div className=›container››
        <Routes>
```

```
          </Routes>
        </div>
      </Router>
  );
}

export default App;
```

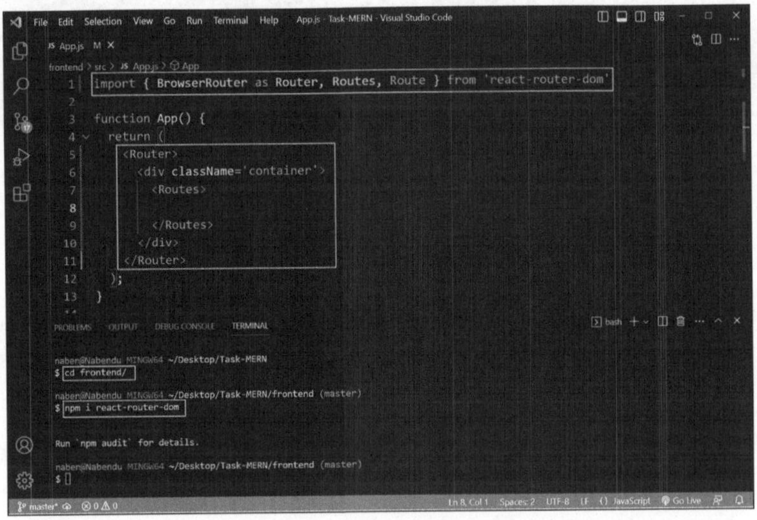

Figure 6.15: *Adding react router*

Next, we will import the three components of **Dashboard**, **Login**, and **Register** in **App.js**. After that, inside the **<Routes>**, we will add the three components with different paths.

```
import Dashboard from './components/Dashboard';
import Login from './components/Login';
import Register from './components/Register';
...
...
<Route path='/' element={<Dashboard />} />
<Route path='/login' element={<Login />} />
<Route path='/register' element={<Register />} />
```

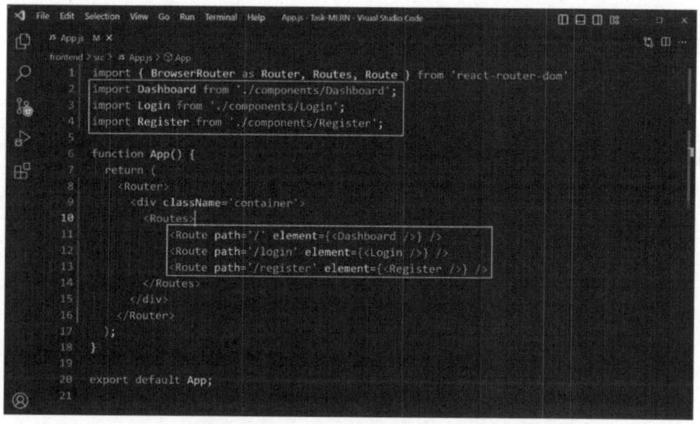

Figure 6.16: *Basic routes*

Now, in http://localhost:3000/ we will see our basic Dashboard component.

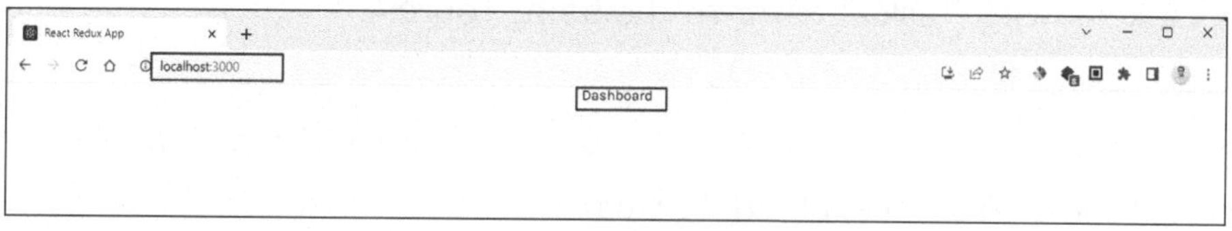

Figure 6.17: *Dashboard route*

In http://localhost:3000/login , we will see our Login component code.

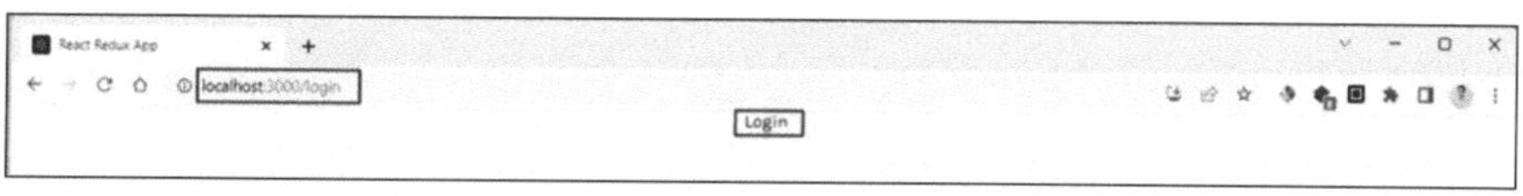

Figure 6.18: *Login route*

And in http://localhost:3000/register we will see our Register component code.

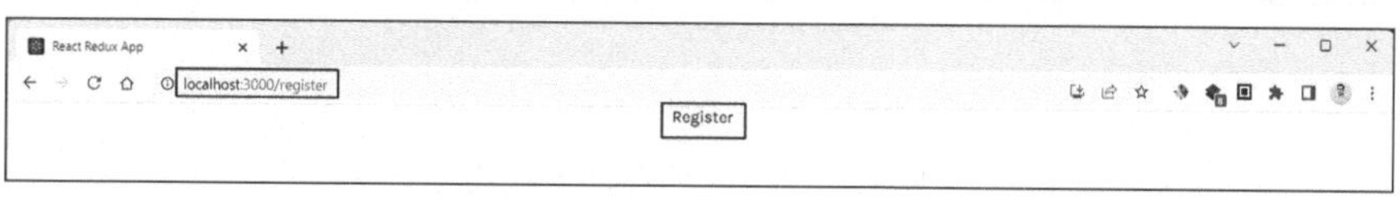

Figure 6.19: *Register route*

Creating Components and Pages

Now, we will create some of the components in our project. First, we will create the common component of the Header, which will be shown on all pages. Following that, we will create the pages for Register and Login.

Header Component

We will first create the common Header component. So, create a file called **Header.js** inside the **components** folder. Here, we have first opened the integrated terminal and installed the icon package of react-icons, using the following command.

```
npm i react-icons
```

Next, we have created the basic structure of the Header component. Here, first, we are importing some icons from react-icons. And we are also importing Link from react-router-dom. Inside the return statement, we have the basic header with a Link showing Task Creator to the home route.

```
import { FaSignInAlt, FaSignOutAlt, FaUser } from 'react-icons/fa'
import { Link } from 'react-router-dom'

const Header = () => {
  return (
    <header className=›header›>
        <div className=»logo»>
            <Link to=›/››Task Creator</Link>
        </div>
    </header>
  )
}

export default Header
```

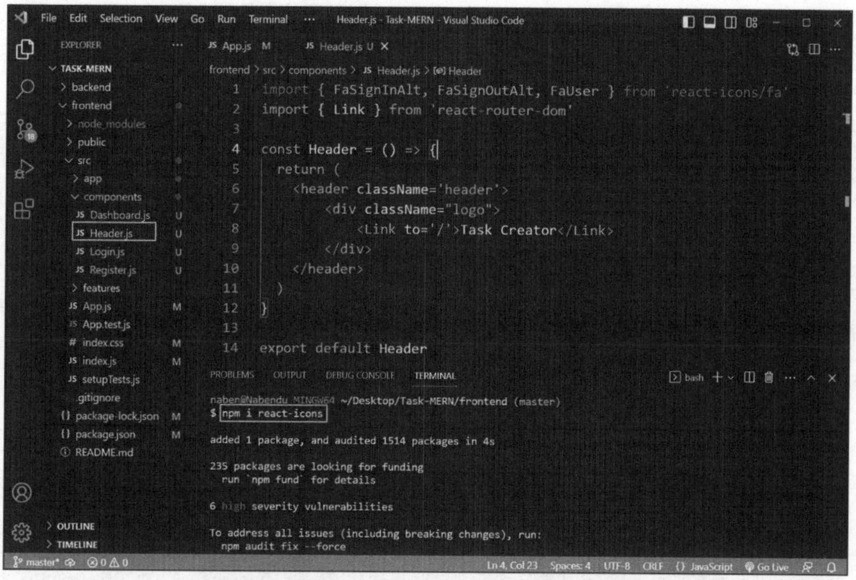

***Figure 6.20**: Creating header component*

Next, in the **Header.js** file, we will also add the other Links for **/login** and **/register** route, inside an ul tag. Here, we are also using the icons imported earlier. Note that on clicking these links, we will be taken to the respective route, showing that component.

```
<ul>
    <li>
        <Link to=›/login››
            <FaSignInAlt /> Login
        </Link>
    </li>
    <li>
        <Link to=›/register››
            <FaUser /> Register
        </Link>
    </li>
</ul>
```

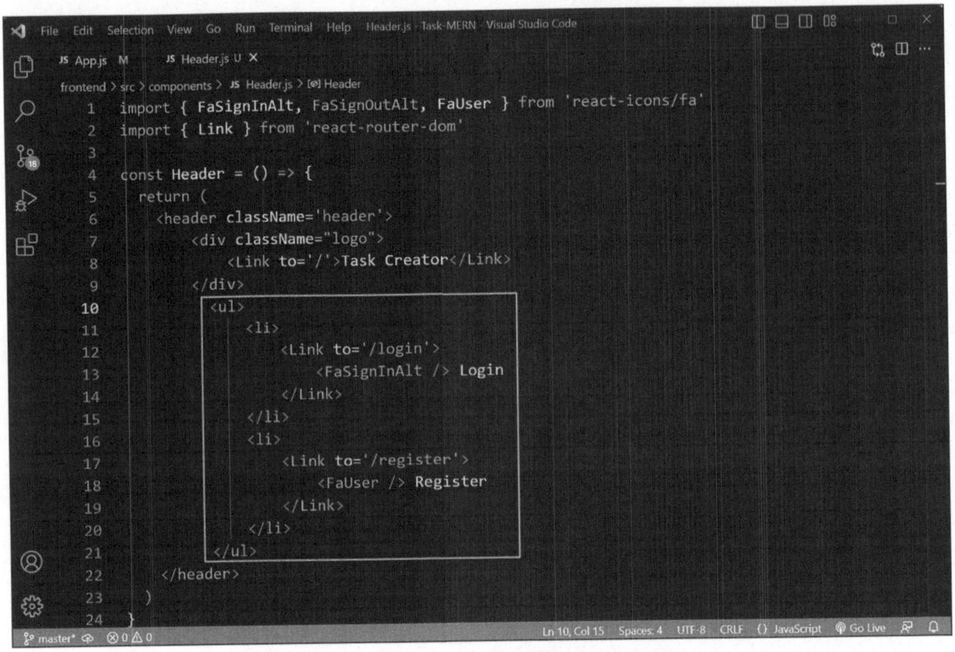

***Figure 6.21**: Adding routes in header component*

We will finally add the Header component inside our **App.js** file. But notice here, we are adding it outside the <**Routes**>. It means that it will be shown on all pages.

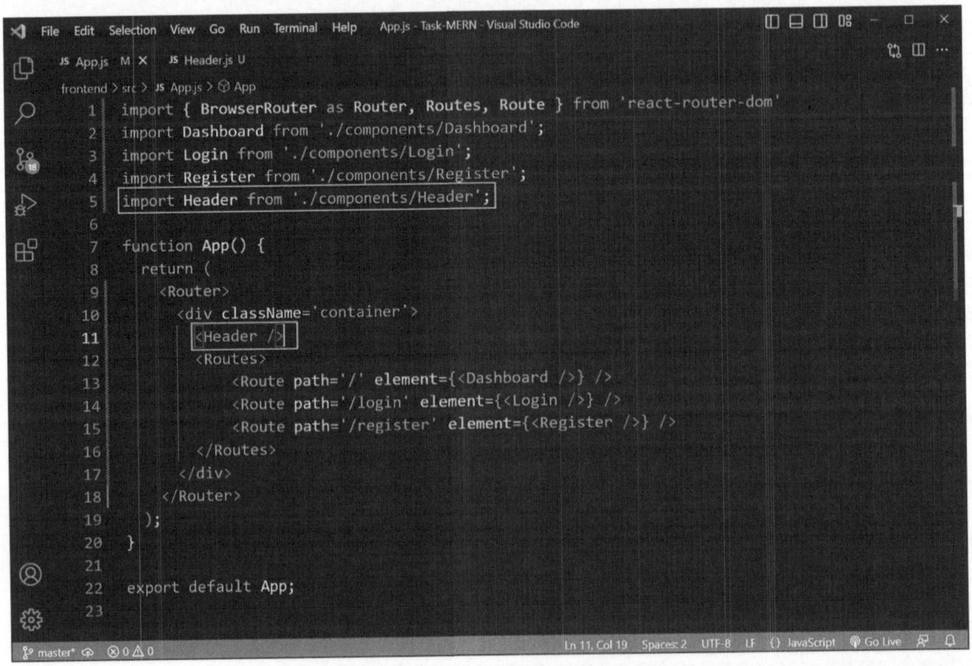

***Figure 6.22**: Adding header component in App.js*

Now, go to http://localhost:3000/ and we will see a nice-looking header with logo, and two icons for Login and Register.

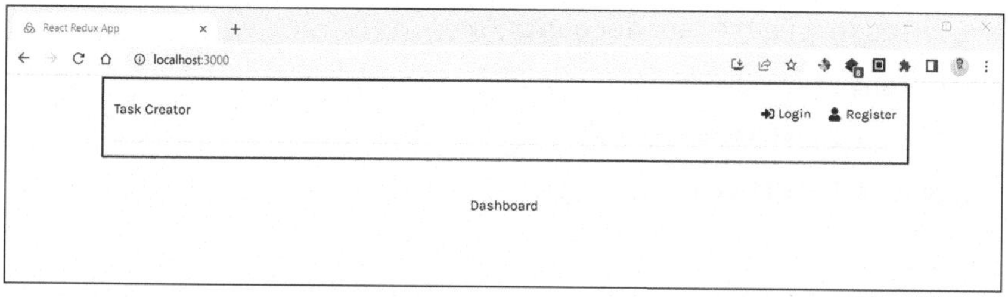

***Figure 6.23**: Header component in browser*

Register Page

Now, we will create our Register page. We can go to this page by clicking the Register logo in the dashboard.

First, replace the basic code with the following code in **Register.js** file. Here, we are first importing **`useState`** and an icon. Next, we are first creating a state variable of formData which will be equal to an object containing **`name`**, **`email`**, **`password`** and **`password2`**.

We are also destructuring the **`formData`**. Inside the return statement, we have a section showing a heading and a paragraph.

Inside the second section, we have a form that we will complete next.

```
import { useState } from "react"
import { FaUser } from 'react-icons/fa'

const Register = () => {
  const [formData, setFormData] = useState({ name: ‹›, email: ‹›,
password: ‹›, password2: ‹› })
  const { name, email, password, password2 } = formData

  const onChange = () => {}

  return (
    <>
```

```
      <section className=›heading››
        <h1><FaUser /> Register</h1>
        <p>Please create an account</p>
      </section>
      <section className=›form››
        <form onSubmit={onSubmit}>
        </form>
      </section>
    </>
  )
}

export default Register
```

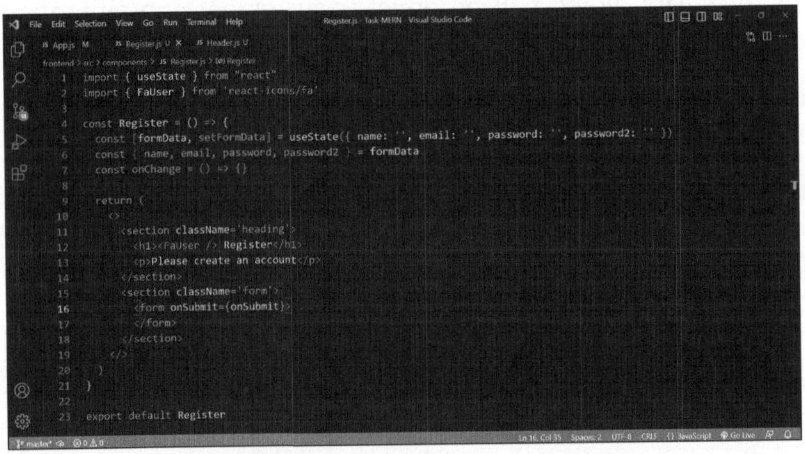

***Figure 6.24**: Creating register component*

Inside the form in **Register.js** file, we will have three input statements for the **`name`**, **`email`**, and **`password`**. These inputs are like what we have in React for input. Also, notice that we have a name tag in all inputs.

```
    <div className=›form-group››
      <input type=›text› className=›form-control› id=›name›
name=›name› value={name} placeholder=›Enter your name› onChange={onChange}
```

```
        />
      </div>
      <div className=›form-group››
        <input type=›email› className=›form-control› id=›email› name=›
email› value={email} placeholder=›Enter your email› onChange={onChange}
        />
      </div>
      <div className=›form-group››
        <input type=›password› className=›form-control› id=›password›
name=›password› value={password} placeholder=›Enter password›
onChange={onChange}
        />
      </div>
```

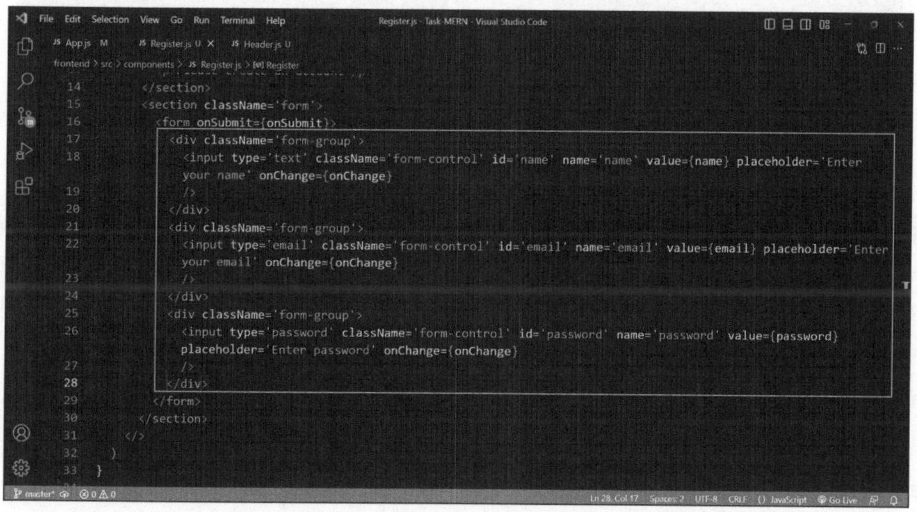

Figure 6.25: *Adding fields in register component*

We will also add the input for **password2**, which is our confirm password field. Also, we added our `Submit` button in **Register.js** file.

```
      <div className=›form-group››
        <input type=›password› className=›form-control› id=›password2›
name=›password2› value={password2} placeholder=›Confirm password›
onChange={onChange}
```

```
    />
  </div>
  <div className=›form-group››
    <button type=›submit› className=›btn btn-block››Submit</button>
  </div>
```

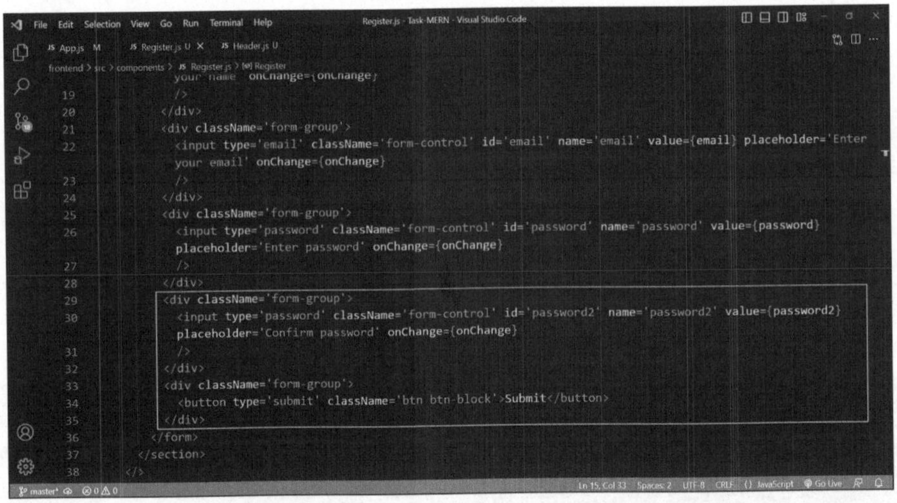

Figure 6.26: *Adding more fields in register component*

Next, we will complete our **onChange** function in the **Register.js** file. Here, we are using **e.target.name** to get all input dynamically. Or else, we would have needed to create different **onChanges** for every input field. The **onSubmit** is now empty, and logic will be added in later chapters.

```
const onChange = e => {
  setFormData(prevState => ({
    ...prevState,
    [e.target.name]: e.target.value
  }))
}

const onSubmit = e => {
  e.preventDefault()
}
```

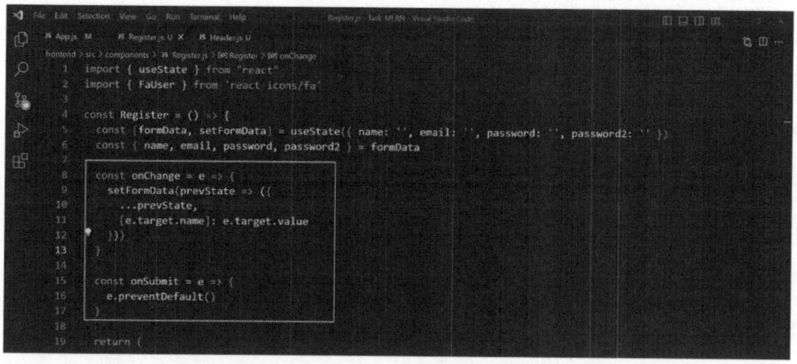

***Figure 6.27**: Adding functions in register component*

On clicking on the register logo, we will be taken to http://localhost:3000/register. And the nice-looking **`Register`** component will be shown.

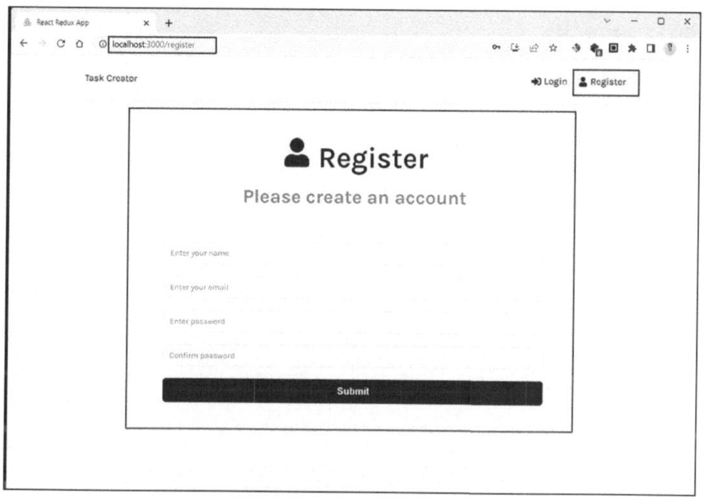

***Figure 6.28**: Register page in browser*

Login Page

Now, we will create the Login page, which is quite similar to the Register page created in the earlier section. First, create a file **Login.js** in the **components** folder and add the following content to it.

Here, we again have the **`formData`**, but with fewer fields of email and password. The onChange and onSubmit are also similar to the Register page.

```
import { FaSignInAlt } from 'react-icons/fa'
import { useState } from "react"
```

```
const Login = () => {
  const [formData, setFormData] = useState({ email: ‹›, password: ‹› })
  const { email, password } = formData
  const onChange = e => {
    setFormData(prevState => ({
      ...prevState,
      [e.target.name]: e.target.value
    }))
  }

  const onSubmit = e => {
    e.preventDefault()
  }

  return (
    <div>Login</div>
  )
}

export default Login
```

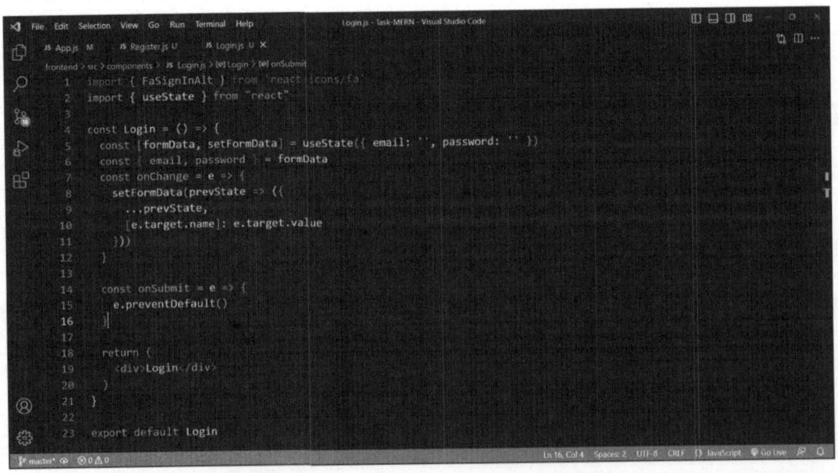

Figure 6.29: *Creating login component*

Now, inside the return statement, we will have a section with a header and another with a form. The form section will only contain an email, password, and button.

```
<>
  <section className=›heading›>
    <h1><FaSignInAlt /> Login</h1>
    <p>Login and start creating tasks</p>
  </section>
  <section className=›form›>
    <form onSubmit={onSubmit}>
      <div className=›form-group›>
        <input type=›email› className=›form-control› id=›email›
name=›email› value={email} placeholder=›Enter your email›
onChange={onChange}
        />
      </div>
      <div className=›form-group›>
        <input type=›password› className=›form-control› id=›password›
name=›password› value={password} placeholder=›Enter password›
onChange={onChange}
        />
      </div>
      <div className=›form-group›>
        <button type=›submit› className=›btn btn-block›>Submit</button>
      </div>
    </form>
  </section>
</>
```

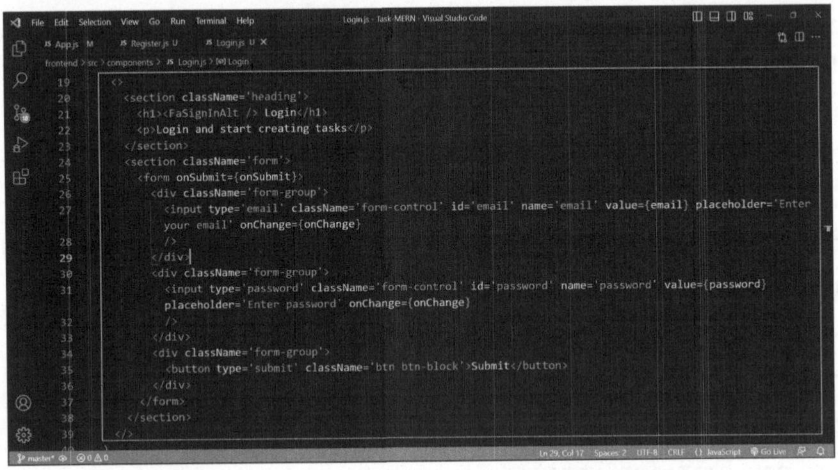

***Figure 6.30**: Adding fields in Login Component*

On clicking o the **`Login`** logo, we will be taken to http://localhost:3000/login. And the nice-looking login component will be shown.

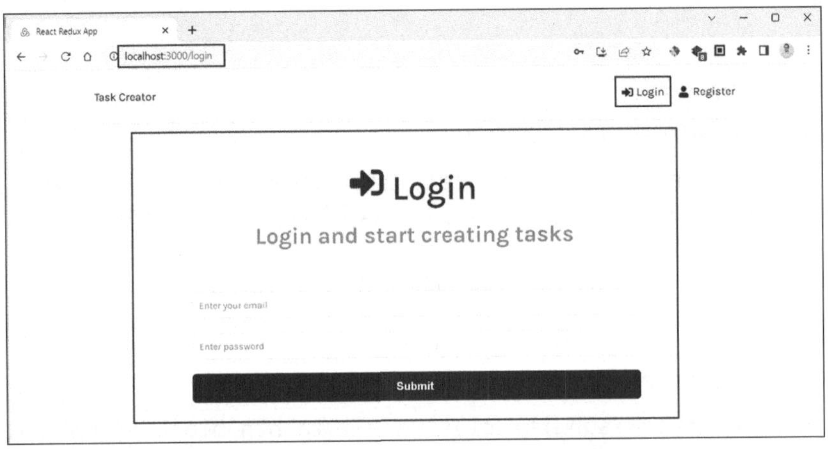

***Figure 6.31**: Login Component in Browser*

Conclusion

In this chapter, we have learned about creating frontends with ReactJS. Here, we had first created a frontend app with the **`create-react-app`** command. Next, we deleted some boiler plate code to do the basic setup in the app.

After that, we did the React router setup in our project. This library is required for routing in our React app. Lastly, we have created the components of Header, Register, and Login in this chapter.

In the next chapter, we will start with the redux setup using slice. Then we are going to complete the User registration along with the Register form.

Points to remember

- We have created a react app with a redux template using the `create-react-app` command.
- Removing unnecessary files when starting with React app, such as **lovo.svg** and **reportWebVitals.js**
- Setting up the react router in the project and showing different components on different paths.
- Creating components using react icons and different form elements of input and button.

Chapter 7
Redux Setup with Slice

Introduction

This chapter covers the implementation of Redux in the project. We will use the latest Toolkit method in Redux to implement a global state in our project. In this chapter, we are also going to set up a reducer for Registration form. Finally, we are also going to test the user registration workflow.

Structure

In this chapter, we are going to discuss the following topics:

- Redux setup with a toolkit
- Auth service and slice
- Registration form hook up
- Testing user registration

Redux setup with a toolkit

To start with Redux with a toolkit, we need to have a slice. Now, traditionally, redux has a separate action creator and reducer. But with the latest toolkit, they have been merged to form the slice. Now, we have the reducer and action creator logic both in slice.

So, create a folder **auth** inside the **features** folder. Inside it, create an **authSlice.js** file and add the following code in it.

Here, we are first importing **createSlice** and **createAsyncThunk** from the redux toolkit. The **createSlice** will be used to create the slice used for reducer and action. And the **createAsyncThunk** will be used for asynchronous actions, which is an API call in our case later on.

After that, we added a variable called **localuser**, which uses local storage to get a user variable. We are going to set this variable later.

Next, we have the **initialState** of our slice, which is an object. Here, we have the **user** key first, which is equal to the **localuser** initially or null if **localuser is** not present. We also have values for **isError**, **isSuccess**, and **isLoading,** which are set as false. These will be used when we do the API call. Lastly, we have a **message** as an empty string.

Next, we are exporting the **authSlice**, which is created using the **createSlice** method. We will complete this method next.

```
import { createSlice, createAsyncThunk } from '@reduxjs/toolkit'

const localuser = JSON.parse(localStorage.getItem('user'))

const initialState = {
    user: localuser ? localuser : null,
    isError: false,
    isSuccess: false,
    isLoading: false,
    message: ''
}

export const authSlice = createSlice({

})
```

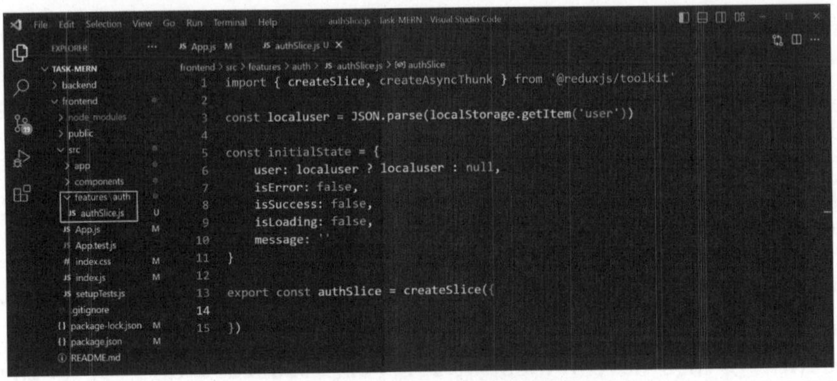

Figure 7.1: *Creating authSlice.js file*

Now, we will write code inside the **`createSlice`** method in the **authSlice.js** file. Here, we are first giving the name of the slice as **`auth`**. Then we are taking the initialState. After that, we have a reducers value, which has a reset. This reset can be used to make the state back to the initial state.

Next, we have an **`extraReducers`** value, which we are going to complete soon. In the end, we are exporting the reset action and also the reducer.

```
export const authSlice = createSlice({
    name: ‹auth›,
    initialState,
    reducers: {
      reset: state => {
        state.isLoading = false
        state.isSuccess = false
        state.isError = false
        state.message = ‹›
      },
    },
    extraReducers: () => {}
})

export const { reset } = authSlice.actions
export default authSlice.reducer
```

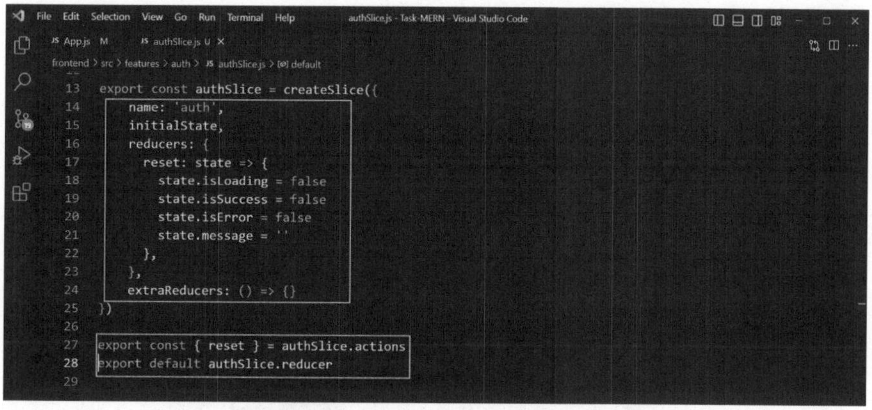

Figure 7.2: *Adding reducers in the authSlice.js file*

Now, we will import the reducer in the **store.js** file. Because of the store in a Redux app, we are able to use the global state in different components.

```
import authReducer from '../features/auth/authSlice'

export const store = configureStore({
  reducer: {
    auth: authReducer
  }
});
```

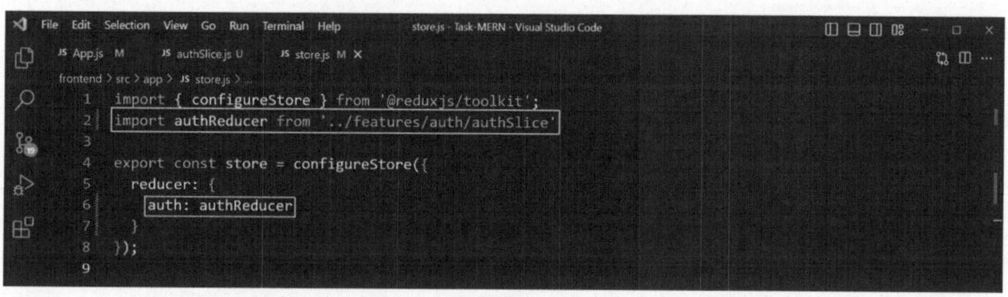

Figure 7.3: *Adding authReducer in store.js file*

Now, we will be using the famous Chrome/Firefox extension of Redux Devtools in our project. Just go to the link and install it in the Chrome/Firefox browser. Since we have already added it, we are getting the `Remove from Chrome` button. Or else we will get `Add to Chrome` button if the extension is not installed.

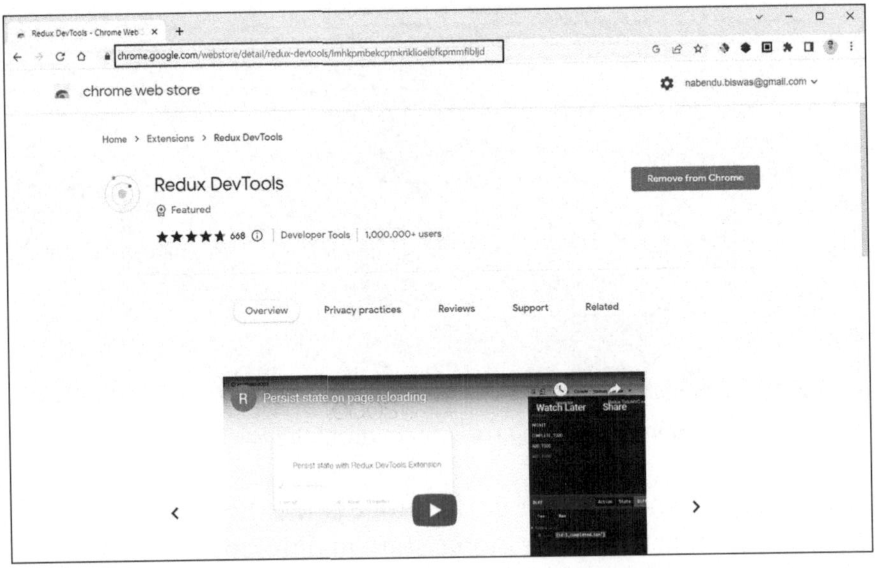

Figure 7.4: *Adding Redux Devtools in Browser*

In the Redux toolkit, we don't need to do any special configurations for this extension. Earlier in redux projects, we needed to install packages and add code for this extension to work. But the redux toolkit comes in-built with it, and no special configuration is required.

So, open the developer tool, and we will see a **Redux** tab. Here, we will see all of our states for auth. This extension is used in almost all production projects since the Redux states can sometimes be difficult to track.

Figure 7.5: *Redux Devtools in Browser*

Auth service and slice

We will create an auth service in this part and also will complete the auth slice started in the previous part. But first, we will install the package of **`axios`** and **`react-toastify`** in our front end.

The package of **`axios`** will be used to do API calls and **`react-toastify`** will be used to show toast messages in case of error.

So, we will add both by opening the integrated terminal and using the following **`npm`** command.

```
npm i axios react-toastify
```

Figure 7.6: *Adding axios and toastify*

Next, we will create the auth service. This service will be used in doing the API call and also saving the result in local storage. So, create a file **authService.js** inside the **auth** folder.

Here, we are first importing `axios` and also creating a variable called **`API_URL`** which is set to **/api/users/**. Next, we have created a register function which is taking the **`userData`**. Inside the function, we are doing a POST call to the **`API_URL`** with the **`userData`**.

The result of the api call, which we get in **`response.data`**, is set in the local storage variable user using **`localStorage.setItem()`** function. We are also returning the response from the function.

Lastly, we are exporting the `register` function.

```
import axios from 'axios'
const API_URL = '/api/users/'
```

```
const register = async (userData) => {
  const response = await axios.post(API_URL, userData)
  if (response.data) {
    localStorage.setItem(‘user’, JSON.stringify(response.data))
  }
  return response.data
}

const authService = { register }

export default authService
```

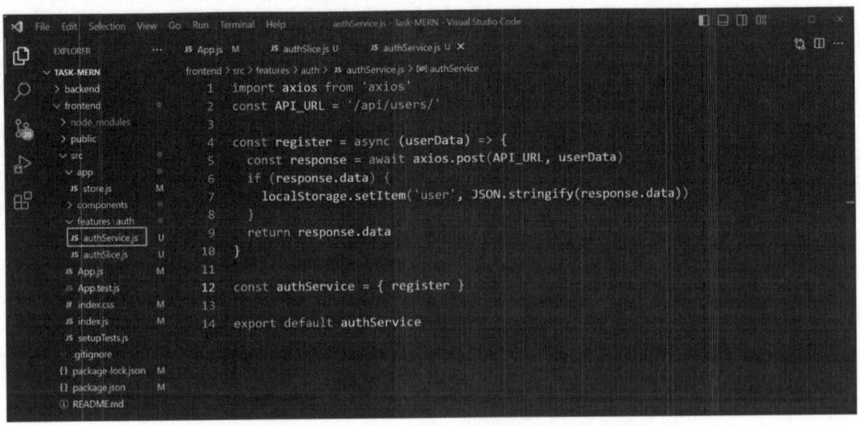

***Figure** 7.7: Creating authService.js file*

Back in the **authSlice.js** file, we will first import the authService. After that, we export a variable register. Here, we are using the **`createAsyncThunk`** function. Again Redux toolkit comes built with a redux thunk, which is a must to do api calls through redux. In the earlier redux versions without a toolkit, we have to manually install the package and do the installation.

Here, the first parameter is the auth/register, which means from the auth folder, take the register function. Next, the parameter is an async arrow function which takes the user and **`thunkAPI`** as a parameter.

Inside the function, we have a try...catch block. From the **`try`** block, we are calling the **`register`** function from the **authService.js** file with the user and returning it.

In the catch part, we are simply catching different kinds of errors and returning them.

```
import authService from './authService'
...
...
export const register = createAsyncThunk(
    'auth/register',
    async (user, thunkAPI) => {
        try {
            return await authService.register(user)
        } catch (error) {
            const message = (error.response && error.response.data &&
error.response.data.message) ||
                error.message ||
                error.toString()
            return thunkAPI.rejectWithValue(message)
        }
    }
)
```

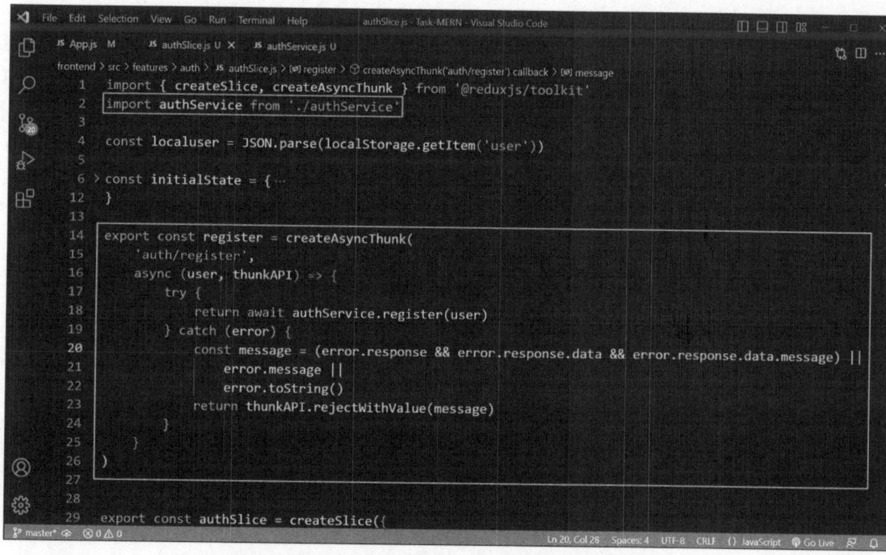

Figure 7.8: *Adding thunk in authSlice.js file*

The api endpoint from the file **authService.js** should go to the backend endpoint of http://localhost:8000 and not to the frontend endpoint of http://localhost:3000 . So, we need to add a proxy variable in the **package.json** file in the **frontend** folder.

```
"proxy": "http://localhost:8000",
```

So, now when we call **`axios.post()`** inside the `register` function in the **authService.js** file, we will go to http://localhost:8000/api/users

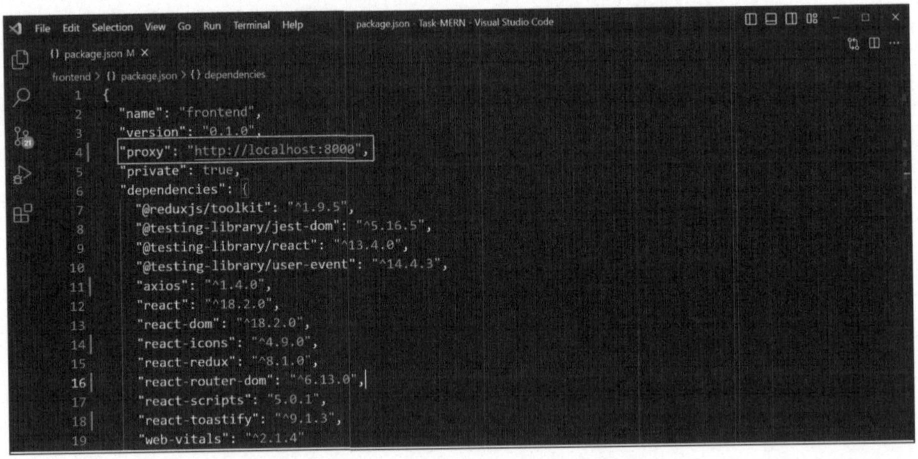

Figure 7.9: *Adding proxy in the package.json file*

Inside our **authSlice.js** file in the **`createSlice`** function, we will add **`extraReducers`**. We generally put the reducer action, which changes the state in these **`extraReducers`**. In the earlier redux versions, we used to do these through the switch statement cases. You can read details for the same in the official redux documentation here.

In our code, we have three cases for pending, fulfilled and rejected cases. Since we are doing an API call to http://localhost:8000/api/users through our register function, we have three states in it. When the API call starts, we have a pending state since the API calls generally take 1–2 seconds. We are making the isLoading state true and will also show a spinner in this state in the front end.

The next state is the fulfilled case, which will happen if our API call is successful. Here, we are making the **`isLoading`** as false and **`isSuccess`** as true and storing the payload which we receive back in the user state.

If, for some reason, the API call is not successful, we have a rejected case. Here, we are making the **`isLoading`** as false and **`isError`** as true. We are also storing the error in the message state, which we will receive in the payload–also making the user state variable null.

```
extraReducers: builder => {
    builder
        .addCase(register.pending, (state) => {
            state.isLoading = true
        })
        .addCase(register.fulfilled, (state, action) => {
            state.isLoading = false
            state.isSuccess = true
            state.user = action.payload
        })
        .addCase(register.rejected, (state, action) => {
            state.isLoading = false
            state.isError = true
            state.message = action.payload
            state.user = null
        })
}
```

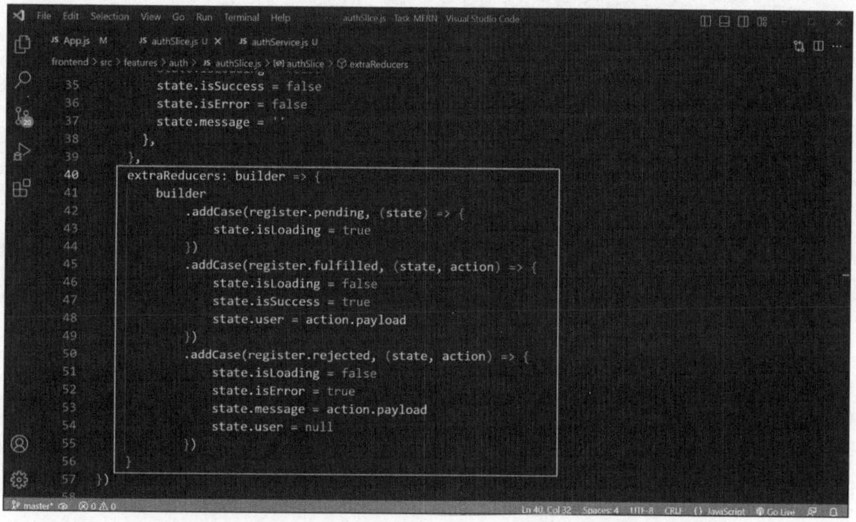

Figure 7.10: *Adding extraReducers in the authSlice.js file*

Registration form hook up

We will now use the slice in our Register component to register a new user. So, head over to the **Register.js** file and add the following imports in it.

Here, we are first importing the custom hooks of **`useSelector`** and **`useDispatch`** from **`react-redux`**. These hooks are used to get the global state of redux and also to dispatch the action creator inside a slice.

After that, we import **`useNavigate`** from **`react-router-dom`**. This custom hook is used to navigate easily to different routes. Next, we are importing **`toast`** from **`react-toastify`**, which will be used to show the toast message.

Lastly, we are importing the **`register`** and **`reset`** from **`authSlice`**, which will be used to call the register and reset action creators.

```
import { useSelector, useDispatch } from 'react-redux'
import { useNavigate } from 'react-router-dom'
import { toast } from 'react-toastify'
import { register, reset } from '../features/auth/authSlice'
```

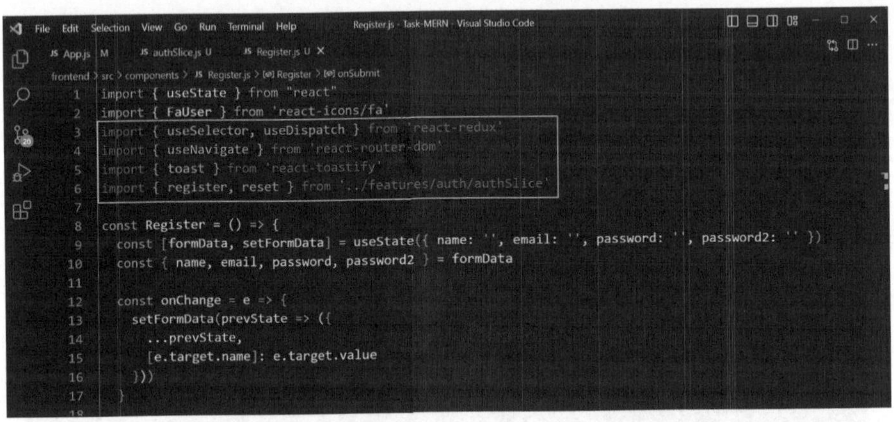

Figure 7.11: *Adding imports in the Register.js file*

Now, to show the **`toast`** message using **`react-toastify`**, we need to do one more configuration. Here, we will first import **`ToastContainer`** from **`react-toastify`**. And will also import a corresponding css file.

We now need to add the **ToastContainer** component after the Routing is done, which is after the <Router> tag.

```
import { ToastContainer } from 'react-toastify'
import 'react-toastify/dist/ReactToastify.css'
...
<ToastContainer />
```

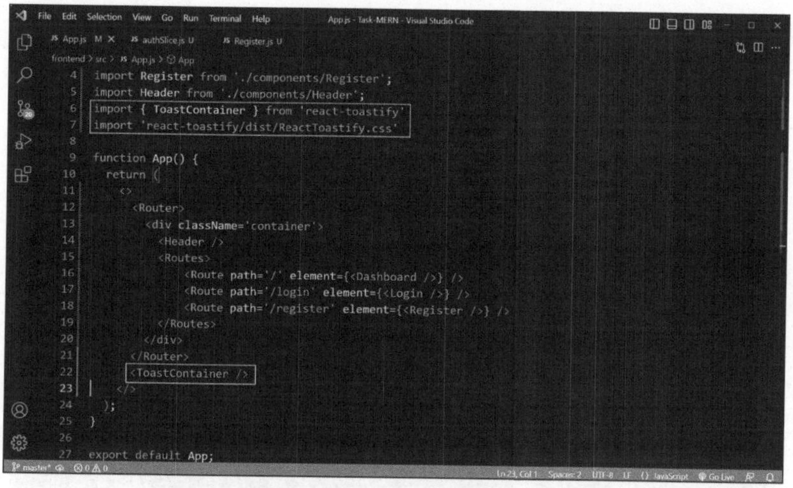

***Figure 7.12**: Configuring toastify in App.js file*

Back in the **Register.js** file, we will create variables for **navigate** and **dispatch** using the **useNavigate** and **useDispatch** hooks.

Next, we will get the global state of the **user**, **isLoading**, **isError**, **isSuccess**, **message** using the **useSelector** hook. Lastly, inside the **onSubmit()** function, we are first checking if the password and the confirm password are different. And showing a toast message of **Passwords are different** in that case.

Else we are taking the name, email and password entered by the user and putting it in a userData variable and, after that dispatching it with the dispatch to the register function in the **authSlice.js** file.

```
const navigate = useNavigate()
const dispatch = useDispatch()

const { user, isLoading, isError, isSuccess, message } = useSelec-
```

```
tor(state => state.auth)
...
...
const onSubmit = e => {
    e.preventDefault()
    if (password !== password2) {
        toast.error('Passwords are different')
    } else {
        const userData = { name, email, password }
        dispatch(register(userData))
    }
}
```

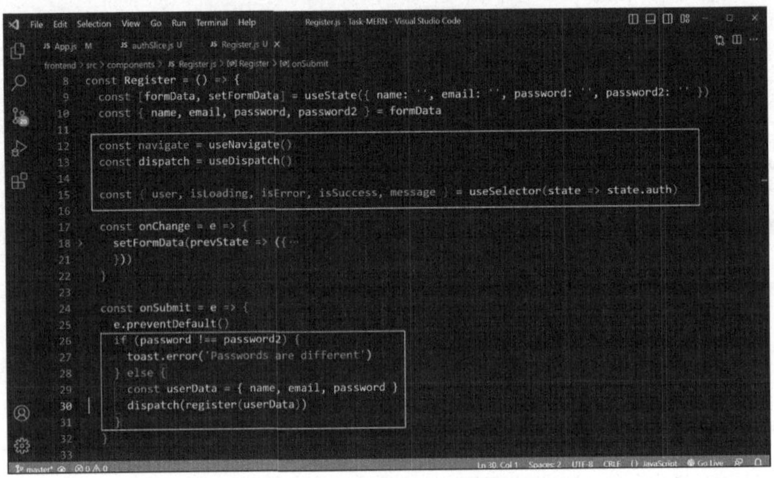

Figure 7.13: *Using hooks in the Register.js file*

Now, in the **Register.js** file, we will add an **`useEffect()`**. This useEffect will run when this component loads or when any of the **`user`**, **`isError`**, **`isSuccess`**, **`message`**, **`navigate`**, dispatch changes.

Inside it, we first check if the state of error is there and show a toast with the error message for that case. Next, if the state is of success or we got the user data, then navigate back to the home route.

If none of the cases is there, we are dispatching the reset to setback everything to initial state values.

```
import { useEffect, useState } from "react"
...
...
useEffect(() => {
    if (isError) toast.error(message)
    if (isSuccess || user) navigate('/')
    dispatch(reset())
}, [user, isError, isSuccess, message, navigate, dispatch])
```

Figure 7.14: *useEffect in Register.js file*

We will also show a loading spinner on our Register page when the user clicks on the Submit button. For this, we will create a Spinner component. So, create a **Spinner.js** file inside the **components** folder and add the following content to it.

Here, we are just using the already defined CSS in our index.css file, which shows the spinner icon.

```
const Spinner = () => {
  return (
    <div className='loadingSpinnerContainer'>
      <div className='loadingSpinner' />
    </div>
  )
}

export default Spinner
```

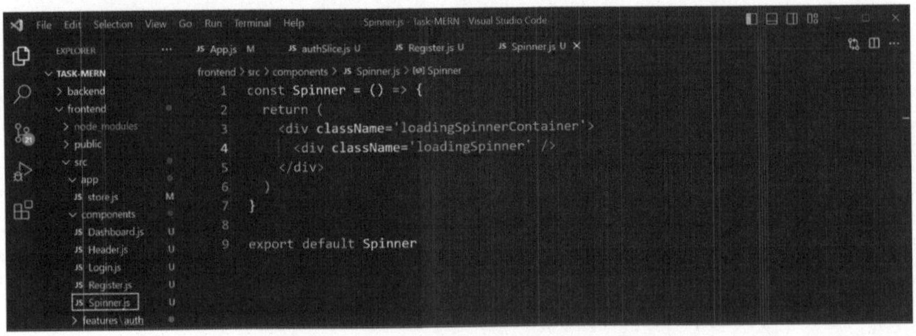

Figure 7.15: *Creating Spinner.js file*

Now, we will first import the **Spinner** in our **Register.js** file.

```
import Spinner from "./Spinner"
```

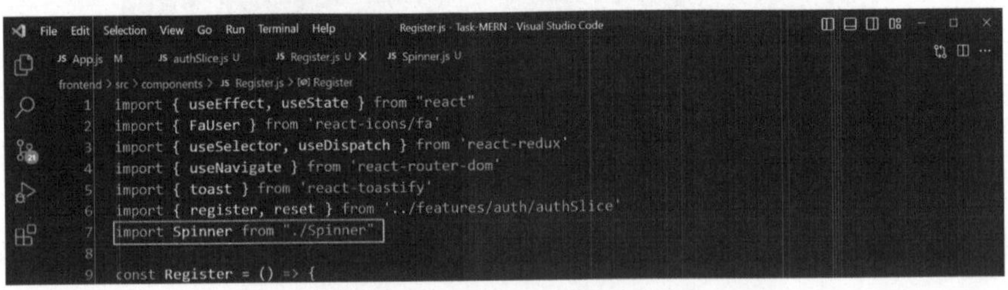

Figure 7.16: *Importing Spinner Component*

Now, we will update the return statement in the **Register.js** file. Here, we are first checking if the **isLoading** state is available and showing the Spinner component if that is the case. Or else we are showing the whole earlier code.

```
isLoading ? <Spinner /> : (
    <>
    <section className='heading'>
        ...
    </section>
    <section className='form'>
        ...
    </section>
  </>
)
```

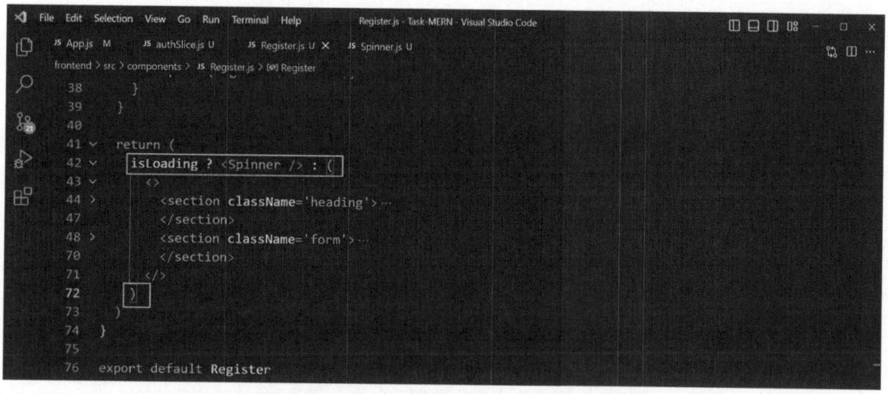

Figure 7.17: *Using Spinner Component*

Testing user registration

Click on the Register button, and you will go to http://localhost:3000/register. We have also opened the Redux dev tools, and here we can notice that reset is called and the user state is set to the initial value.

Here, we have entered all the required fields.

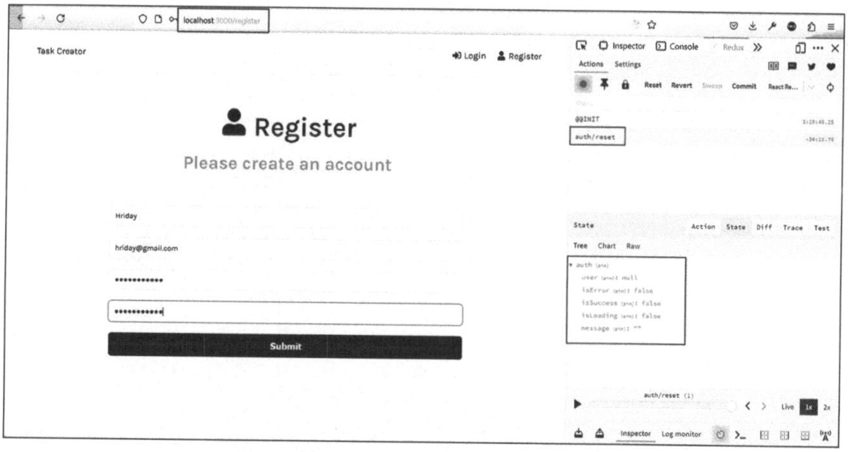

Figure 7.18: *Initial states in the register*

We have intentionally given the confirmed password as wrong. Here, a toast message of **`Passwords are different`** is shown, which automatically disappears after 5 seconds.

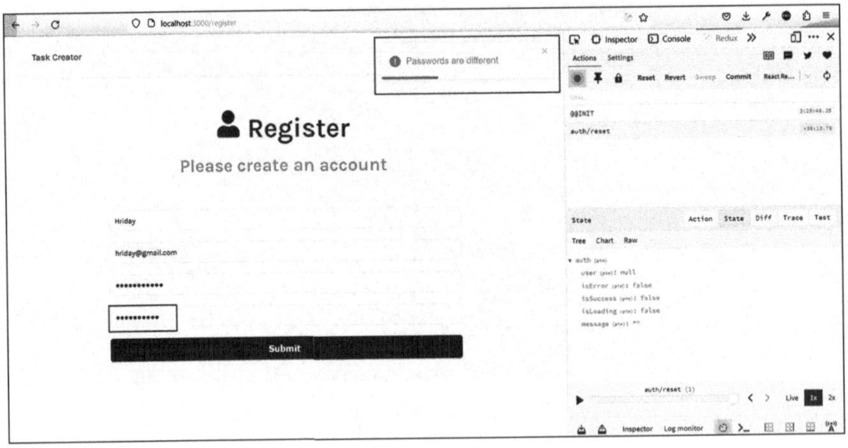

***Figure 7.19**: Toast message in register*

We have, this time, given the same passwords in both fields and hit the **Submit** button. Here, we have been taken to the home page of the Dashboard. But also notice that different actions have been done in the Redux devtools.

Here, first, the pending action ran from the **extraReducers** in the authSlice.js file. Here, the **isLoading** was set to true, and the rest states were kept as it was earlier.

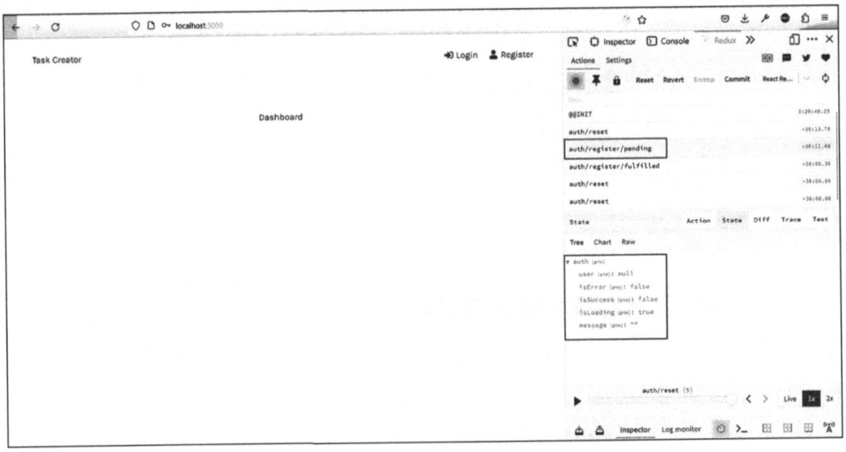

***Figure 7.20**: Pending state in the register*

Since the API call to the backend was successful, the fulfilled action had run. This has made the **isLoading** false and **isSuccess** as true. And the user state was set to the payload received from the backend. This payload consists of **_id**, **name**, **email**, and **token**.

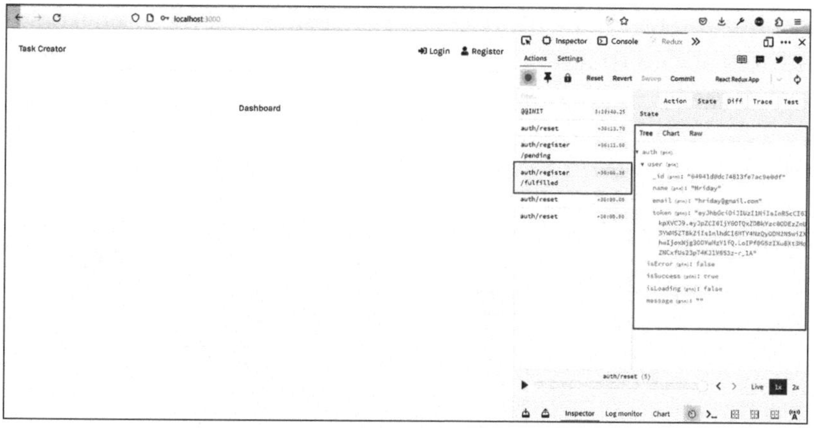

Figure 7.21: *Fulfilled state in the register*

The reset was run again, and it set everything back to an earlier state, but the user was kept intact.

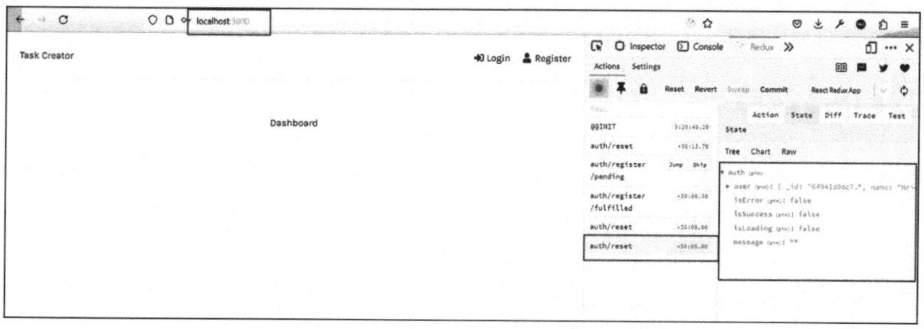

Figure 7.22: *Reset state in the register*

The user data was also saved in the Local Storage of the browser, containing all the fields of the user object.

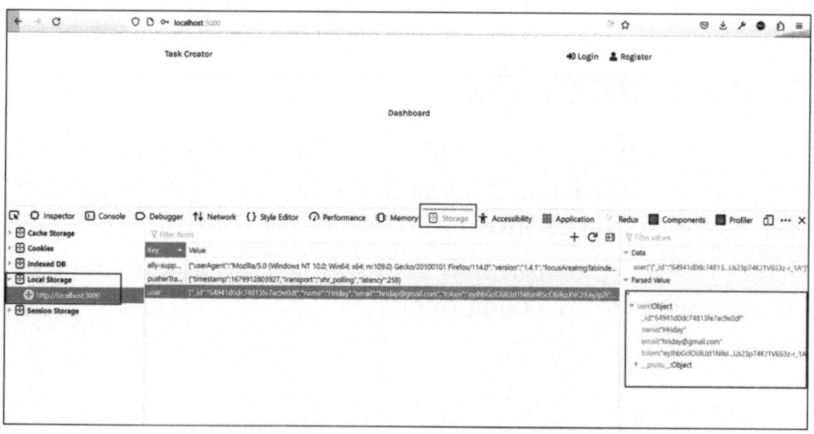

Figure 7.23: *Local Storage in Browser*

Finally, we checked the value for users in the connected MongoDB database, and a new field was added to it.

Figure 7.24: *Record in Database*

Conclusion

In this chapter, we have learned about implementing Redux in our project through the toolkit. Here, we first created a slice for auth, which is a combination of reducer and action creator. We had also hooked it up with auth service to help do api calls to the backend endpoint.

Finally, we have completed our Register user functionality from the front end using the slice. And we were able to Register a user by submitting a form from the front end.

In the next chapter, we will implement the login and logout functionalities.

Points to remember

- Implementing the Redux toolkit in a project using slice and services.
- Using a slice in the latest Redux toolkit, we combine the functionalities of reducer and action creator.
- Getting global state through redux in a component. And dispatching action creators from a component.

Chapter 8
Login and Logout Functionalities

Introduction

This chapter covers the implementation of Logout and Login functionalities in the project. We will be going to use logic similar to the previous chapter to set both of them. In this chapter, we are also going to set up a reducer for the Login form. Finally, we are also going to test the user login workflow.

Structure

In this chapter, we are going to discuss the following topics:

- Implementing Logout
- Implementing Login
- Login form hook up
- Testing user login

Implementing Logout

In the previous chapter, we have implemented the Register functionality. Now, the logout functionality will be much simpler than it. Here, on click of a new Logout button, we have removed all tokens.

So, first, in the **authSlice.js** file, create a new function called logout. Similar to the register function, it uses the `createAsyncThunk` function. But it is much simpler than the register function of the previous chapter.

Here, the first parameter is the auth/login, which means from the auth folder, take the login function. We are going to create this function next in the authService.js file. Next, the parameter is an async arrow function calling the **`logout()`** from the authService.js file.

```
export const logout = createAsyncThunk('auth/logout', async () => await authService.logout())
```

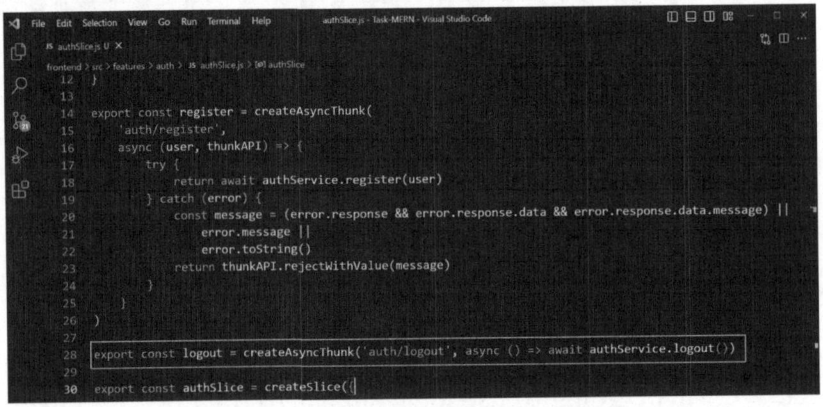

Figure 8.1: *Creating logout in authSlice.js file*

Now, in the authService.js file, we will create our logout function. Again notice that here it's much simpler than the register function created in the earlier chapter.

Here, we are just removing the user from the local storage using the **`localStorage.removeItem()`** method. After that, we are also exporting the logout function.

```
const logout = () => localStorage.removeItem('user')
```

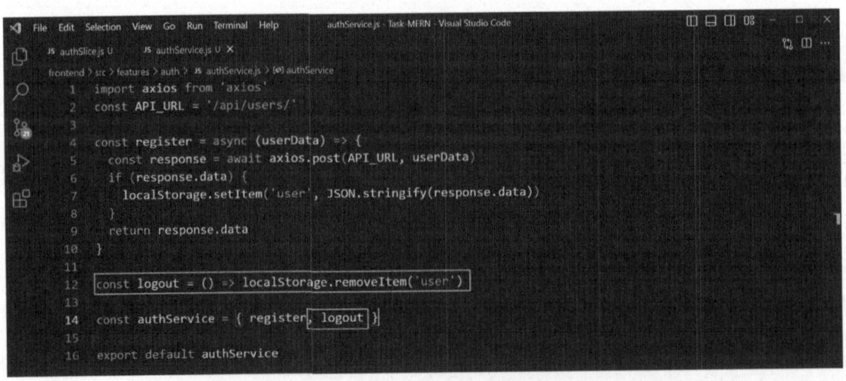

Figure 8.2: *Creating logout in authService.js file*

We don't have a Logout button in our project. This Logout button will be created in the Header component. So, head over to the Header.js file and import **useNavigate** from react-router-dom.

We are also importing **useSelector** and **useDispatch** from react-redux. Next, we import logout and reset from the **authSlice** file.

Inside the Header, we have created a **navigate** variable using the **useNavigate** hook. Then we created a **dispatch** variable using the **useDispatch** hook. And we are also accessing the global state of the **user** using the **useSelector** hook.

```
import { Link, useNavigate } from 'react-router-dom'
import { useSelector, useDispatch } from 'react-redux'
import { logout, reset } from '../features/auth/authSlice'
...
...
const navigate = useNavigate()
const dispatch = useDispatch()
const { user } = useSelector(state => state.auth)
```

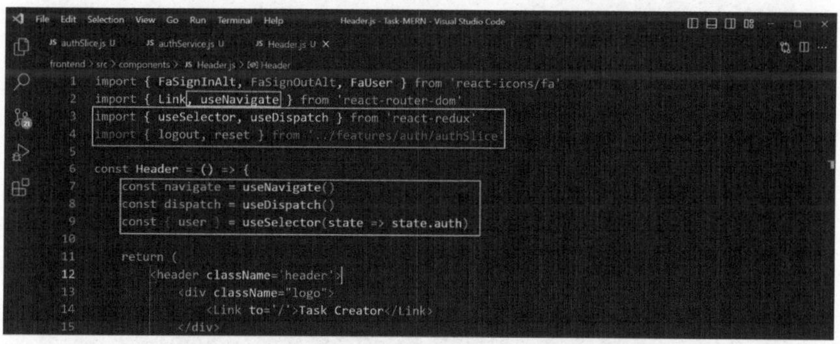

Figure 8.3: *Adding imports in the Header.js file*

We will update our logic to show buttons in the **Header.js** file. Earlier, we were just showing the Login and Register buttons inside the `<ul>` through two `<li>`

But now we have updated the logic and are using a ternary operator. Earlier we were only showing the pair or **Login** and **Register** button. But now if user is available, we are showing the **Logout** button. Or else the **Login** and **Register** buttons.

```
{user ? (
    <li>
        <button className=›btn››>
            <FaSignOutAlt /> Logout
        </button>
    </li>
) : (
    <>
        <li>
            <Link to=›/login››<FaSignInAlt /> Login</Link>
        </li>
        <li>
            <Link to=›/register››<FaUser /> Register</Link>
        </li>
    </>
)}
```

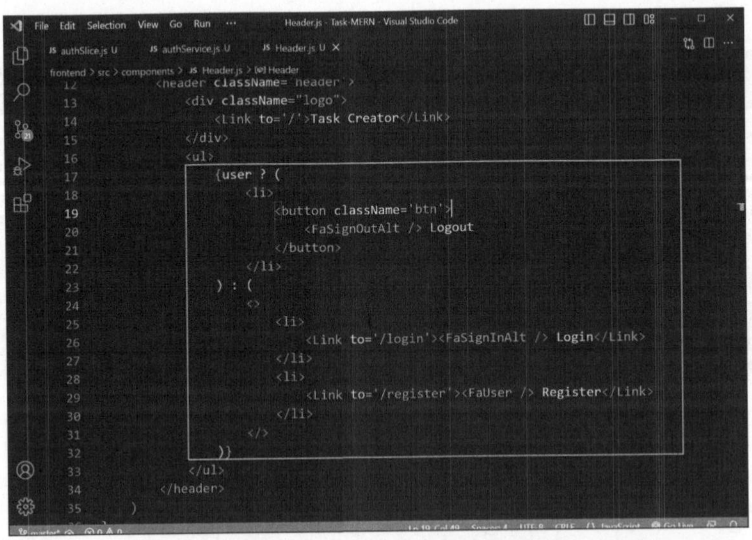

Figure 8.4: *Adding Logout button in Header.js file*

Now, we will add an **`onClick`** handler to the Logout button in the **Header.js** file. The onClick handler is calling a function **`logoutFn`**.

We have created the **`logoutFn`** function, which is first dispatching the **`logout()`** from the **authSlice.js** file. Next, it dispatches the **`reset()`** from the **authSlice.js** file. Afterwards, we navigate back to the home route using **`navigate()`**.

```
const logoutFn = () => {
    dispatch(logout())
    dispatch(reset())
    navigate(‹/›)
}
...
...
{user ? (
    <li>
        <button className=›btn› onClick={logoutFn}>
            <FaSignOutAlt /> Logout
        </button>
    </li>
) : (
    <>
      ...
    </>
)}
```

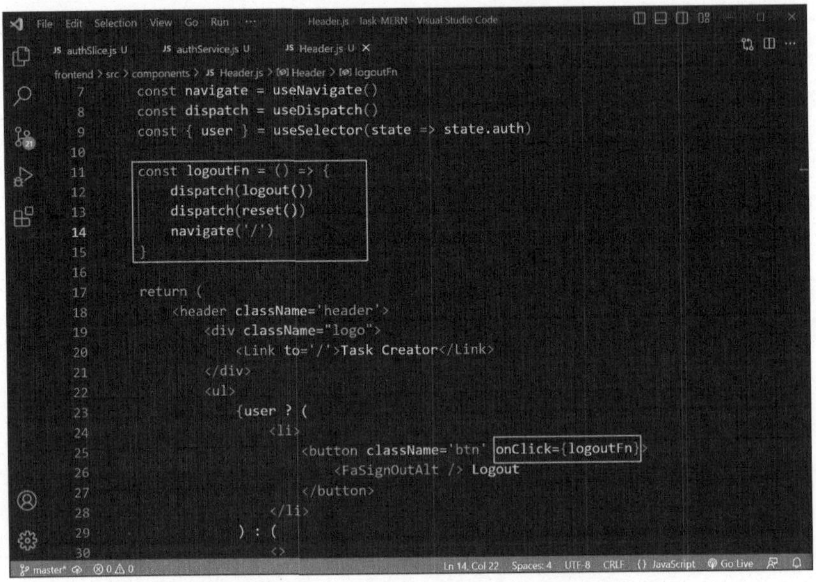

***Figure 8.5**: Adding Logout function in Header.js file*

As in the case of register, we need to add a case in the **`extraReducers`** in the **authSlice.js** file. In the register, we had three cases because we were doing the API call.

But here, we have only one case of **`fulfilled`** in which we are making the user state null.

```
.addCase(logout.fulfilled, (state) => {
    state.user = null
                                         })
```

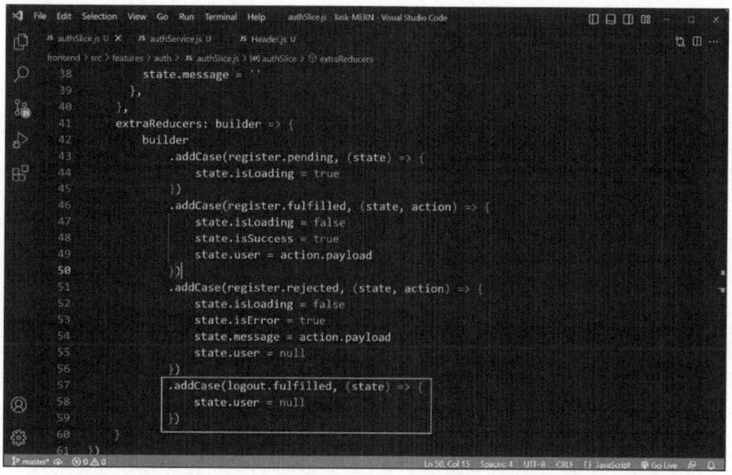

Figure 8.6: *Adding logout case function in authSlice.js file*

Now, go to http://localhost:3000/ from the Chrome/Firefox browser and open the redux devtools. Log in to the app if not already done.

If logged in, we will see the Logout button. And also, in Redux Devtools, we will see the **`INIT`** state with the user and other states.

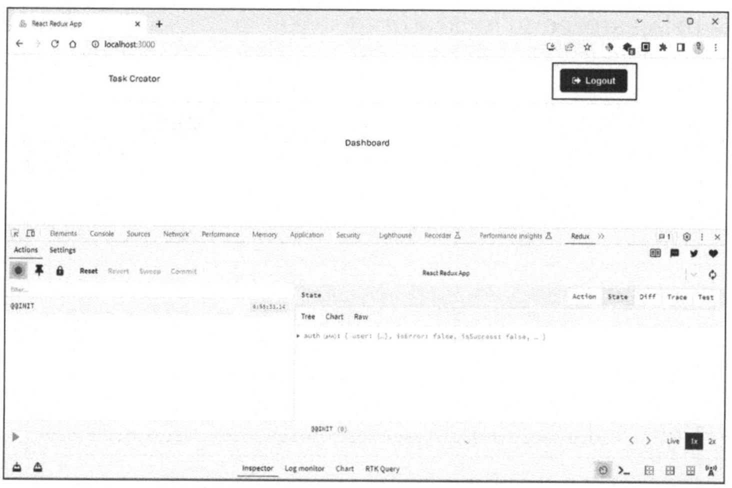

Figure 8.7: *Logout button in localhost*

Once we click on the Logout button in the preceding screenshot, we see three states have been changed. We have a logout/pending, reset and finally, the logout/fulfilled states.

Since, in the Header.js in **`logoutFn()`** we are also calling the **`reset()`** from the **authSlice.js** file, these two additional states are being called.

We can see in the fulfilled state that the user is set to null.

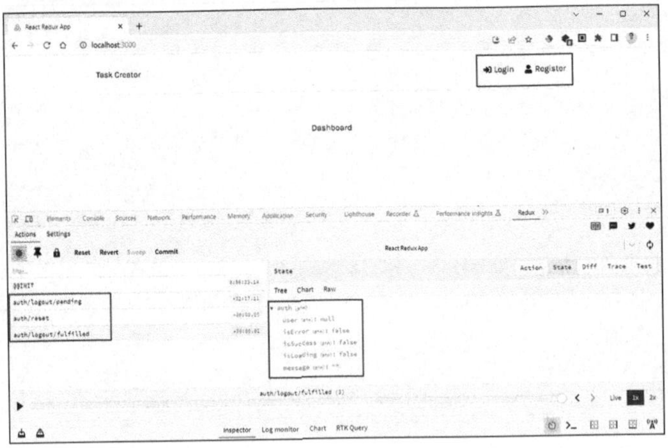

Figure 8.8: *On clicking the Logout button in localhost*

When they Logout, the user's data is also deleted from the local storage. To check the same, Login again and go to the Application tab in Chrome or Storage tab in Firefox.

Here, click on Local Storage and then http://localhost:3000/ . Here, we will see the user data being stored in local storage.

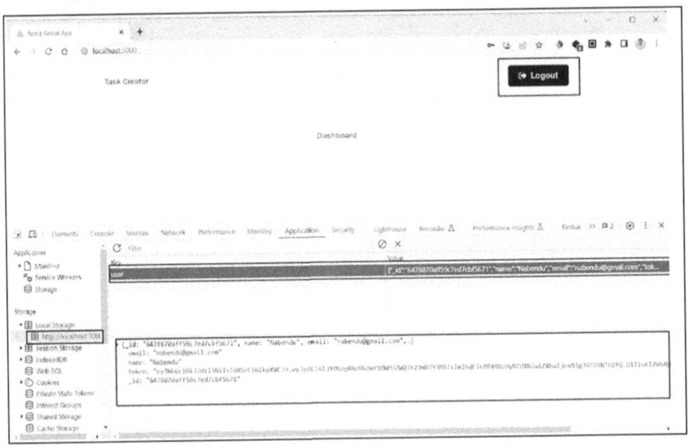

Figure 8.9: *Login in localhost showing the user in local storage*

Now, click on the Logout button, and we will see that the user data has been deleted from the **`Local Storage`**.

This happens because when we click on the **`LocalStorage`** button, then the function **`localStorage.removeItem('user')`** in **authService.js** is executed. And this removes the user from local storage.

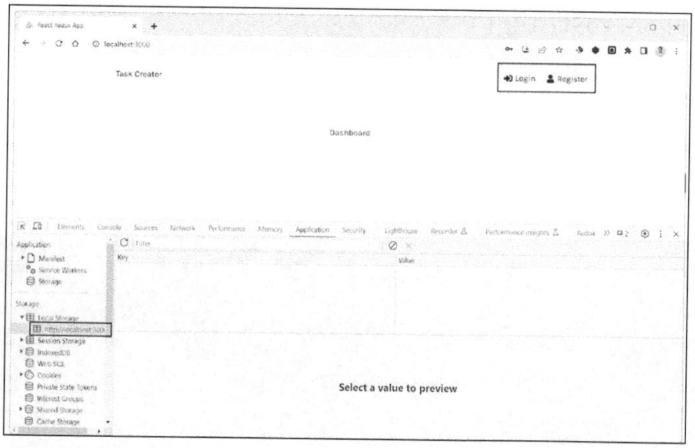

Figure 8.10: *Logout in localhost removing user in local storage*

Implementing Login

Now, we will implement the Login functionality. This is quite similar to the Register functionality in the previous chapter.

Back in the **authSlice.js** file, we are exporting a variable login. Here, we are using the **createAsyncThunk** function.

Here, the first parameter is the auth/login, which means from the auth folder, take the login function. Next, the parameter is an async arrow function which takes the user and **thunkAPI** as a parameter.

Inside the function, we have a **try...catch** block. From the **try** block, we are calling the **login** function from the **authService.js** file with the user and returning it. In the **catch** part, we are simply catching different kinds of errors and returning them.

```
export const login = createAsyncThunk('auth/login', async (user, thunkAPI)
=> {
    try {
        return await authService.login(user)
    } catch (error) {
        const message =
            (error.response && error.response.data && error.response.
data.message) ||
            error.message ||
```

```
            error.toString()
        return thunkAPI.rejectWithValue(message)
    }
})
```

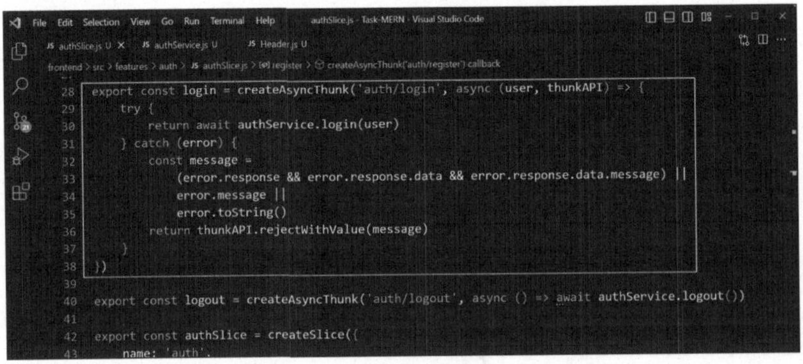

***Figure 8.11**: Adding thunk in authSlice.js file*

Next, we have created a **login** function in the **authService.js** file, which takes the **userData**. Inside the function, we are doing a POST call to the **API_URL** plus **login** with the **userData**.

The result of the api call, which we get in **response.data**, is set in the local storage variable user using **localStorage.setItem()** function. We are also returning the response from the function.

Lastly, we are exporting the **login** function.

```
const login = async (userData) => {
  const response = await axios.post(API_URL + 'login', userData)
  if (response.data) {
    localStorage.setItem('user', JSON.stringify(response.data))
  }
  return response.data
}
```

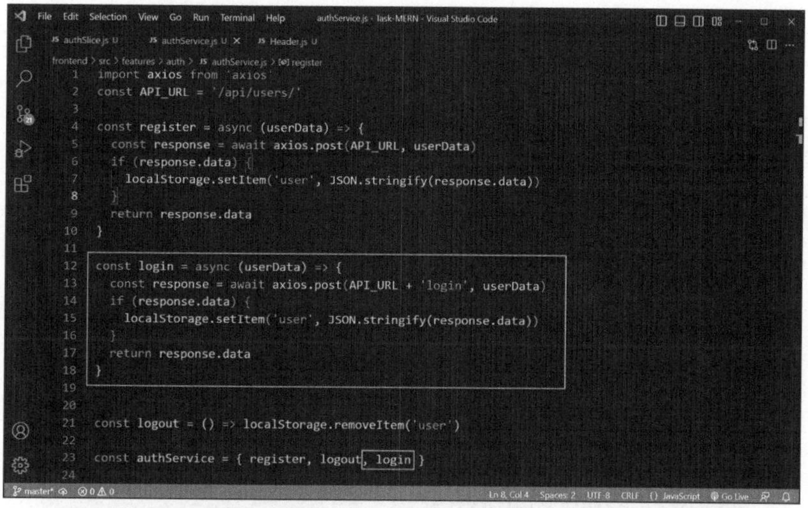

Figure 8.12: *Adding login functionalities in the authService.js file*

Next, similar to the register, we will add three cases in the **authSlice.js** file. In our code, we have three cases for pending, fulfilled and rejected cases. Since we are doing an API call to http://localhost:8000/api/users/login through our login function, we have three states in it. When the API call starts, we have a pending state since the API calls generally take 1–2 seconds. Again, we are making the **`isLoading`** state to true and will also show a spinner in this state in the front end.

The next state is the fulfilled case, which will happen if our API call is successful. Here, we are making the **`isLoading`** as false and **`isSuccess`** as true and storing the payload which we receive back in the user state.

If, for some reason, the API call is not successful, we have a rejected case. Here, we are making the **`isLoading`** as false and **`isError`** as true. We are also storing the error in the message state, which we will receive in the payload–also making the user state variable null.

```
.addCase(login.pending, (state) => {
    state.isLoading = true
})
.addCase(login.fulfilled, (state, action) => {
    state.isLoading = false
    state.isSuccess = true
    state.user = action.payload
```

```
})
.addCase(login.rejected, (state, action) => {
    state.isLoading = false
    state.isError = true
    state.message = action.payload
    state.user = null
})
```

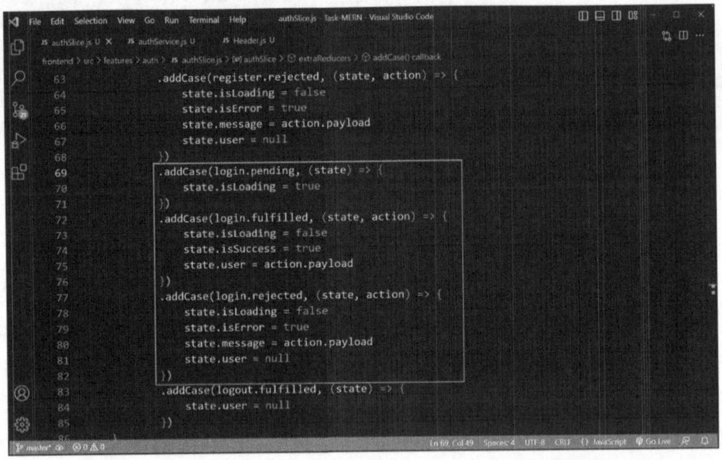

Figure 8.13: *Adding cases for login in the authSlice.js file*

Login form hook up

We will now use the Slice in our Login component to log in a user. So, head over to the **Login.js** file and add the following imports in it.

Here, we are first importing the **`useEffect`** hook custom, which will be used to dispatch the reset function soon. Next, we are importing hooks of **`useSelector`** and **`useDispatch`** from **`react-redux`**. These hooks are used to get the global state of redux and also to dispatch the action creator inside a slice.

After that, we import **`useNavigate`** from **`react-router-dom`**. This custom hook is used to navigate easily to different routes. Next, we are importing **`toast`** from **`react-toastify`**, which will be used to show the toast message.

Next, we are importing **`login`** and **`reset`** from **`authSlice`**, which will be used to call the login and reset action creators. Lastly, we are importing the Spinner component, which will be used to show the Spinner when the API call starts.

Next, we will create variables for **`navigate`** and **`dispatch`** using the **`useNavigate`** and **`useDispatch`** hooks.

Next, we will get the global state of the **`user`**, **`isLoading`**, **`isError`**, **`isSuccess`**, **`message`** using the **`useSelector`** hook.

```
import { useState, useEffect } from “react”
import { useSelector, useDispatch } from ‘react-redux’
import { useNavigate } from ‘react-router-dom’
import { toast } from ‘react-toastify’
import { login, reset } from ‘../features/auth/authSlice’
import Spinner from “./Spinner”
...
const navigate = useNavigate()
const dispatch = useDispatch()


const { user, isLoading, isError, isSuccess, message } = useSelector(state => state.auth)
```

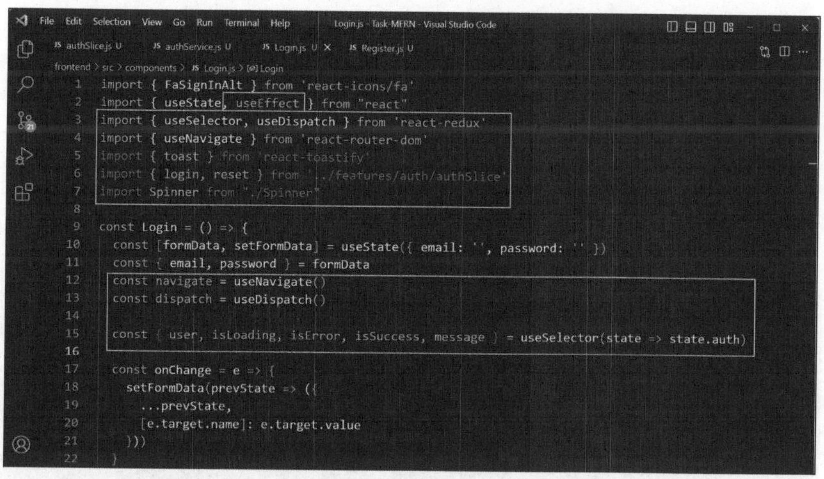

Figure 8.14: *Adding imports in the Login.js file*

Now, in the **Login.js** file, we will add an **`useEffect()`**. This **`useEffect`** will run when this component loads or when any of the **`user`**, **`isError`**, **`isSuccess`**, **`message`**, **`navigate`**, dispatch changes.

Inside it, we are first checking if the state of error is there and show a toast with the error message for that case. Next, if the state is of success or we got the user data, then navigate back to the home route.

If none of the cases is there, we are dispatching the reset to setback everything to initial state values.

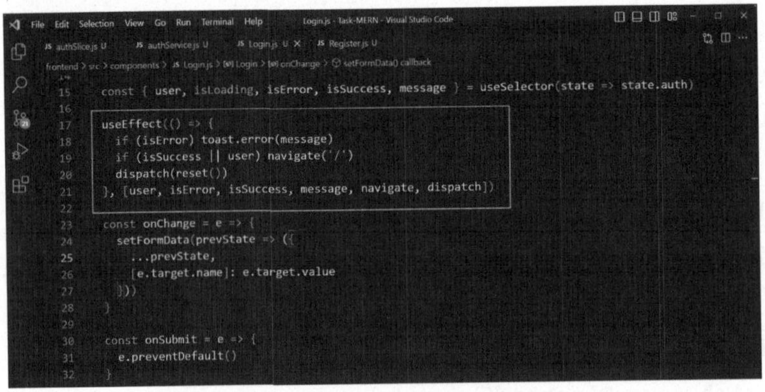

Figure 8.15: *Adding useEffect in Login.js file*

Now in the **Login.js** file, inside the **`onSubmit()`** function, we are taking the email and password entered by the user and putting it in a **`userData`** variable and, after that dispatching it with the dispatch to the login function in the **authSlice.js** file.

```
const onSubmit = e => {
    e.preventDefault()
    const userData = { email, password }
    dispatch(login(userData))
}
```

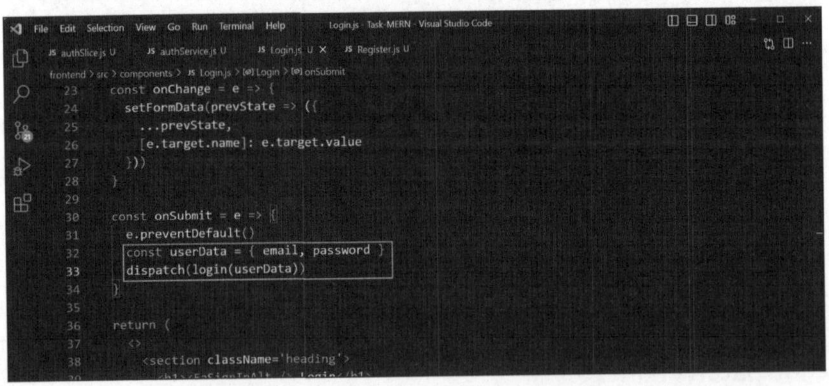

Figure 8.16: *Adding submit logic in the Login.js file*

Now, we will update the return statement in the **Login.js** file. Here, we are first checking if the **`isLoading`** state is available and showing the Spinner component if that is the case. Or else we are showing the whole earlier code.

```
isLoading ? <Spinner /> : (
    <>
    <section className=’heading’>
        ...
    </section>
    <section className=’form’>
        ...
    </section>
  </>
)
```

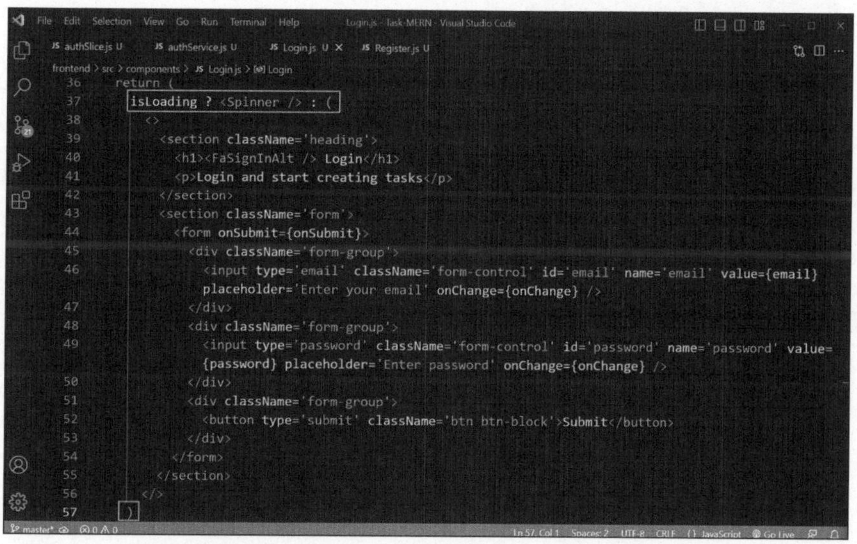

***Figure 8.17**: Adding Spinner in Login.js file*

Testing user login

Click on the Login button, and you will go to http://localhost:3000/login . We have also opened the Redux dev tools, and here we can notice that reset is called and the user state is set to the initial value.

Here, we have entered all the required fields.

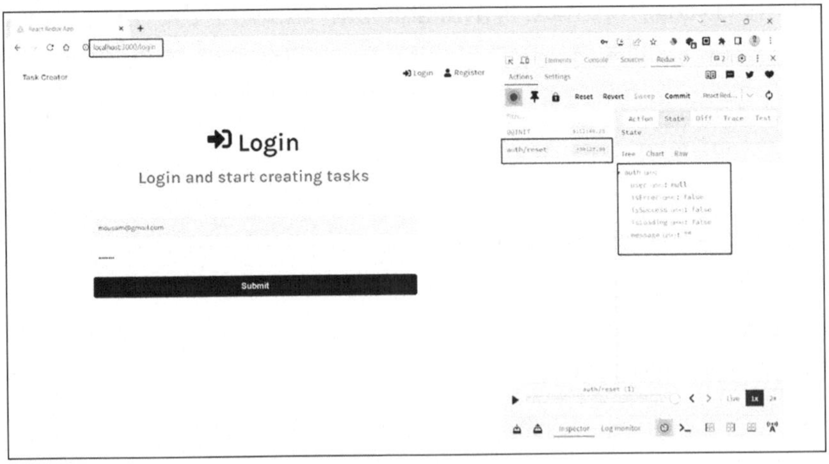

Figure 8.18: *Initial states in the login*

We have intentionally given the password as wrong. Here, a toast message of **`Invalid data`** is shown, which automatically disappears after 5 seconds.

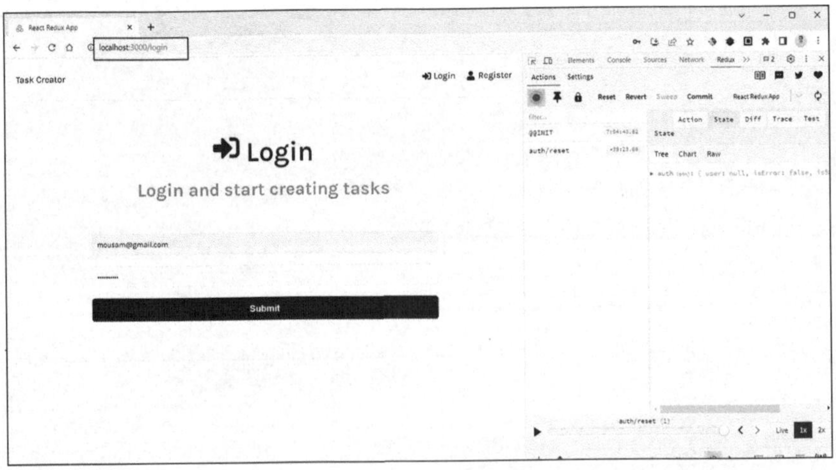

Figure 8.19: *Toast message in the login*

We have, this time, given the correct password and hit the **`Submit`** button. Here, we have been taken to the home page of the dashboard. But also notice that different actions have been done in the Redux devtools.

Here, first, the pending action ran from the **`extraReducers`** in the **authSlice.js** file. Here, the **`isLoading`** was set to true, and the rest states were kept as it was earlier.

***Figure 8.20**: Pending state in the login*

Since the API call to the backend was successful, the fulfilled action had run. This has made the **`isLoading`** false and **`isSuccess`** as true. And the user state was set to the payload received from the backend. This payload consists of **`_id`**, **`name`**, **`email`** and **`token`**.

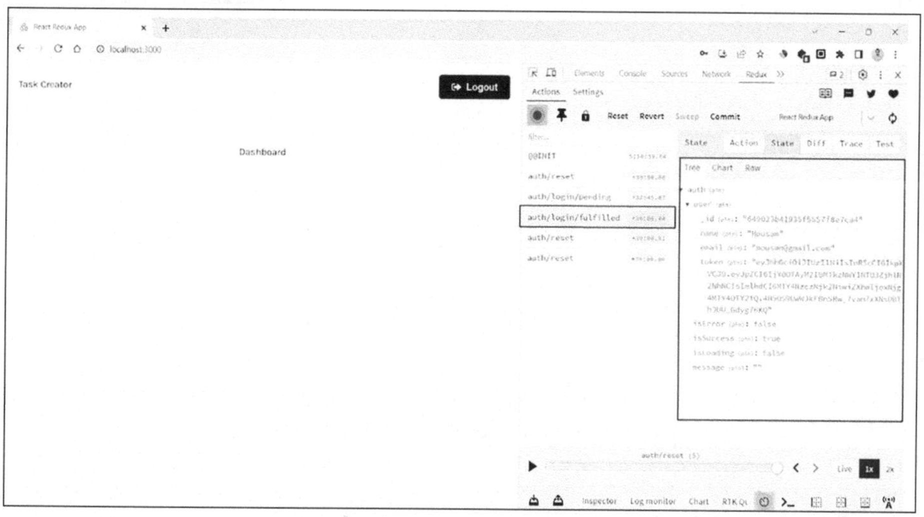

***Figure 8.21**: Fulfilled state in the login*

The reset was run again, and it set everything back to an earlier state, but the user was kept intact.

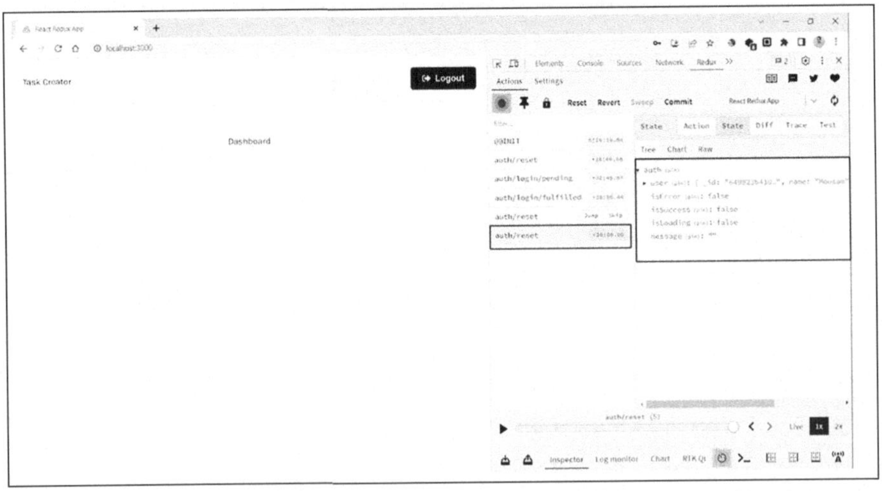

Figure 8.22: *Reset state in the login*

The user data was also saved in the Local Storage of the browser, containing all the fields of the user object.

Figure 8.23: *Local Storage in Browser*

Conclusion

In this chapter, we have learned about implementing Logout in our project through the toolkit. The logout was implemented by simply removing the user from local storage and making its state null. We also created the logic logout button to be shown if the user is logged in.

After that, we created the Login functionalities, which were quite similar to Register in the previous chapter. Finally, we were able to log in as a user by submitting a form from the front end.

In the next chapter, we will implement the restriction of the dashboard and the creation of a Task form.

Points to remember

- How to show a logout button if the user is logged in.
- Using a Slice in the latest Redux toolkit, we combine the functionalities of reducer and action creator.
- How to get global state from Redux in a component and also dispatch action creators from a component.

CHAPTER 9

Dashboard Creation and Task Form

Introduction

This chapter covers the implementation of the Dashboard in the frontend. We will also restrict the dashboard to authorized users. In this chapter, we are also going to create the Task slice in Redux. Finally, we are also going to create the Task Form.

Structure

In this chapter, we are going to discuss the following topics:

- Changing Dashboard logic
- Creating Task Slice
- Creating Task Form

Changing Dashboard Logic

Our Dashboard page was accessible to everyone in the earlier chapter. We are going to change the logic so that only logged-in users can see the dashboard page.

In the **Dashboard.js** file, we are first importing `useEffect` from react, because we will do an async task through it. Next, we are importing `useNavigate` hook from react-router-dom, which will be used to navigate to the login page.

Also, the **`useSelector`** is imported from react-redux. It will be used to access the global state of the user. Inside the Dashboard component, we are first creating the variables of navigate and user through the **`useNavigate`** and **`useSelector`** hooks, respectively.

After that, from within an **`useEffect`**, which will run when the user navigates change, we are checking if a user is not available. If that is the case, we are navigating the user to the /login route.

```
import { useEffect } from ‘react’
import { useNavigate } from ‘react-router-dom’
import { useSelector } from ‘react-redux’

const Dashboard = () => {
  const navigate = useNavigate()
  const { user } = useSelector(state => state.auth)

  useEffect(() => {
    if (!user) navigate(‹/login›)
  }, [user, navigate])

  return (
    <div>Dashboard</div>
  )
}

export default Dashboard
```

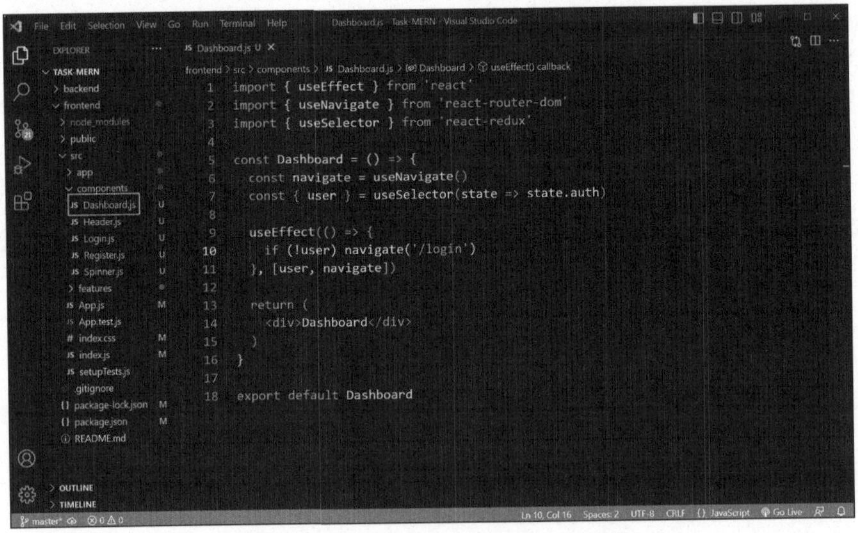

Figure 9.1: *Updating Dashboard.js file*

Now, in the browser type http://localhost:3000/ and hit *enter*.

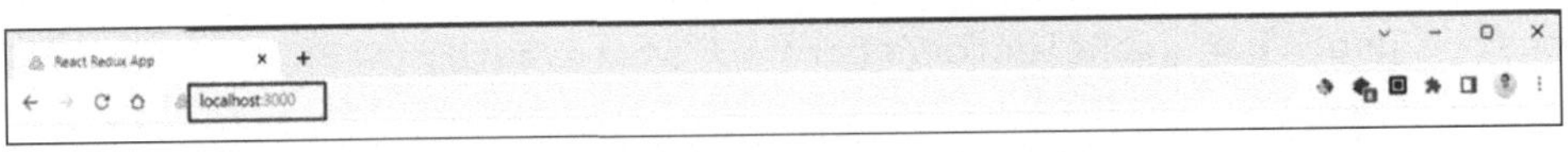

Figure 9.2: *Visiting localhost in browser*

We will be redirected to http://localhost:3000/login because of the new code in **Dashboard.js** file. We don't have a user state yet.

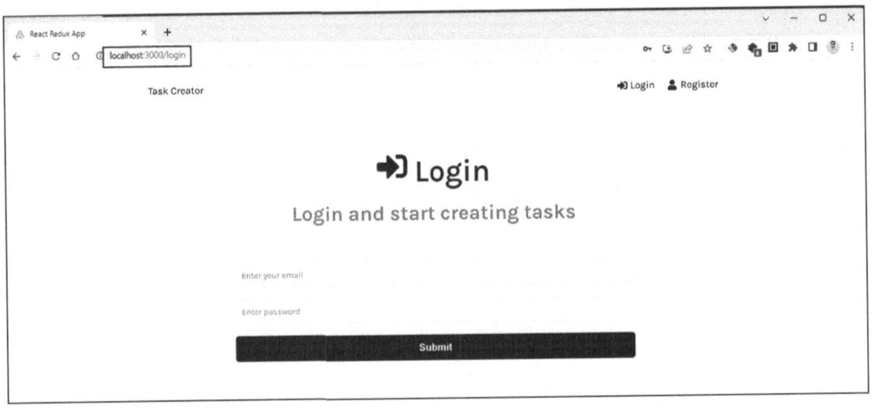

Figure 9.3: *Dashboard route changing to login route*

Now, in the preceding screen login with a valid email and password. And we will be redirected to the Dashboard page.

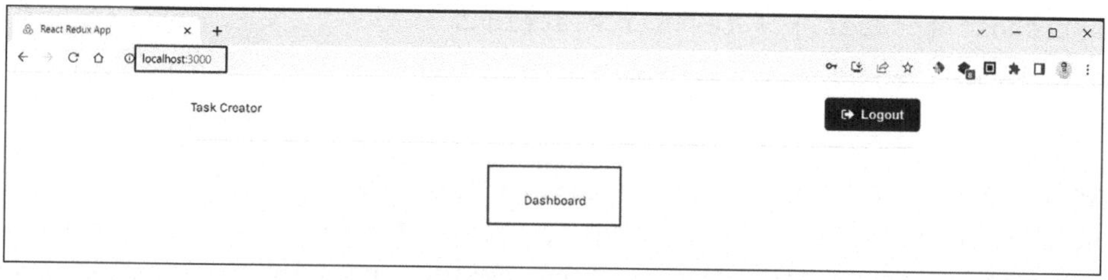

***Figure 9.4**: Dashboard shown only after logging*

Creating Task Slice

Now, we will create the task slice and service which will be used in the dashboard to create tasks. Similar to the auth logic, we will create a folder called **tasks** inside the **features** folder.

Now, create a file **taskSlice.js** and **taskService.js** inside the **tasks** folder. Inside the **taskSlice.js** file, put the following code:

```
import { createSlice, createAsyncThunk } from ‘@reduxjs/toolkit’

const initialState = {
    tasks: [],
    isError: false,
    isSuccess: false,
    isLoading: false,
    message: ‹›
}

export const taskSlice = createSlice({
    name: ‹task›,
    initialState,
    reducers: {
      reset: state => initialState
    }
})
```

```
export const { reset } = taskSlice.actions
export default taskSlice.reducer
```

Here, we are first importing **createSlice** and **createAsyncThunk** from redux toolkit. The **createSlice** will be used to create the slice used for reducer and action. And the **createAsyncThunk** will be used for asynchronous actions, which is an API call in our case later on.

Next, we have the **initialState** of our slice which is an object. Here, we have **tasks** key first which is equal to an empty array. We also have values for **isError**, **isSuccess**, and **isLoading** which are set as false. These will be used when we do the API call. Lastly, we have a **message** as an empty string.

Next, we are exporting the **taskSlice**, which is created using the **createSlice** method. Here, we are first giving the name of the slice as a **task**. Then we are taking the **initialState**. After that, we have a reducers value, which has a reset. This reset can be used to restore the state to its initial state.

At the end, we are exporting the reset action and the reducer.

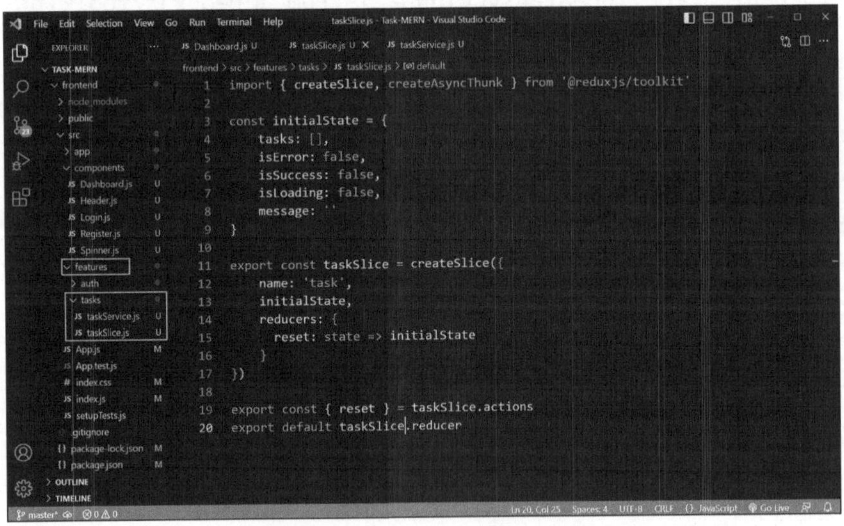

Figure 9.5: *Basic taskSlice.js file*

Now, we will import the task reducer in the **store.js** file. Because of the store in a Redux app, we are able to use global state in different components. So, now we will be able to access the tasks state in various components.

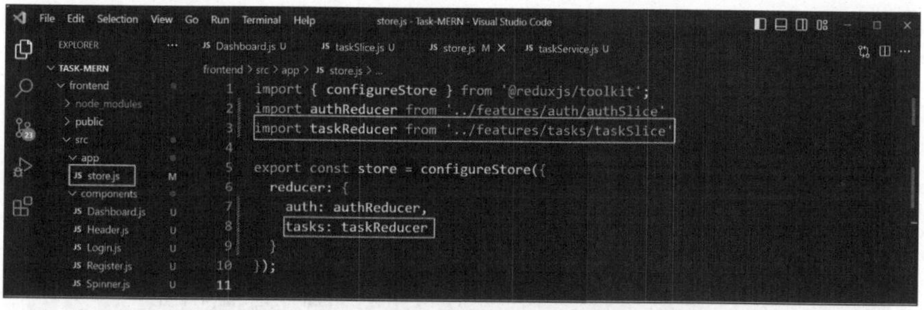

***Figure 9.6**: Adding tasks state in store.js file*

Now, back in http://localhost:3000/ after logging in we will see the initial state of tasks in the Redux devtools tab of the developer console.

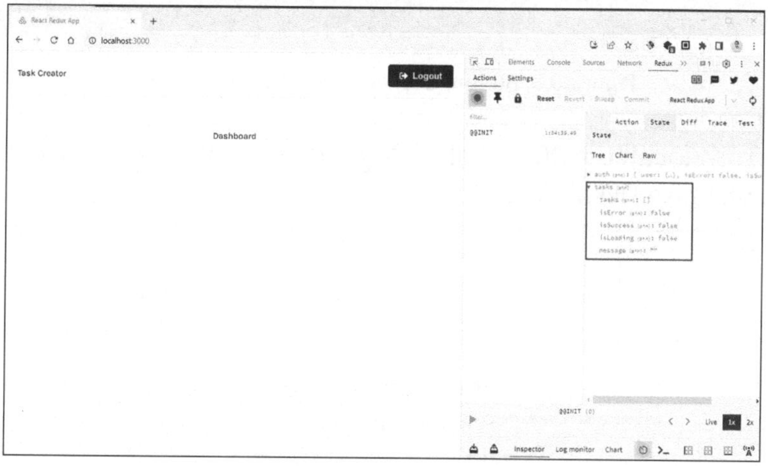

***Figure 9.7**: Initial tasks state in Redux devtools*

Back in the **Dashboard.js** file, we will show a Welcome message now. Here, we are showing the user name also from the user global state. Since we should be successfully logged in when reaching this component, we will get this user name.

```
<>
  <section className=›heading›>
    <h1>Welcome {user && user.name}</h1>
    <p>Tasks Dashboard</p>
  </section>
</>
```

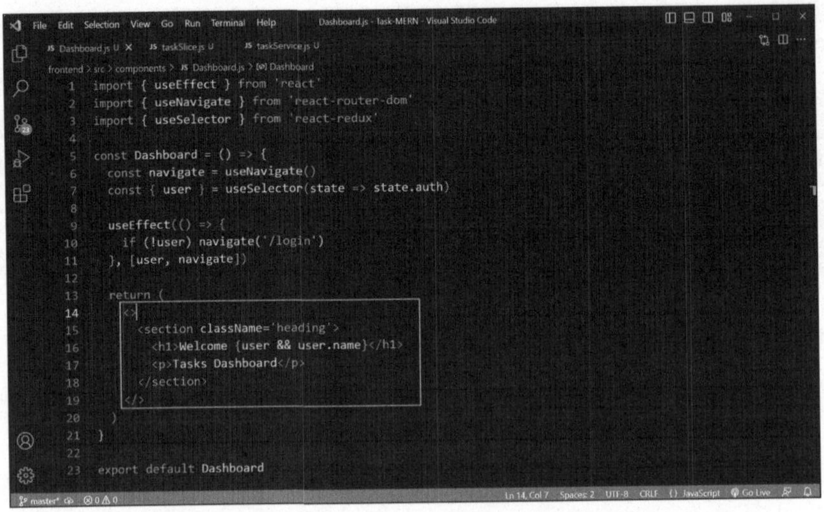

***Figure 9.8**: Adding Username in Dashboad.js file*

Back in http://localhost:3000/ after logging, we will see the user name also, with a text of Tasks Dashboard.

***Figure 9.9**: Showing Username in localhost*

Creating Task Form

Now, we will create a Task Form, which will be used to take the user input in the Dashboard for tasks. So, first create a file **TaskForm.js** inside the **components** folder.

Here, we are first importing the **`useState`** from react and the **`useDispatch`** hook from react-redux. Next, we have a basic **`TaskForm`** functional component, showing the text **`TaskForm`** inside a div.

```
import { useState } from ‘react’
```

```
import { useDispatch } from ‘react-redux’

const TaskForm = () => {
  return (
    <div>TaskForm</div>
  )
}

export default TaskForm
```

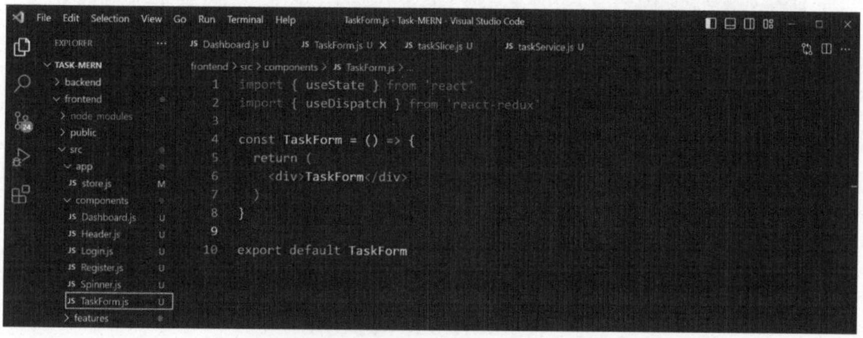

***Figure 9.10**: Creating TaskForm.js file*

Now, we will import this **TaskForm** component in our Dashboard.js file. Here, we are first using an import statement for the TaskForm component. After that, we are adding it after the section.

```
import TaskForm from ‘./TaskForm’
...
...
<>
  <section className=›heading›>
    <h1>Welcome {user && user.name}</h1>
    <p>Tasks Dashboard</p>
  </section>
  <TaskForm />
</>
```

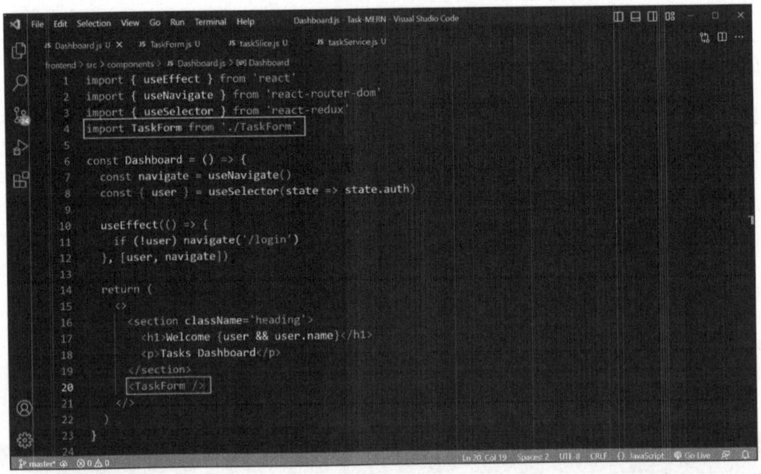

***Figure 9.11**: Adding TaskForm component in Dashboard.js file*

Back in http://localhost:3000/ we will see the **TaskForm** div being shown.

***Figure 9.12**: Showing TaskForm component in localhost*

Next, we will complete the **TaskForm** component by adding the following code in **TaskForm.js** file:

```
const TaskForm = () => {
    const [text, setText] = useState(‹›)

    const onSubmit = (e) => {
        e.preventDefault()
        setText(‹›)
    }
```

```
    return (
        <section className=›form›>
            <form onSubmit={onSubmit}>
                <div className=›form-group›>
                    <label htmlFor=›text›>Task</label>
                    <input type=›text› id=›text› value={text}
onChange={e => setText(e.target.value)}
                    />
                </div>
                <div className=›form-group›>
                    <button className=›btn btn-block› type=›submit›>Add
Task</button>
                </div>
            </form>
        </section>
    )
}
```

Here, inside the TaskForm function, we are first having a state of text using the useState hook. Next, we have a submit function which is using `e.preventDefault()`, to prevent the page from refreshing when we hit the Add Task button. We are also setting the text state back to an empty screen here.

Inside the return, we have a section with a class of form. These styles are already there in the **index.css** file. Next, we have a form with an onSubmit handler which is calling the onSubmit function created earlier.

Next, we have a div with a class of **form-group**. Inside it, we have a label and an input box. This input box is changing the state of the text when the user types in it.

In the next div, we have a button with the class name for styles. Since this button is inside a form, it is of type submit. When we click this `Add Task` button, it will trigger the `onSubmit` handler of the form.

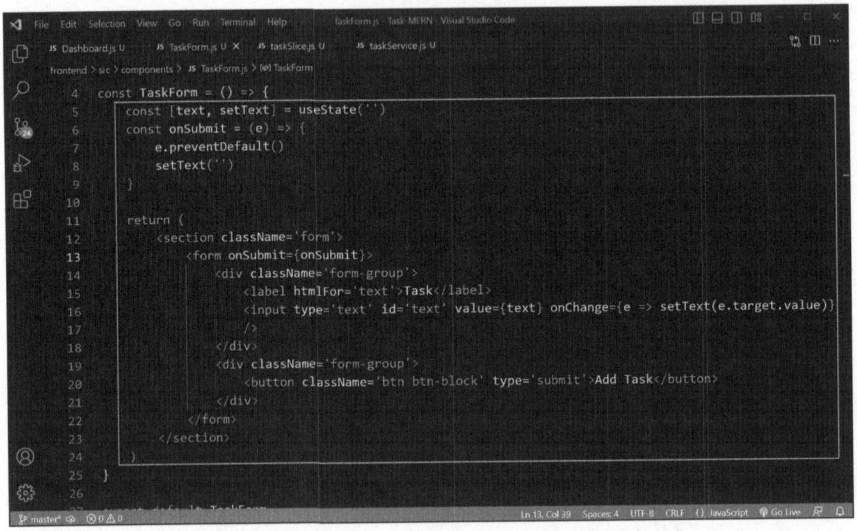

Figure 9.13: *Adding login TaskForm.js file*

Going back to http://localhost:3000/ will show us a nice form in the Dashboard, with input box and a button.

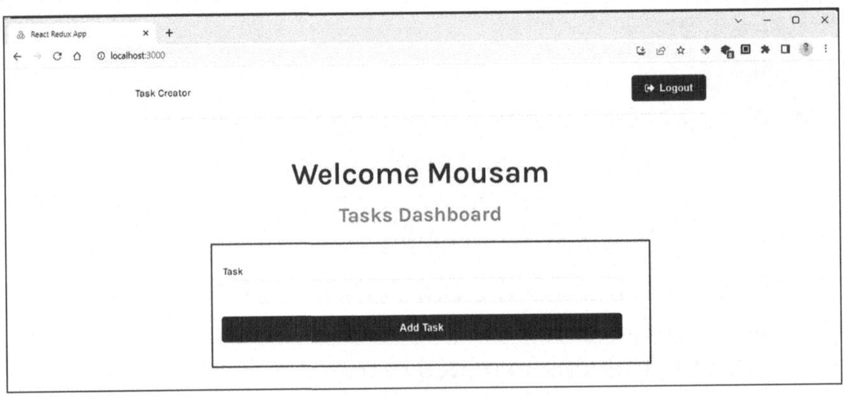

Figure 9.14: *Updated TaskForm component in localhost*

Lastly, in the **TaskForm.js** file, we will first import the **`createTask`** method from **taskSlice.js** file. We have not yet created this method, and will be created in the next chapter.

After that, inside the **`TaskForm`** function, we are first creating a dispatch variable by using the **`useDispatch()`** hook. Next, we are using the dispatch variable inside the **`onSubmit`** function. Here, we are using the dispatch variable to call the **`createTask`** method with the text state.

```
import { useState } from ‘react’
import { useDispatch } from ‘react-redux’
import { createTask } from ‘../features/tasks/taskSlice’

const TaskForm = () => {
    const [text, setText] = useState(‹›)
    const dispatch = useDispatch()

    const onSubmit = (e) => {
        e.preventDefault()
        dispatch(createTask({ text }))
        setText(‹›)
    }

    return (
      ...
    )
}
```

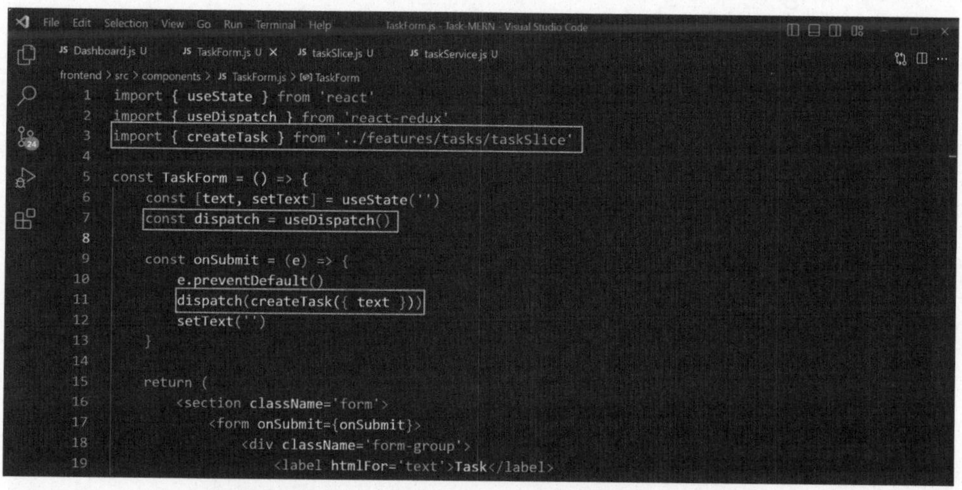

Figure 9.15: *Adding dispatch login in TaskForm.js file*

Conclusion

In this chapter, we learned about changing the Dashboard logic in our project. Here, we have restricted the dashboard to the logged in user. After that, we created the task slice, which will be used to create tasks. We also created a Task Form. In this form, we can take the user input to create a task.

In the next chapter, we will complete the task functionalities. And also fetch the tasks from the server and display them in Dashboard. We will also add the delete tasks logic.

Points to Remember

- Implementing logic for only logged-in users to see the dashboard.
- Using a slice to create the global task state.
- Creating a form in React for the input of tasks.

Multiple Choice Questions

1. What does the `useNavigate` hook do?
   a. Navigate to home route
   b. Navigate to any provided route
   c. Navigate to login route
   d. There is nothing like `useNavigate` hook
2. What does the `useSelector` hook do?
   a. Access the local state
   b. Access the component state
   c. There is nothing like `useSelector` hook
   d. Access the global state
3. In the redux toolkit the slice is a combination of ....
   a. store and reducer
   b. store and action
   c. action and reducer
   d. Reducer only

4. How to set a local state in a Functional React component?
    a. Using **`useEffect`** hook
    b. Using **`useState`** hook
    c. Using **`this.state`**
    d. State is not in functional components
5. What does the useDispatch hook do?
    a. Used to **`dispatch`** action to Slice
    b. Used to **`dispatch`** state to Slice
    c. Used to get global state from Slice
    d. There is nothing like **`useDispatch`** hook

Answers

1. b.
2. d.
3. c.
4. b.
5. a.

CHAPTER 10

Using Thunk and Completing App

Introduction

This chapter covers the implementation of Thunk in our Task workflow. We will also fetch the tasks from the server. This chapter also completes our app, in which we will add logic to display the tasks and also delete them.

Structure

In this chapter, we are going to cover the following topics:

- Creating task with Async Thunk
- Fetching tasks from the server
- Displaying tasks
- Deleting tasks

Creating task with Async Thunk

Back in the **taskSlice.js** file, which we created in our previous chapter, we will first import the taskService. Next, we are exporting a variable **`createTask`**. Here, again we are using the **`createAsyncThunk`** function. We don't need to import Thunk because the redux toolkit comes in-built with Thunk.

In the **`createAsyncThunk`** function, the first parameter is the **`tasks/create`**, which means from the **`tasks`** folder, take the **`create`** function. Next, the parameter is an async arrow function which takes the **`taskData`** and **`thunkAPI`** as a parameter.

Inside the function, we have a **try...catch** block. From the **try** block, we are first getting the token using the getState() method. Next, we call the **createTask** function from the **taskService.js** file with the taskData and token and then return it.

In the **catch** part, we are simply catching different kinds of errors and returning them. Note that the catch block will only execute if there is an error in the try block.

```
import taskService from './taskService'
...
export const createTask = createAsyncThunk(
  'tasks/create',
  async (taskData, thunkAPI) => {
      try {
      const token = thunkAPI.getState().auth.user.token
      return await taskService.createTask(taskData, token)
      } catch (error) {
      const message =
      (error.response && error.response.data && error.response.data.
message)
      || error.message
      || error.toString()
      return thunkAPI.rejectWithValue(message)
      }
  }
)
```

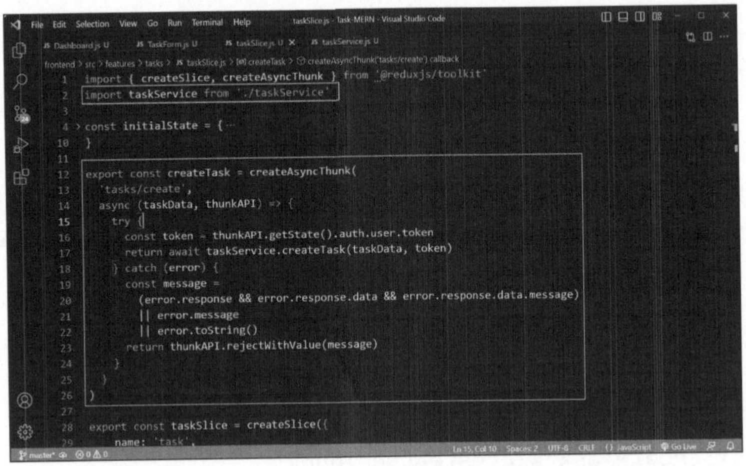

Figure 10.1: *Creating createTask in taskSlice.js file*

Next, we will create the task service. This service will be used to save the task data in the database. But since only the logged-in user should be able to do this, we will use a token also. So, create a file **taskService.js** inside the **tasks** folder.

Here, we are first importing **axios** and also creating a variable called **API_URL** which is set to **/api/tasks/**. Next, we have created a **createTask** function which takes the **taskData** and the **token**. Note that this only is the function which we are calling from our taskSlice.js file.

Inside the function, we have a **config** object first, where we are creating a **headers** key. The value of it is an object, which has a key of Authorization and a value of "Bearer token". Note that it is mandatory to add the keyword Bearer to the token while doing a POST call with the token.

Next, we are doing a **POST** call to the **API_URL** with the **taskData** and **config**. The result of the api call which we get in response.data and returning back the response from the function. Lastly, we are exporting the **createTask** function.

```
import axios from ‘axios’

const API_URL = ‘/api/tasks/’

const createTask = async (taskData, token) => {
       const config = {
       headers: {
```

```
        Authorization: `Bearer ${token}`,
      }
    }
    const response = await axios.post(API_URL, taskData, config)
    return response.data
}

const taskService = { createTask, getTasks, deleteTask }

export default taskService
```

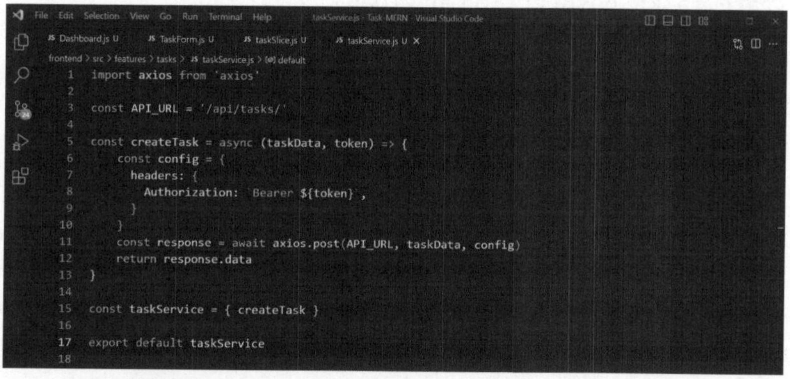

Figure 10.2: *Creating createTask in taskService.js file*

Inside our **taskSlice.js** file in the `taskSlice` function, we will add `extraReducers`. We will put the reducer action, which changes the state in these `extraReducers`.

In our code, we have three cases for pending, fulfilled and rejected cases. Since we are doing an API call to http://localhost:8000/api/tasks through our `createTask` function, we have three states in it. When the API call starts, we have a pending state since the API calls generally take 1–2 seconds. In the pending state, isLoading will be made to true, and we will also show a spinner in this state in the front end.

The next state is the fulfilled case, which will happen if our API call is successful. Here, we are making the isLoading as false and isSuccess as true and storing the payload which we receive back in the `tasks` state.

If, for some reason, the API call is not successful, we have a rejected case. Here, we are making the isLoading as false, isError as true. We are also storing the error in the **message** state, which we will receive in the payload.

```
extraReducers: (builder) => {
  builder
      .addCase(createTask.pending, (state) => {
        state.isLoading = true
      })
      .addCase(createTask.fulfilled, (state, action) => {
        state.isLoading = false
        state.isSuccess = true
        state.tasks.push(action.payload)
      })
      .addCase(createTask.rejected, (state, action) => {
        state.isLoading = false
        state.isError = true
        state.message = action.payload
      })
}
```

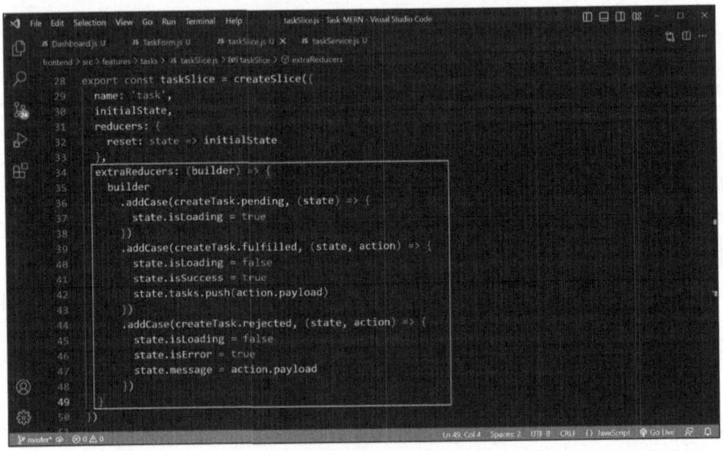

Figure 10.3: *Creating extraReducers in taskSlice.js file*

Now in Chrome/Firefox browser, go to http://localhost:3000/ and log in if not done. Also, open the Redux devtools to see the redux states. We will see the initial login states of auth and tasks in the redux devtools.

Here, add anything in the **Task** input box and click the **Add Task** button.

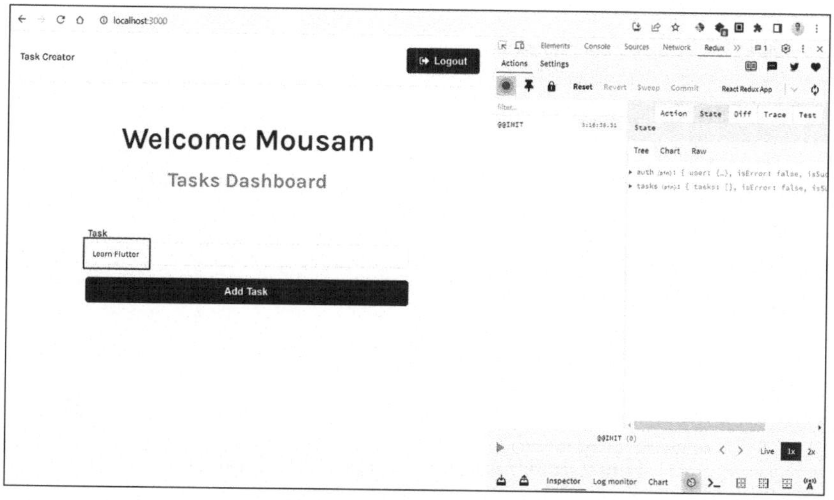

***Figure 10.4**: Adding text in Frontend*

Here, first, the pending action ran from the extraReducers in the **taskSlice.js** file. Here, the **isLoading** was set to true, and the rest states were kept as it was earlier.

Next, the API call to the backend was successful, so the fulfilled action had run. This has made the isLoading as false, isSuccess as true and **isError** as false. And the tasks state was set to the payload received from the backend. This payload consists of **text**, **user**, **_id**, **createdAt**, and **updatedAt**.

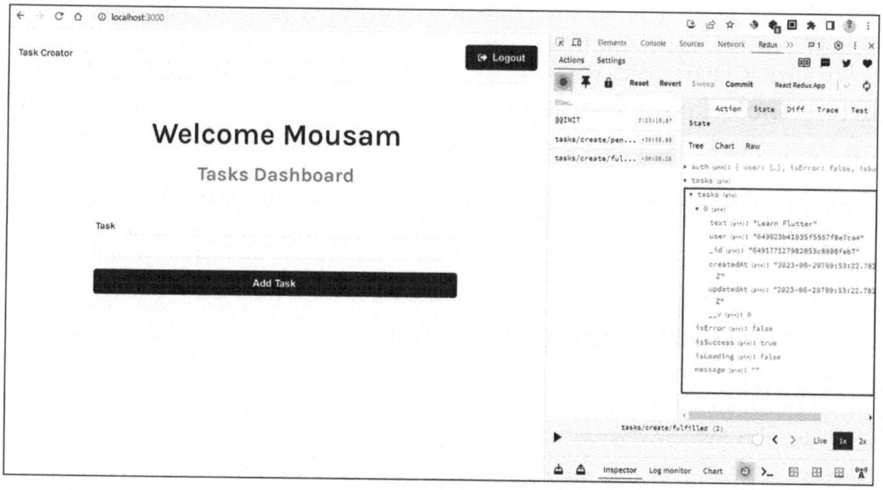

***Figure 10.5**: Task been added in Redux*

Finally, we checked the value for tasks in the connected MongoDB database, and a new field was added to it.

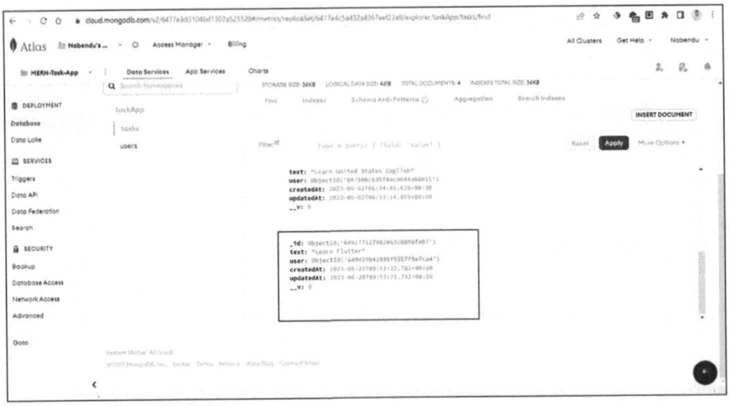

***Figure 10.6**: Task been added to the database*

Fetching tasks from server

Now, we will fetch all tasks from the server. For this, in the **taskSlice.js** file, we will create a getTasks variable. Here, we are again using the **createAsyncThunk** function.

In the **createAsyncThunk** function, the first parameter is the **tasks/getAll**, which means from the **tasks** folder, take the **getAll** function. Next, the parameter is an async arrow function which takes **_** and **thunkAPI** as a parameter. This is a common JavaScript way to say that no parameter is `required`.

Inside the function, we have a **`try…catch`** block. From the **`try`** block, we are first getting the token using the **`getState()`** method. Next, we call the **`getTasks`** function from the **taskService.js** file with the token and then return it.

In the **`catch`** part, we are simply catching different kinds of errors and returning them.

```
export const getTasks = createAsyncThunk(
  'tasks/getAll',
  async (_, thunkAPI) => {
    try {
      const token = thunkAPI.getState().auth.user.token
      return await taskService.getTasks(token)
```

```
    } catch (error) {
      const message =
        (error.response && error.response.data && error.response.data.message)
        || error.message
        || error.toString()
      return thunkAPI.rejectWithValue(message)
    }
  }
)
```

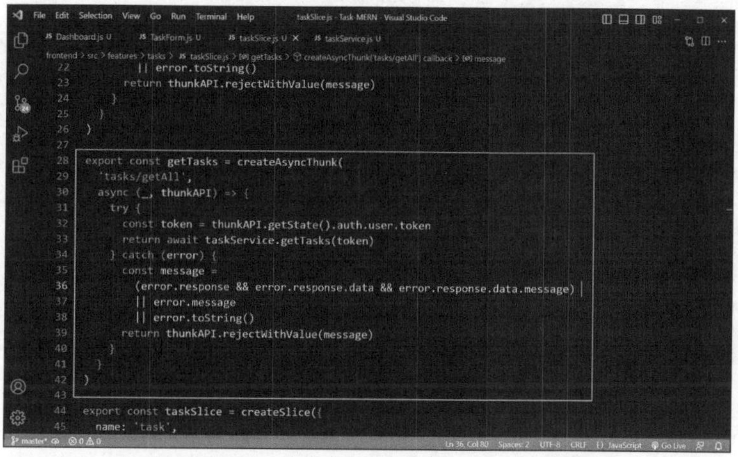

Figure 10.7: *getTasks function in taskSlice.js file*

Back in the **taskService.js** file, we have created a **`getTasks`** function which takes the **`token`** as a parameter. This is the function which we are calling from our **taskSlice.js** file.

Inside the function, we have a **config** object first, similar to the one created in the **`createTask`** function earlier in the chapter.

Next, we are doing a **`GET`** call to the **`API_URL`** with the **config**. The result of the api call which we get in **`response.data`** and returning back the response from the function. Lastly, we are exporting the **`getTasks`** function.

```
const getTasks = async token => {
  const config = {
```

```
      headers: {
        Authorization: `Bearer ${token}`,
      }
    }
    const response = await axios.get(API_URL, config)
    return response.data
}

const taskService = { createTask, getTasks }
```

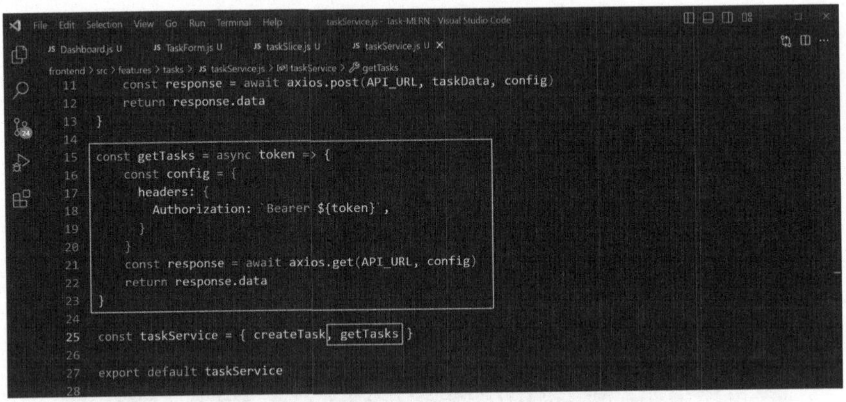

Figure 10.8: *getTasks function in taskService.js file*

Inside our **taskSlice.js** file in the **`taskSlice`** function, we will add the new cases in the **`extraReducers`**.

In our code, we have three cases for pending, fulfilled and rejected cases. Since we are doing an API GET call to http://localhost:8000/api/tasks through our **`getTasks`** function, we have three states in it. When the API call starts, we have a pending state. In the pending state, isLoading will be made to true.

The next state is the fulfilled case, which will happen if our API call is successful. Here, we are making the isLoading as false and isSuccess as true and storing the payload which we receive back in the **`tasks`** state.

If, for some reason, the API call is not successful, we have a rejected case. Here, we are making the **`isLoading`** as false, isError as true. We are also storing the error in the message state, which we will receive in the payload.

```
.addCase(getTasks.pending, (state) => {
  state.isLoading = true
})
.addCase(getTasks.fulfilled, (state, action) => {
  state.isLoading = false
  state.isSuccess = true
  state.tasks = action.payload
})
.addCase(getTasks.rejected, (state, action) => {
  state.isLoading = false
  state.isError = true
  state.message = action.payload
})
```

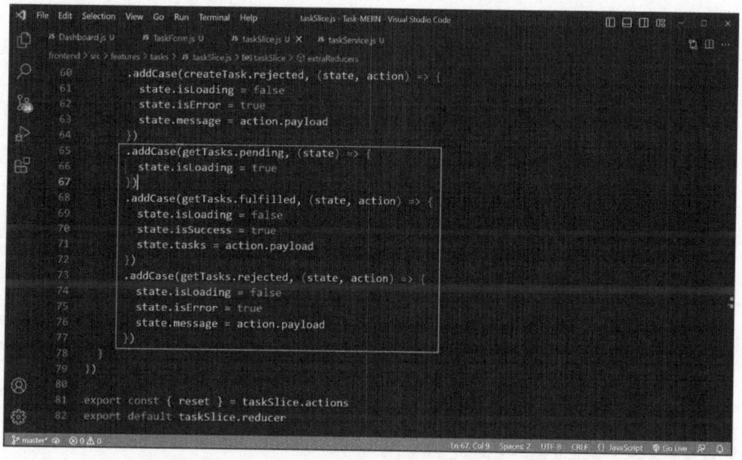

Figure 10.9: *extraReducer cases in taskSlice.js file*

Now, in the **Dashboard.js** file, we will show a button instead of the earlier text. In the next part, we will add logic to show all tasks from a new component when we click this button.

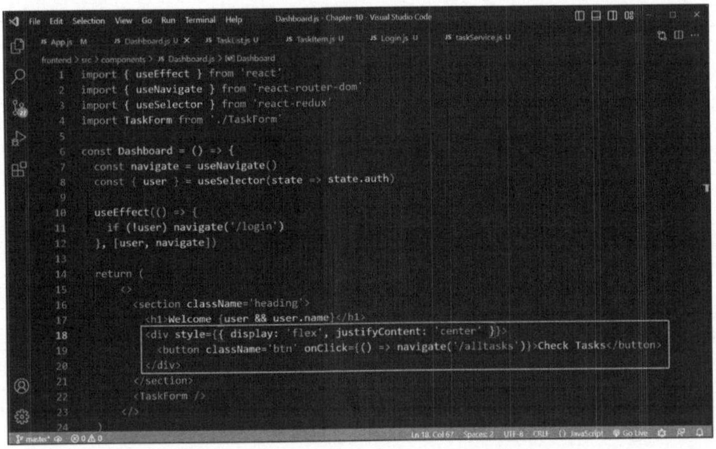

Figure 10.10: *Adding button in Dashboard.js file*

Back in the browser at http://localhost:3000/, we will see the button for all tasks.

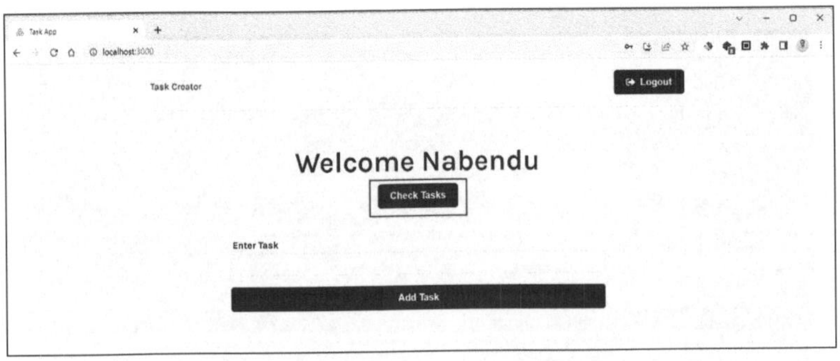

Figure 10.11: *Button in localhost*

Displaying the tasks

Now, we will display the tasks for which we have created the logic in the previous part. Here, in the **App.js** file, we will add a new route to show all tasks.

For this, we are adding a <Route> with the path as **/alltasks** and which will call the **TaskList** component. We are also importing this **TaskList** component, which we are going to create next.

```
import TaskList from './components/TaskList';
```

```
...
...
<Route path='/alltasks' element={<TaskList />} />
```

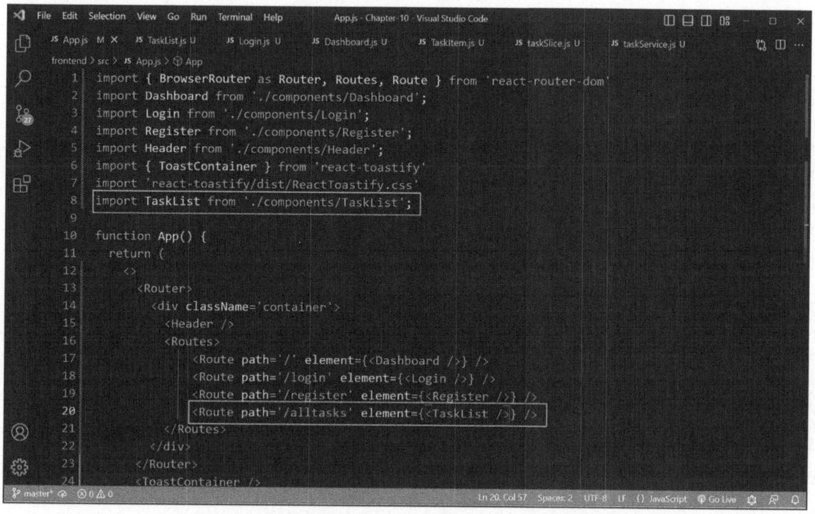

***Figure 10.12**: Adding new route in App.js file*

Next, create a new file **TaskList.js** in the **components** folder. Here, we are first importing the **useEffect** hook from react, which will be used to do the async task of calling different action creators through dispatch. Next, we import **useSelector** and **useDispatch** hooks from **react-redux**. As earlier, they will be used to access the global state and dispatch the action creator.

Next, we are importing the recently created **getTasks** function from the task slice and also importing the reset function. We are also importing a TaskItem component, which we have not created yet and the Spinner component from showing a Spinner. Lastly, we are importing the useNavigate hook, which will be used in our **useEffect**.

Now, inside the **TaskList** function, we are first creating a variable of dispatch and navigating using the **useDispatch** and **useNavigate** hooks, respectively. After that, using the **useSelector** hook, we get the global state of tasks. Also, notice that we are destructuring it to get the **tasks**, **isLoading**, **isError**, and **message**.

Next, inside the **useEffect** hook, we are first checking for errors and console logging it. If there are no errors, then we are calling the **getTasks** method through the **dispatch** function. We also have an unmounting state dispatching the reset method. The **useEffect** method also has a second parameter as an array of **navigate**, **isError**,

message and **dispatch**. This means the useEffect will be fired whenever these will change. Lastly, the return statement is only showing a div, which we will update next.

```
import { useEffect } from 'react'
import { useSelector, useDispatch } from 'react-redux'
import { getTasks, reset } from '../features/tasks/taskSlice'
import TaskItem from './TaskItem'
import Spinner from './Spinner'
import { useNavigate } from 'react-router-dom'

const TaskList = () => {
    const dispatch = useDispatch()
    const navigate = useNavigate()
    const { tasks, isLoading, isError, message } = useSelector(state =>
state.tasks)

    useEffect(() => {
        if (isError) console.log(message)
        dispatch(getTasks())
        return () => dispatch(reset())
    }, [navigate, isError, message, dispatch])

    return (
      <div>TaskList</div>
    )
}

export default TaskList
```

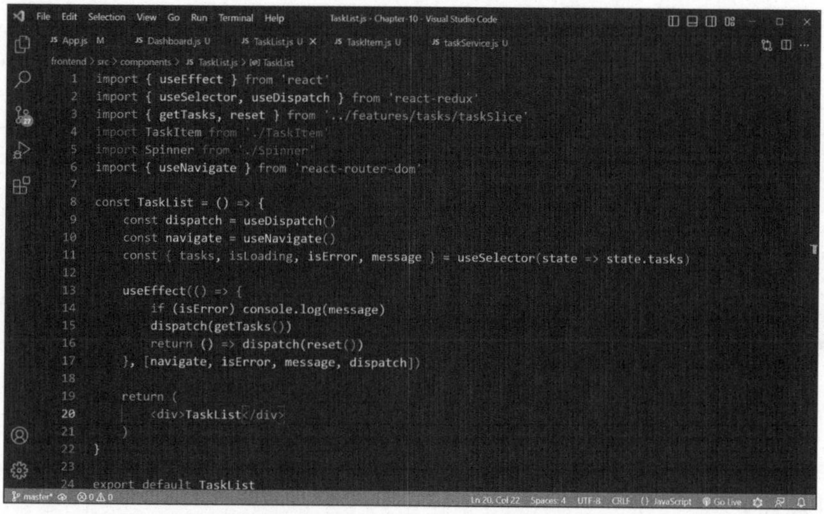

***Figure 10.13**: The TaskList.js file*

Next, we will update the return statement inside the **TaskList.js** file. Here, we are using the ternary operator and checking if the isLoading is true, then showing the Spinner component. Or else the other part is executed. Here, we are first checking if the tasks array length is greater than zero.

If it is the case, then we are looping through the tasks variable and sending each task to the **`TaskItem`** component.

```
isLoading ? <Spinner /> : (
  <section className='content'>
      {tasks.length > 0 && (
          <div className='tasks'>
              {tasks.map(task => <TaskItem key={task._id} task={task}
/>)}
          </div>
      )}
  </section>
)
```

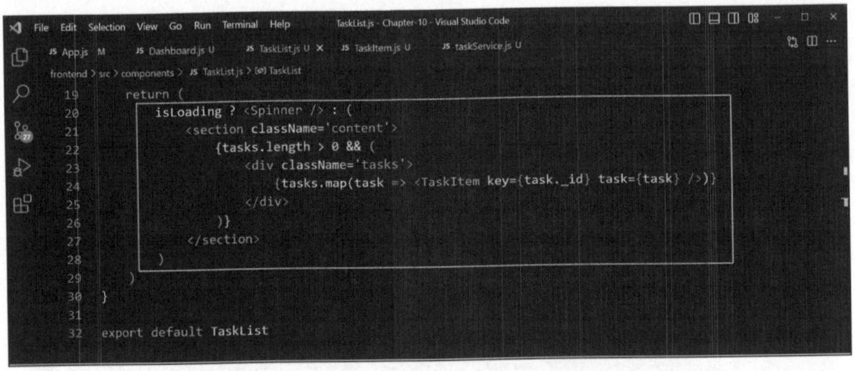

***Figure 10.14**: Adding return logic in TaskList.js file*

Next, create the **TaskItem.js** file in the **components** folder. Here, we are first importing the useDispatch hook from react-redux, which we are going to use later while creating delete functionalities.

Inside the **`TaskItem`** function, we are first destructuring the props of the task. Next, we show the **`createdAt`** and **`text`** inside a div and h2, respectively. Also, notice that the createdAt is changed to the proper format using the new **`Date()`** and **`toLocaleString('en-US')`**.

```
import { useDispatch } from ‘react-redux’

const TaskItem = ({ task }) => {
    return (
        <div className=’task’>
            <div>{new Date(task.createdAt).toLocaleString(‘en-US’)}</
div>
            <h2>{task.text}</h2>
        </div>
    )
}

export default TaskItem
```

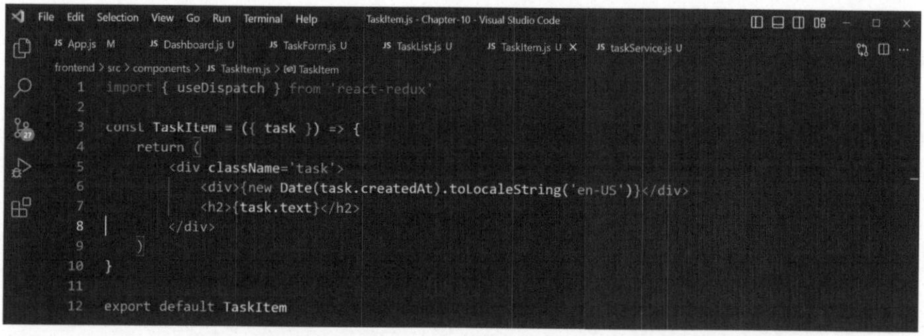

***Figure 10.15**: Creating TaskItem.js file*

We will also update the **TaskForm.js** file to navigate to the **/alltasks** route and hence show the **TaskList** component. Here, we are first importing the useNavigate hook from react-router-dom.

After that, we use it to create a variable called navigate inside the TaskForm function. After that, in the **`onSubmit()`** method, which is called after the user clicks on the **`Add Tasks`** button, we add navigate() at the end to go to **`/alltasks`**.

Also, we are changing a bit of the text style of Enter Text using inline styling.

```
import { useNavigate } from ‘react-router-dom’

const TaskForm = () => {
    const navigate = useNavigate()

    const onSubmit = (e) => {
        e.preventDefault()
        dispatch(createTask({ text }))
        setText(‘’)
        navigate(‘/alltasks’)
    }

    return (
        <section className=’form’>
            <form onSubmit={onSubmit}>
                <div className=’form-group’>
```

```
                    <label htmlFor='text' style={{ fontWeight:
'bolder'}}>Enter Task</label>
                </div>
            </form>
        </section>
    )
}
```

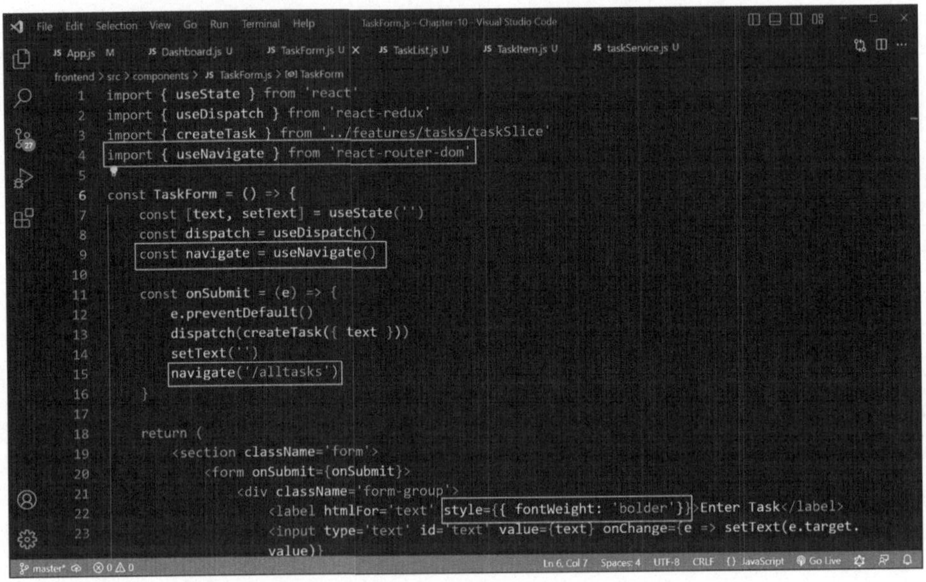

Figure 10.16: *Updating navigation in TaskForm.js file*

Now, in the Chrome/Firefox browser, directly open http://localhost:3000/alltasks or click on the **`Check Tasks`** button to go there. Also, open the Redux devtools in the browser. Here, we will first see the pending case for getAll tasks.

In this state, since the API call has been going on, we will see the isLoading as true. The tasks will be an empty array, and the isError and isSuccess will be false. Also, the message will be an empty string.

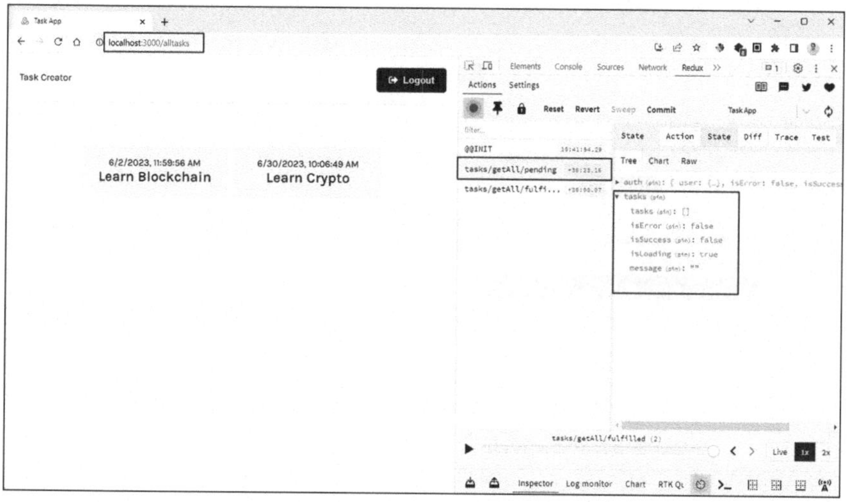

Figure 10.17: *Pending state for all tasks*

Once the API call is successful, we will see the tasks array is filled with data from the backend. It contains the text and the **`createdAt`** field, which we are showing in the browser.

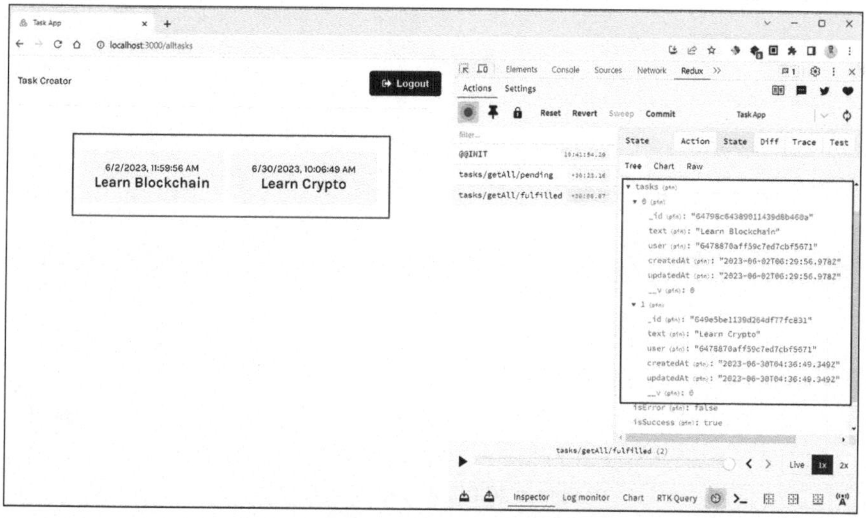

Figure 10.18: *Fulfilled state for all tasks*

Now, back in http://localhost:3000/, enter a task and click on the **`Add Task`** button. Notice that when we came here, the reset case was running, and it made all states its initial value.

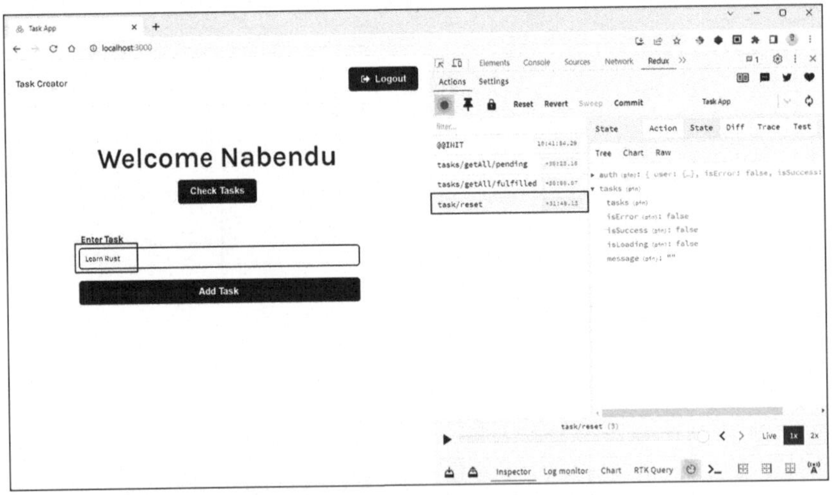

Figure 10.19: *Reset before adding tasks*

On clicking on the `Add Task`, we are taken to http://localhost:3000/alltasks and the new task is added. Also, notice the new task is added in the tasks state in Redux devtools.

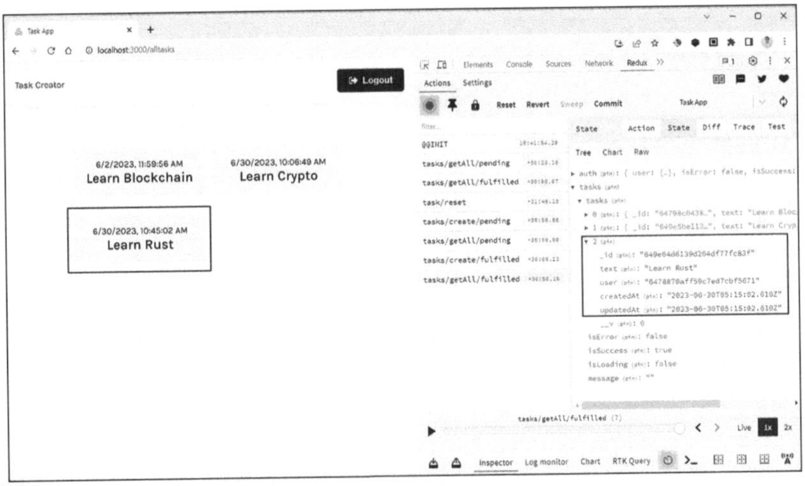

Figure 10.20: *Added new task*

Now, let's also see the tasks for another user. Here, we have logged in with another user's login and then clicked on the `Check Tasks` button.

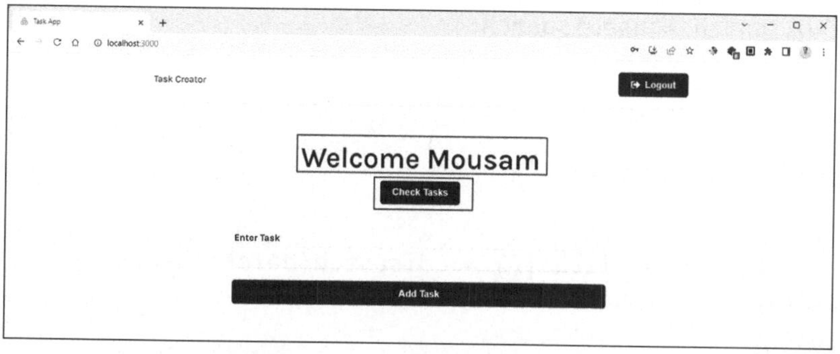

***Figure 10.21**: Checking tasks for different user*

Here, notice that different tasks are shown for the user in the http://localhost:3000/alltasks link.

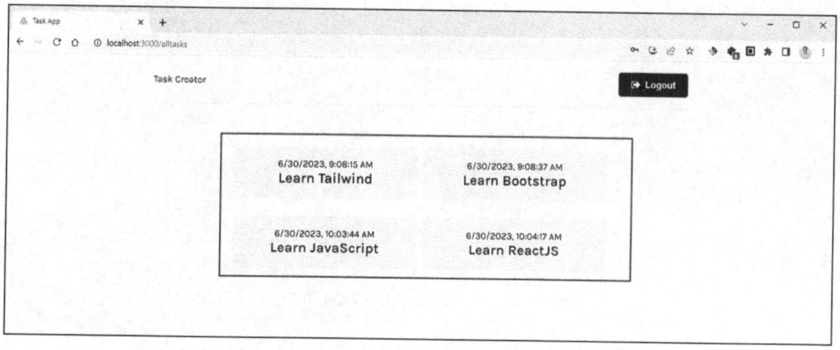

***Figure 10.22**: Tasks for different user*

Deleting tasks

Now, we will add the last functionality in our project, which is to delete a task. So in the **TaskItem.js** file, we will first import the **`useDispatch`** hook from **`react-redux`**. Next, we are also importing the **`deleteTask`** from **taskSlice**, which we will create next.

Inside the **`TaskItem`**, we are creating a dispatch variable which will use the useDispatch. Next, we have added a button which will dispatch the **`deleteTask()`** with the task id.

```
import { useDispatch } from 'react-redux'
import { deleteTask } from '../features/tasks/taskSlice'

const TaskItem = ({ task }) => {
```

```
    const dispatch = useDispatch()

    return (
        <div className='task'>
            ...
            <button onClick={() => dispatch(deleteTask(task._id))}
className='close'>X</button>
        </div>
    )
}
```

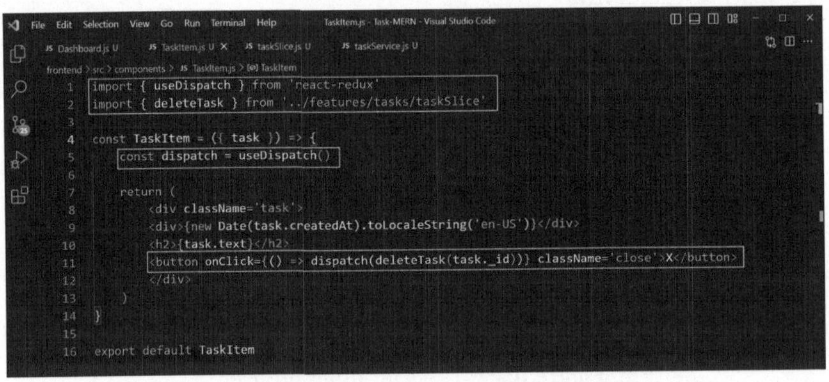

***Figure 10.23**: Adding button to delete task*

Now, in the **taskSlice.js** file, we will create a **`deleteTask`** variable. Here, we are again using the **`createAsyncThunk`** function.

In the **`createAsyncThunk`** function, the first parameter is the **tasks/delete**, which means from the **tasks** folder, take the **`delete`** function. Next, the parameter is an async arrow function which takes **id** and **thunkAPI** as a parameter.

Inside the function, we have a **`try...catch`** block. From the **`try`** block, we are first getting the token using the **`getState()`** method. Next, we call the **`deleteTask`** function from the **taskService.js** file with the **`id`** and the **`token`** and then return it.

In the catch part, we are simply catching different kinds of errors and returning them.

```
export const deleteTask = createAsyncThunk(
  'tasks/delete',
```

```
  async (id, thunkAPI) => {
    try {
      const token = thunkAPI.getState().auth.user.token
      return await taskService.deleteTask(id, token)
    } catch (error) {
      const message =
        (error.response && error.response.data && error.response.data.message)
        || error.message
        || error.toString()
      return thunkAPI.rejectWithValue(message)
    }
  }
)
```

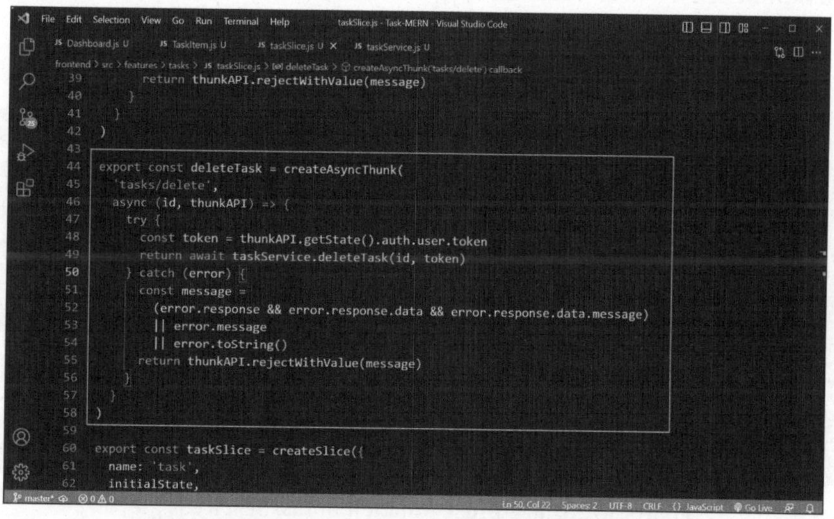

Figure 10.24: *deleteTask function in taskSlice.js file*

Back in the **taskService.js** file, we have created a **deleteTask** function which takes the **id** and **token** as a parameter. This is the function which we are calling from our taskSlice.js file.

Inside the function, we have a **config** object first, similar to the one created in the **getTasks** function earlier in the chapter.

Next, we are doing a DELETE call to the **`API_URL`** plus **`id`** with the **`config`**. The result of the api call which we get in **`response.data`** and returning back the response from the function. Lastly, we are exporting the **`deleteTask`** function.

```
const deleteTask = async (id, token) => {
  const config = {
    headers: {
      Authorization: `Bearer ${token}`,
    }
  }
  const response = await axios.delete(API_URL + id, config)
  return response.data
}

const taskService = { createTask, getTasks, deleteTask }
```

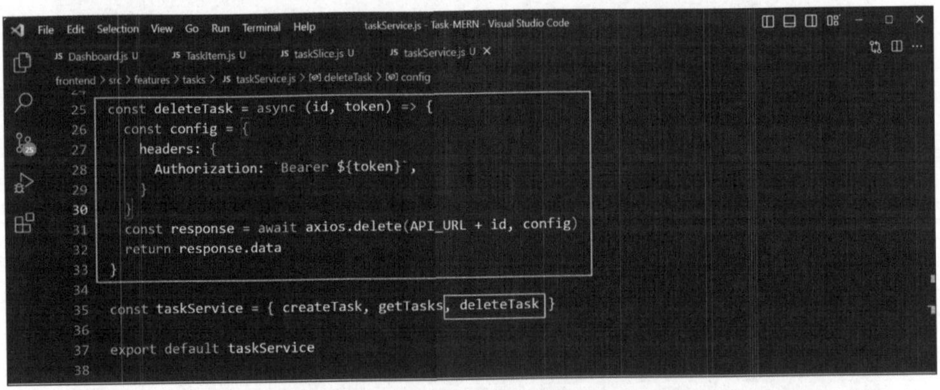

Figure 10.25: *deleteTask function in taskService.js file*

Now, in our **taskSlice.js** file in the **`taskSlice`** function, we will add the new cases in the **`extraReducers`**.

In our code, we have three cases for pending, fulfilled and rejected cases. Since we are doing an API DELETE call to http://localhost:8000/api/tasks through our **`deleteTask`** function, we have three states in it. When the API call starts, we have a pending state. In the pending state, **`isLoading`** will be made to true.

The next state is the fulfilled case, which will happen if our API call is successful. Here, we are making the **`isLoading`** as false and isSuccess as true and then filtering the tasks state to remove the passed task and update the tasks state.

If, for some reason, the API call is not successful, we have a rejected case. Here, we are making the **`isLoading`** as false, **`isError`** as true. We are also storing the error in the **`message`** state, which we will receive in the payload.

```
.addCase(deleteTask.pending, (state) => {
  state.isLoading = true
})
.addCase(deleteTask.fulfilled, (state, action) => {
  state.isLoading = false
  state.isSuccess = true
  state.tasks = state.tasks.filter(task => task._id !== action.payload.
id)
})
.addCase(deleteTask.rejected, (state, action) => {
  state.isLoading = false
  state.isError = true
  state.message = action.payload
})
```

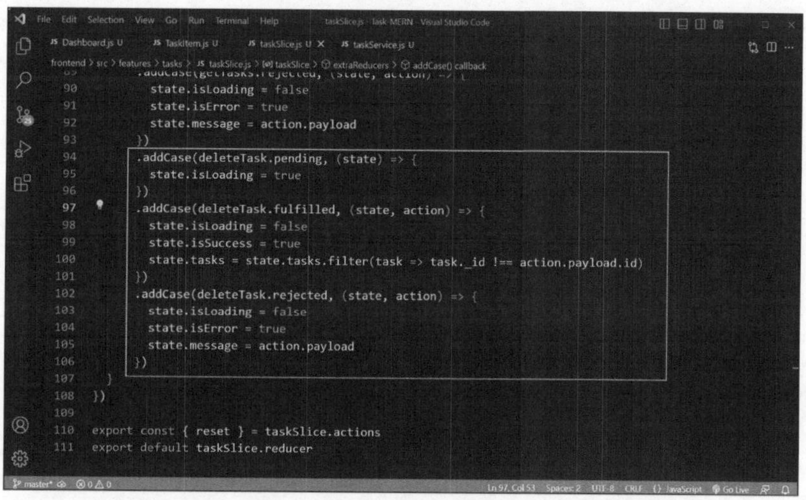

Figure 10.26: *extraReducers for delete in taskSlice.js file*

Now, go back to http://localhost:3000/alltasks, and we will see the X button. We can see that there are four tasks here and also notice the task in the Redux devtools.

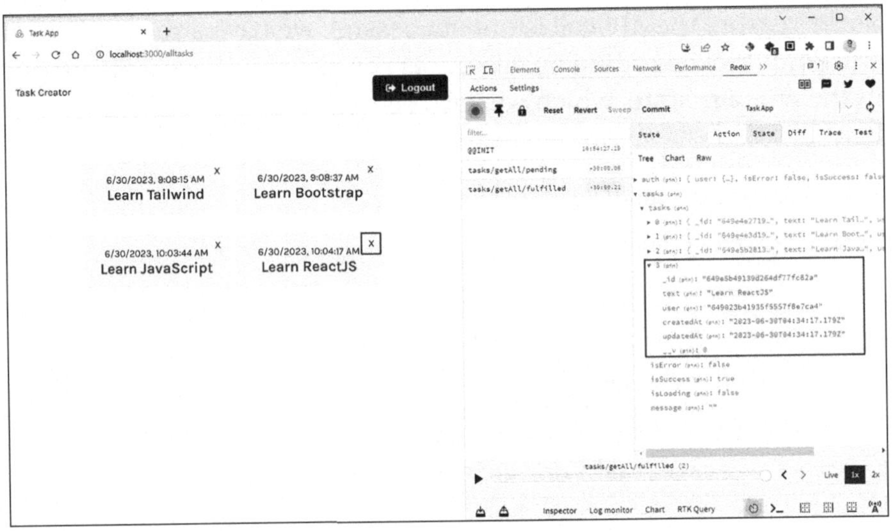

Figure 10.27: *All tasks for a user in localhost*

Once we click on the X button in http://localhost:3000/alltasks, we will first see the pending case for delete tasks.

In this state, since the API call has been going on, we will see the isLoading as true. The isError will be false, and the isSuccess will be true. Also, the message will be an empty string. The tasks array will still contain four elements.

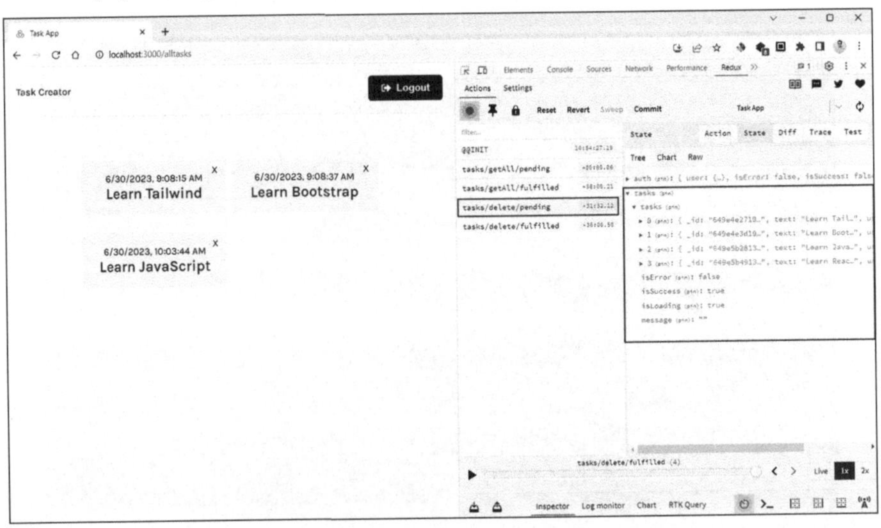

Figure 10.28: *Pending state for delete in localhost*

Once the API call is successful, we will see the fulfilled case for delete tasks. Also, the tasks state will now contain three elements.

In the browser also, we will see the `Learn ReactJS` element being deleted.

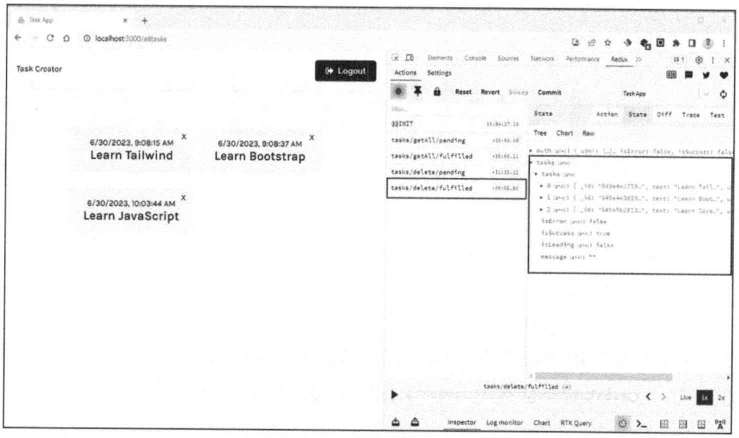

***Figure 10.29**: Fulfilled state for delete in localhost*

Conclusion

In this chapter, we have learned about implementing Thunk in our Task workflow. Here, we have also fetched all tasks from the database. After that, we displayed all tasks in the front end.

Next, we have also learned to delete the task from the front end and database.

In the next chapter, we will test the front end made in React using Jest and React Testing Library.

Points to remember

- Implementing tasks with async Thunk
- Displaying all tasks on the front end
- Deleting a task from the front end and database

CHAPTER 11

Frontend Testing

Introduction

This chapter covers the testing of our frontend using Jest and React Testing Library. These two libraries are in-built in React and help us do unit testing in our frontend code.

It's generally the developer's responsibility to do unit testing of code. Unit testing helps catch errors early, and in a lot of companies, the unit testing code coverage should be 80%. Unit testing involves some type of coding, which is again a developer domain. The testers generally do end-to-end testing using manual or automated testing, which is different than the unit testing done by developers.

Structure

In this chapter, we are going to discuss the following topics:

- Setup testing in Frontend
- Task Slice and Service test with Jest
- Testing with React Testing Library
- Configuring and Checking Coverage

Setup testing in Frontend

We don't need to do much setup for testing, as the react app created using create-react-app comes in-built with the testing library of Jest and also React Testing Library(RTL). We can check the same in **package.json** on our frontend.

```
"@testing-library/jest-dom": "^5.16.5",
```

```
"@testing-library/react": "^13.4.0",
"@testing-library/user-event": "^14.4.3"
```

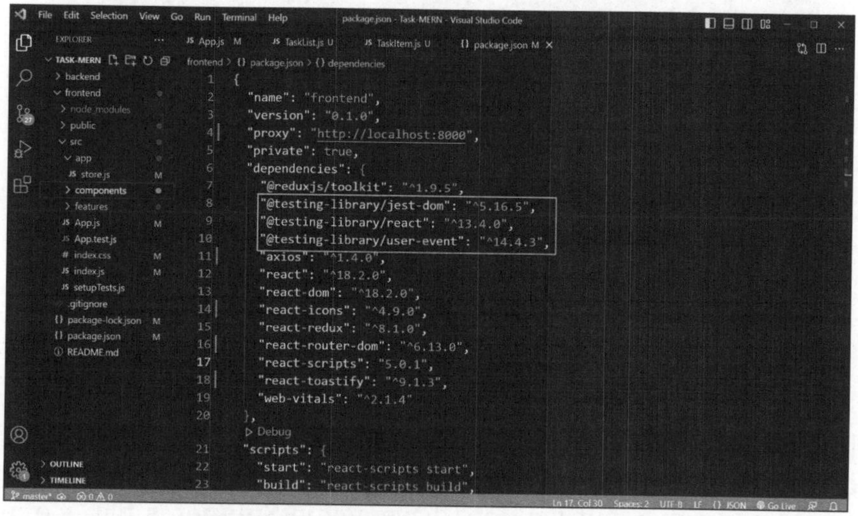

Figure 11.1: *Checking React testing libraries*

Now, from the terminal go to the frontend folder and run the npm test. It will fail since we have made a lot of changes in the **App.js** file.

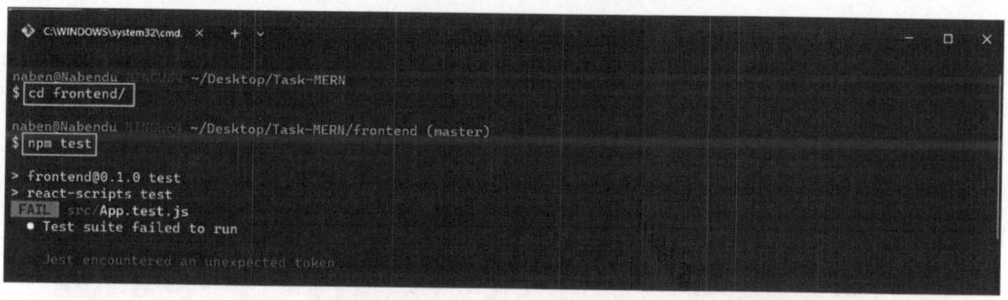

Figure 11.2: *Running tests*

Now, we will remove the **App.test.js** file as it will cause errors in our tests.

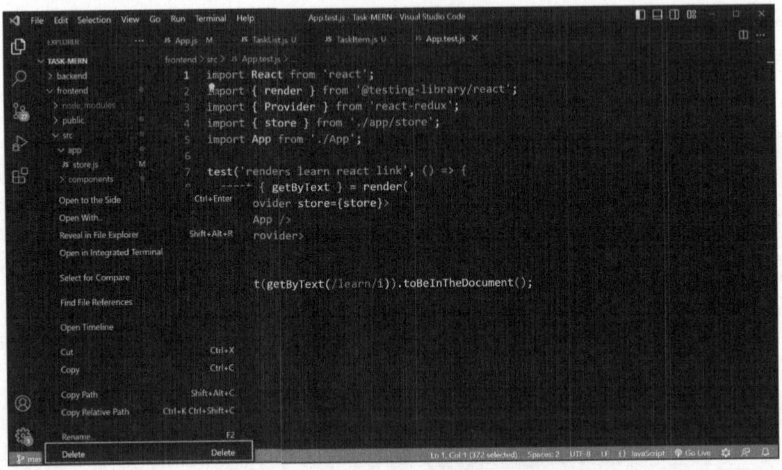

Figure 11.3: *Deleting App.test.js file*

We will write our first Jest test for the **Spinner.js** file. For this, we have also created a **Spinner.test.js** file. In Jest testing, we need to identify any element with something unique, but we don't have any in **Spinner.js** file. So, we have added the attribute of **data-testid** in both divs.

```
      <div className='loadingSpinnerContainer' data-testid=
"spin-container">
          <div className='loadingSpinner' data-testid="inner-container"
/>
      </div>
```

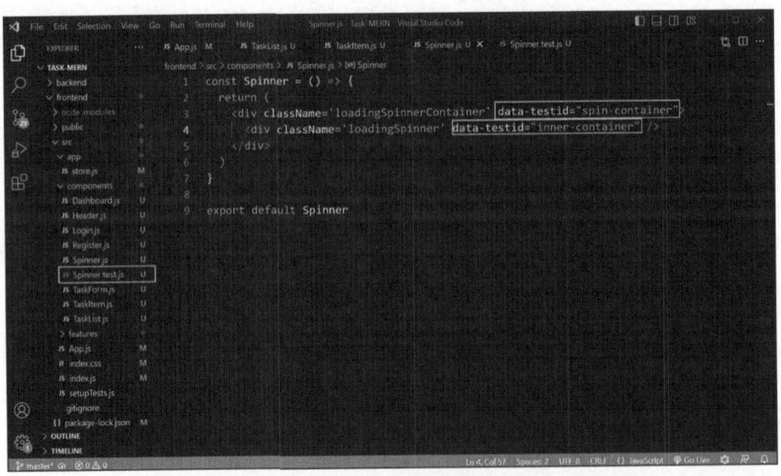

Figure 11.4: *Adding data-testid in Spinner.js file*

Finally, we will write our first test in the **Spinner.test.js** file. Here, we will first import the render and screen from the testing library. We will also import the Spinner component.

In jest testing, we have a 'describe' block wrapping all of our tests. Here, the first parameter is a string and the second is an arrow function. Next, we have a single test. Here, also the first parameter is a string which is "render correctly" in our case. The second parameter is an arrow function in which we will write the test statements.

Here, we are first rendering the Spinner component with the render method. Next, we created a variable called **`containerDiv`**, and with **`screen.getByTestId()`** got the first div with the name **`spin-container`**. Here, we are testing it with the **`expect()`** function and **`toBeInTheDocument()`**.

We are repeating the same for the **`inner-container`**.

```
import { render, screen } from "@testing-library/react";
import Spinner from "./Spinner";

describe("Spinner", () => {
      test("render correctly", () => {
      render(<Spinner />);

      const containerDiv = screen.getByTestId("spin-container");
      expect(containerDiv).toBeInTheDocument();

      const innerDiv = screen.getByTestId("inner-container");
      expect(innerDiv).toBeInTheDocument();
      })
})
```

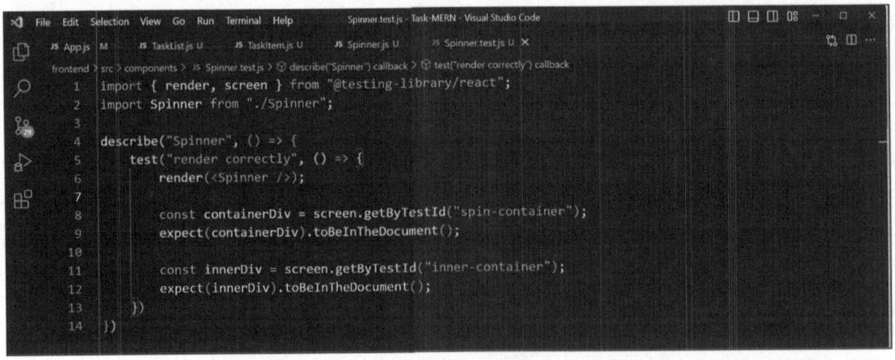

Figure 11.5: *Writing test in Spinner.test..js file*

Now, on running the tests with **npm test**, the test in **Spinner.test.js** will pass.

Figure 11.6: *Running successful test from Spinner.test..js*

Task Slice and Service Test with Jest

We will now test the **taskSlice.js** and **taskService.js** files. The tests for these components are a bit complicated because we need to test them using mock data.

For this, we will install the library of `axios-mock-adapter` with the following command. This library helps us to mock axios calls. Note that we are installing the same dev dependency as we don't need it in production.

```
npm i -D axios-mock-adapter
```

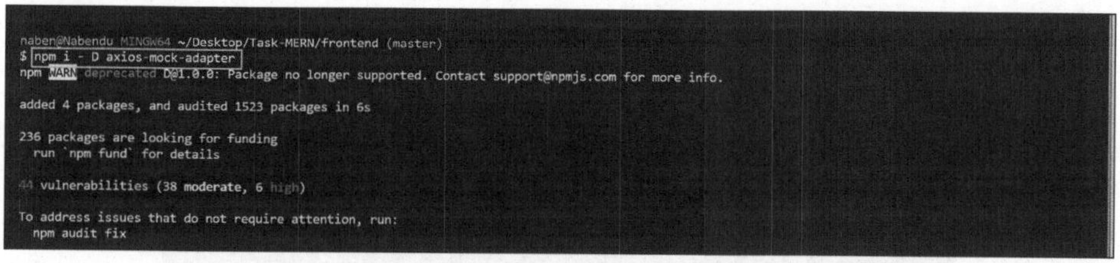

***Figure 11.7**: Installing axios-mock-adapter package*

Next, we will install **`redux-mock-store`** in our frontend app. This library will mock the redux store in our app. We will install it with the following command:

```
npm i redux-mock-store
```

***Figure 11.8**: Installing redux-mock-store package*

We also need to add a new **.babelrc** in the root directory of the frontend, and add the content for presets in it. Besides this, we need to install **`babel-jest`** and **@babel/preset-env** as dev dependency.

```
npm install --save-dev babel-jest @babel/preset-env
{
        "presets": [
        "@babel/preset-env"
        ]
}
```

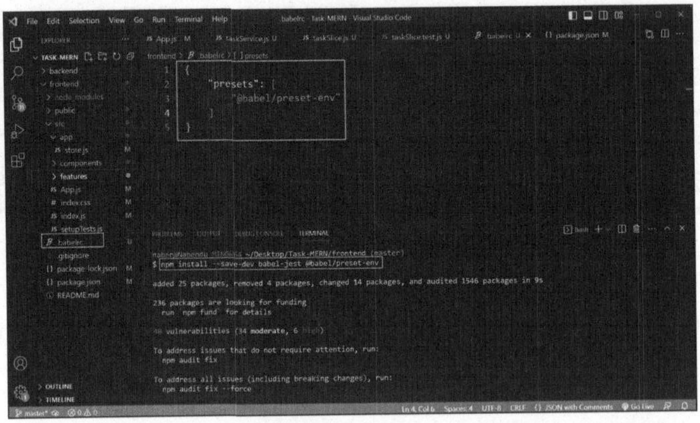

Figure 11.9: *Changing babel configurations*

We also need to do a setup in the **package.json** file. Here, we are using **babel-jest** to transform the js or jsx files. And we are also ignoring the **node_modules** and axios.

```
«jest»: {
    "transform": {
    "^.+\\.jsx?$": "babel-jest"
    },
    "transformIgnorePatterns": [
    "node_modules/(?!axios)/"
    ]
}
```

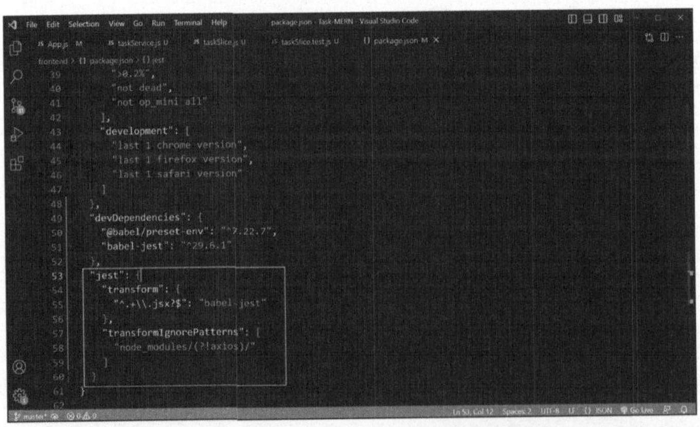

Figure 11.10: *Adding babel config in package.json file*

Now, we will create a **taskSlice.test.js** file inside the **tasks** folder. Here, we will first import **configureMockStore** from redux-mock-store, which will help us to mock redux. Next, we will import thunk middleware from **redux-thunk**.

We will import the **MockAdapter** from **axios-mock-adapter** which will help us mock **axios**. Next, we will also import axios which is used to do API calls in React. We will also import **getTasks** and **taskService**.

Lastly, we will create a variable of **mockStore** and use the **configureMockStore** and pass thunk in it. And we will also create a variable of mock and use the **MockAdapter** and pass axios in it.

```
import configureMockStore from ‘redux-mock-store’;
import thunk from ‘redux-thunk’;
import MockAdapter from ‘axios-mock-adapter’;
import axios from ‘axios’;
import { getTasks } from ‘./taskSlice’;
import taskService from ‘./taskService’;

const mockStore = configureMockStore([thunk]);
const mock = new MockAdapter(axios);
```

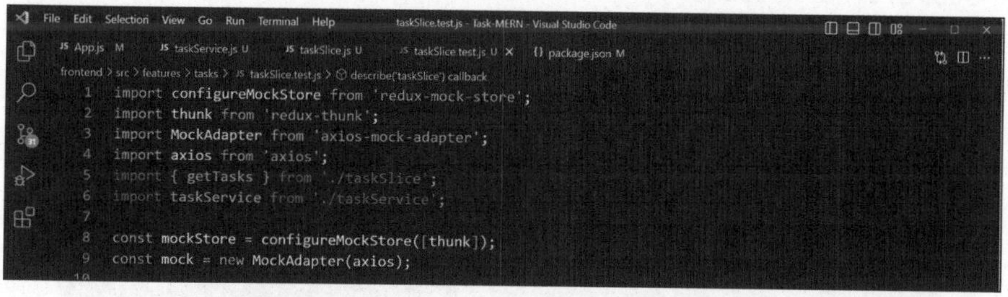

Figure 11.11: *Writing imports in taskSlice.test.js file*

Next, in the **taskSlice.test.js** file, inside a describe block, we will first create a variable store. We will have **beforeEach()** and **afterEach()** functions. These functions run before and after every test.

In the beforeEach, we are using **mockStore** to mock our initial task state as per the taskSlice.js file. Also, we need to use a mock user token, as it is used in the taskSlice.js file.

In the **afterEach**, we are resetting the mock and the store.

```
describe('taskSlice', () => {
  let store;
  beforeEach(() => {
      store = mockStore({
      task: {
      tasks: [],
      isError: false,
      isSuccess: false,
      isLoading: false,
      message: '',
      },
      auth: {
       user: { token: 'mock_token' },
      },
      });
   });
   afterEach(() => {
      mock.reset();
      store.clearActions();
  });
});
```

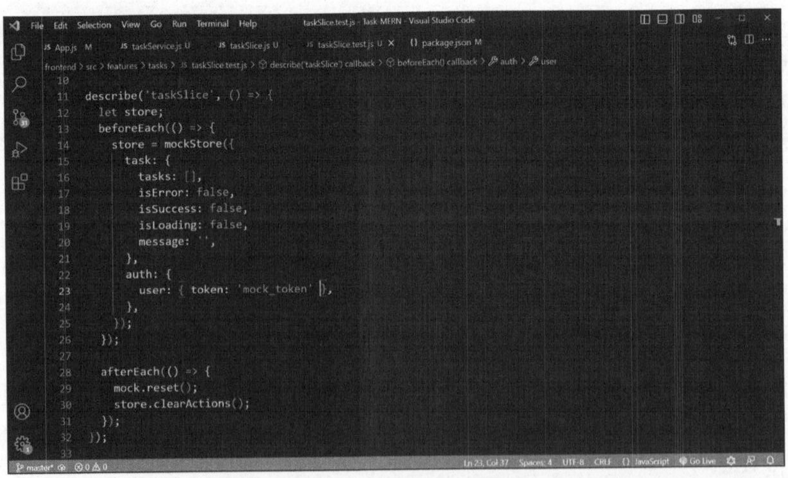

Figure 11.12: *Writing describe in taskSlice.test.js file*

Now, we will write our test in the **taskSlice.test.js** file. Here, we have a test function, where we first use the **mock_token**. Next, we have taken a dummy task which is an array of objects. Here, we have given some dummy fields.

Next, we created a constant variable called **getTaskSpy**. Here, using the **jest.spyOn()** which takes the first parameter as **taskService** and the second as **getTasks**. This should be resolved to the tasks.

Next, we are dispatching the **getTasks()** from **taskSlice.js** file. Finally, we are expecting the **getTasksSpy** to be called using the token.

```
test(‹calls the taskService to fetch tasks›, async () => {
    const token = 'mock_token';
    const tasks = [
    {
        _id: '649e4e271947362dc297436a',
        text: 'Learn Tailwind',
        user: '649023b41935f5557f8e7ca4',
        createdAt: '2023-06-30T03:38:15.287Z',
        updatedAt: '2023-06-30T03:38:15.287Z',
        __v: 0
    }
    ];

    const getTasksSpy = jest.spyOn(taskService, 'getTasks').mock-
ResolvedValue(tasks);
    await store.dispatch(getTasks());
    expect(getTasksSpy).toHaveBeenCalledWith(token);
});
```

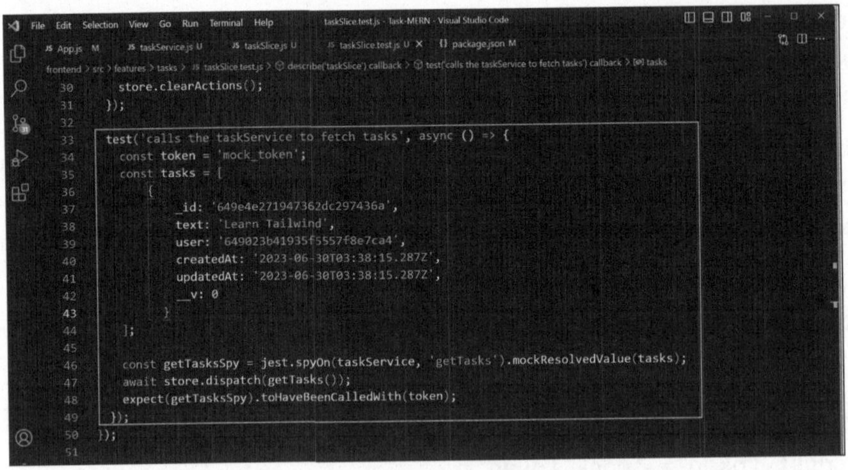

Figure 11.13: *Writing tests in taskSlice.test.js file*

Now, on running the test with npm test our **taskSlice.test.js** file will pass.

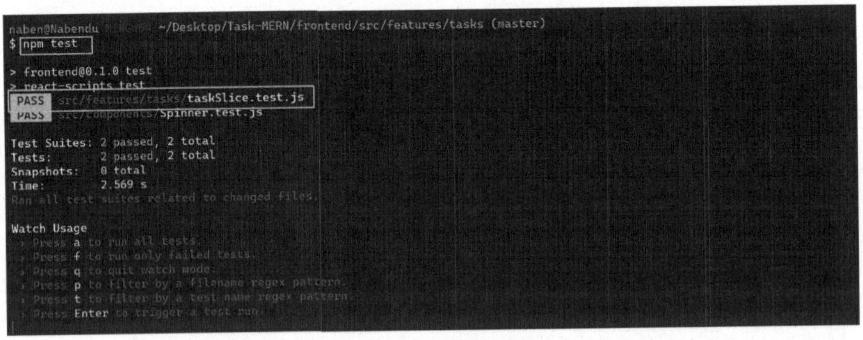

Figure 11.14: *Running tests for taskSlice.test.js file*

Now, we will write the test for the task service component. So, create a **taskService.test.js** file inside the **tasks** folder. Here, we are first importing axios for API calls. Then we are importing MockAdapter for mocking axios. Lastly, we are importing the `taskService` component. We also created a mock variable using `MockAdapter` and passed the axios.

```
import axios from 'axios';
import MockAdapter from 'axios-mock-adapter';
import taskService from './taskService';

const mock = new MockAdapter(axios);
```

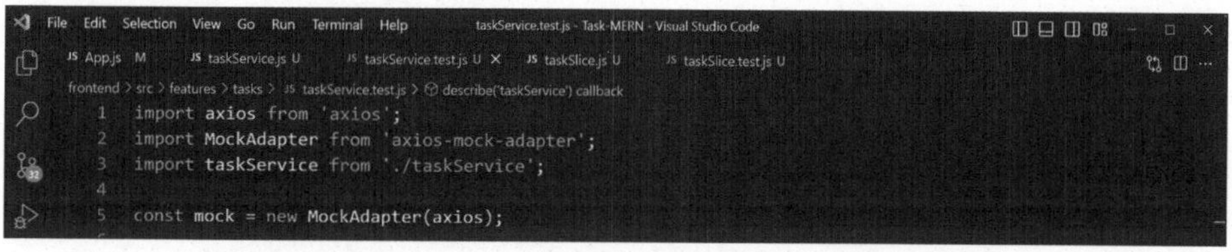

Figure 11.15: *Writing imports for taskService.test.js file*

Now, we will create a describe block in the **taskService.test.js** file. Here, we have first the **`afterEach()`** which will reset the mock after every test. Next, inside the test, we first have a token constant of token. Then we have a tasks array with an object containing a task.

Now, we are using the **`mock.onGet()`** to hit the API endpoint of /api/tasks using the token. Here, we expect the reply to have 200 and the tasks array. Next, we are calling the **`taskService`** file **`getTasks`** function using the token. The response is expected to be the tasks array.

```
describe('taskService', () => {
  afterEach(() => {
       mock.reset();
  });

  test(‹fetches tasks successfully›, async () => {
       const token = 'mock_token';
       const tasks = [
        {
              _id: '649e4e271947362dc297436a',
              text: 'Learn Tailwind',
              user: '649023b41935f5557f8e7ca4',
              createdAt: '2023-06-30T03:38:15.287Z',
              updatedAt: '2023-06-30T03:38:15.287Z',
              __v: 0
        }
       ];

       mock.onGet('/api/tasks/', { headers: { Authorization: `Bearer
```

```
${token}` } }).reply(200, tasks);
      const response = await taskService.getTasks(token);
      expect(response).toEqual(tasks);
  });
});
```

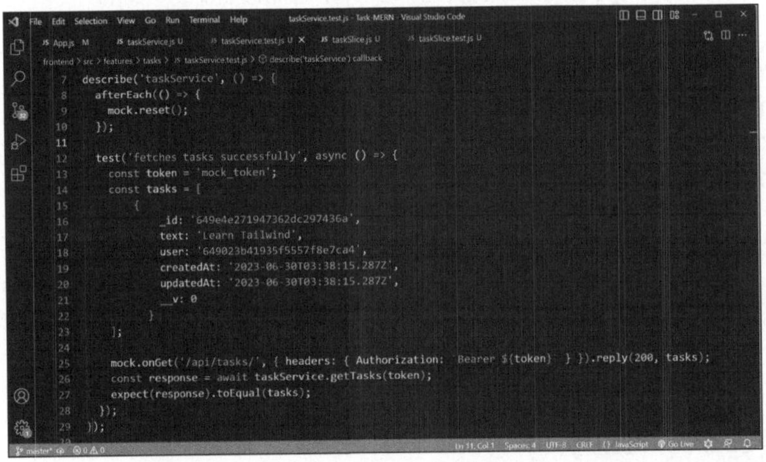

Figure 11.16: *Writing test for taskService.test.js file*

- On running the **npm** test again, the test in **taskService.test.js** file passes.

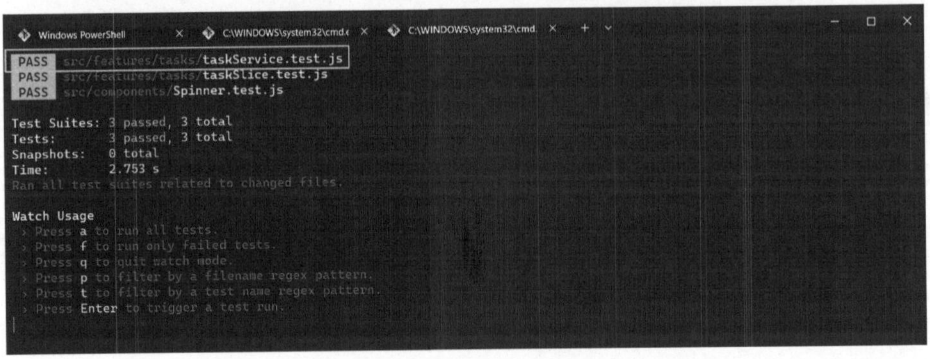

Figure 11.17: *Running test for taskService.test.js file*

Testing with React Testing Library

In this section, we will test the Task Item and Store components. So, first, create a file **TaskItem.test.js** in the **components** folder and add the following code in it. Here, we will first import the render and Provider. Next, we are importing the **configureMockStore** from **redux-mock-store**, which will help us to mock redux.

We are also importing the component of **`TaskItem`** for testing. Now, inside a describe block, we have first created a task, with dummy data.

Lastly, we will create a variable of **`mockStore`** and use the configureMockStore and pass an empty array in it. And we will also create a variable of the store and call the **`mockStore`**.

```
import { render } from '@testing-library/react';
import { Provider } from 'react-redux';
import configureStore from 'redux-mock-store';
import TaskItem from './TaskItem';

describe('TaskItem', () => {
  const task = {
      _id: 'task-123',
      createdAt: '2023-07-09T10:00:00',
      text: 'Learn Blockchain',
  };

  const mockStore = configureStore([]);
  const store = mockStore({});
});
```

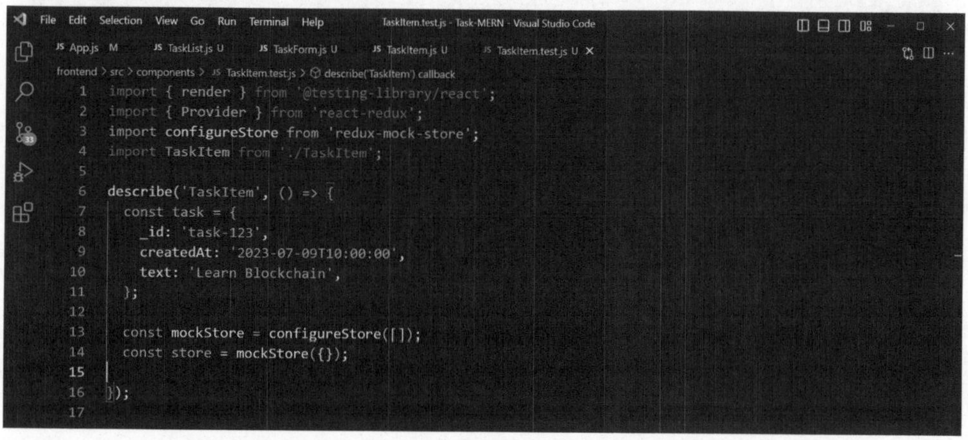

Figure 11.18: *Writing imports & describe for TaskItem.test.js file*

Next, we will add tests in the **TaskItem.test.js** file, inside the describe block. Here, we are rendering the `TaskItem` component, in which we are passing our dummy task. We are also wrapping it with the redux Provider. The redux provider is taking our mock store.

We are extracting the `getByText` from the render function, through which we are doing our tests. Now, we have two expected tests in which we are checking if the text and createdAt is in the document.

```
test(‹renders task details correctly›, () => {
    const { getByText } = render(
    <Provider store={store}>
    <TaskItem task={task} />
    </Provider>
    );

    expect(getByText(task.text)).toBeInTheDocument();
    expect(getByText(new Date(task.createdAt).toLocal-
eString(‘en-US’))).toBeInTheDocument();
});
```

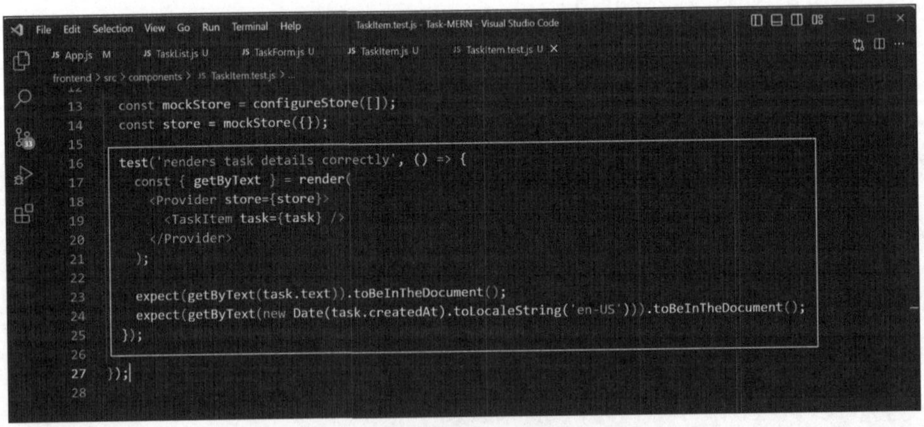

Figure 11.19: *Writing test for TaskItem.test.js file*

On running the `npm` test again, the test in **TaskItem.test.js** file passes.

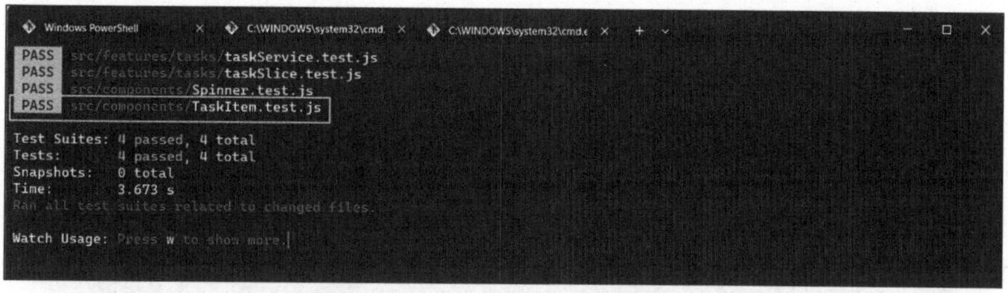

***Figure 11.20**: Running test for TaskItem.test.js file*

Now, we will write the tests for our **store.js** file. So, create a **store.test.js** file and add the following content in it. Here, we are first importing the configureStore from redux toolkit. Next, we are also importing the **authReducer** and **taskReducer** from the respective slice files.

Now, inside a describe block we are writing out a test to create the store with correct reducers. Here, again we have a store variable created with configureStore. Inside it we are passing the reducer with auth and tasks. Notice that it is similar to what we are doing in the **store.js** file.

Next, we get the state of the reducers with the **getState()** and storing it in a **storeReducers** variable. Finally, we are checking whether this **storeReducers** have the properties of auth and tasks.

```
import { configureStore } from ‘@reduxjs/toolkit’;
import authReducer from ‘../features/auth/authSlice’;
import taskReducer from ‘../features/tasks/taskSlice’;

describe(‘store’, () => {
  test(‹creates the store with the correct reducers›, () => {
      const store = configureStore({
      reducer: {
      auth: authReducer,
      tasks: taskReducer
      }
      });

      const storeReducers = store.getState();
```

```
    expect(storeReducers).toHaveProperty('auth');
    expect(storeReducers).toHaveProperty('tasks');
  });
});
```

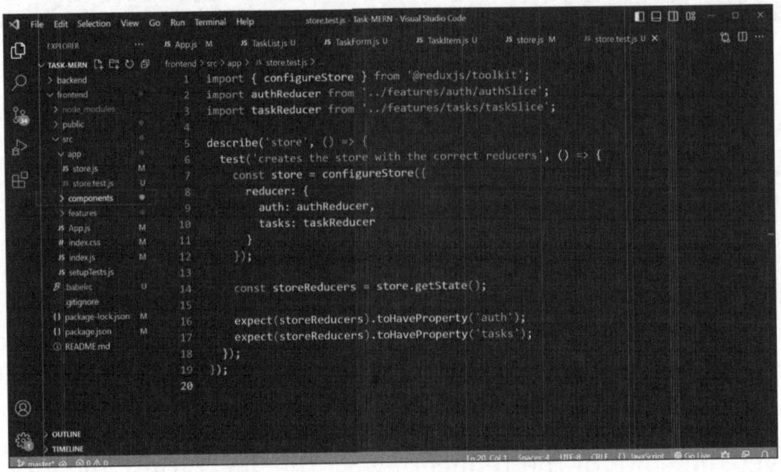

Figure 11.21: *Writing test for store.test.js file*

On running the npm test again, the test in **store.test.js** file passes.

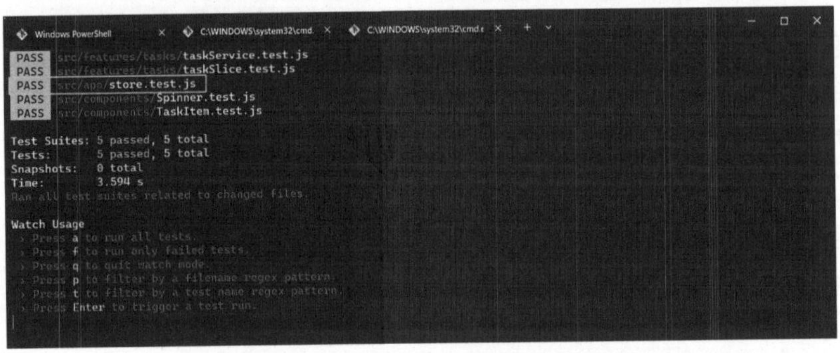

Figure 11.22: *Running test for store.test.js file*

Now, we will write the tests for our **index.js** file. So, create an **index.test.js** file and add the following content in it. Here, we are first importing the required things, which include `render`, `Provider`, `store`, and the `App` component.

Next, we have written a simple test in which we are extracting a container variable from the `render` function. Inside the render, we are passing the `App` component, wrapped with the `Provider` component, where we are passing the store. This is similar to what we are doing in the **index.js** file.

Now, we have a variable called **`rootComponent`** in which we are storing the **`firstChild`**. This is actually the **`App`** component. Next, we are testing and expecting this **`rootComponent`** to be in the document.

Also, when we run this test with the **`npm run test`**, it will pass.

```
import React from ‘react’;
import { render } from ‘@testing-library/react’;
import { Provider } from ‘react-redux’;
import { store } from ‘./app/store’;
import App from ‘./App’;

test(‘renders the root component correctly’, () => {
  const { container } = render(
      <Provider store={store}>
        <App />
      </Provider>
  );

  const rootComponent = container.firstChild;
  expect(rootComponent).toBeInTheDocument();
});
```

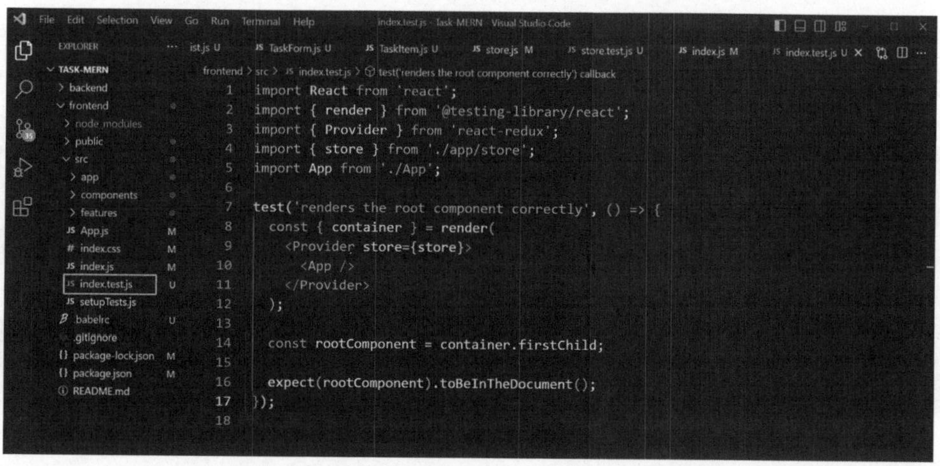

Figure 11.23: *Writing test for index.test.js file*

Configuring and Checking Coverage

In this section, we will learn to configure our frontend app to include coverage. After that, we will check the coverage for our app. In a lot of production scenarios, it is expected to provide 80% coverage.

First, in the **package.json** file, we will add the following line in scripts. Here, the test will be known as coverage and it will run the npm test with options of coverage and **`watchAll`**.

```
"coverage": "npm test -- --coverage --watchAll"
```

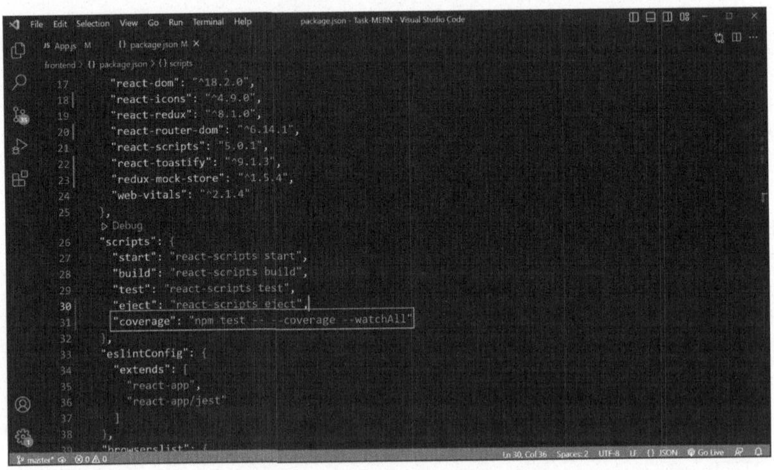

Figure 11.24: *Adding coverage command in package.json file*

After that, open a terminal and run the command **`npm run coverage`**. It will first test all the test files. We will notice that all of them passed.

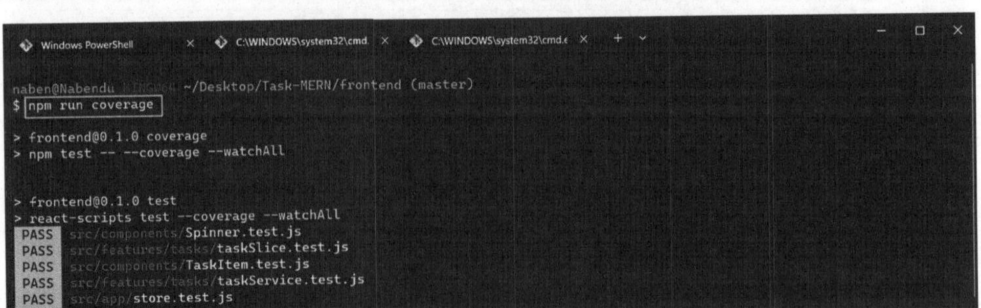

Figure 11.25: *Running coverage command*

Once the tests are done, we will get coverage for all files. The coverage checks how many lines of code are covered in all files. We see a lot of red because in this app, we didn't do extensive testing and covered all the files.

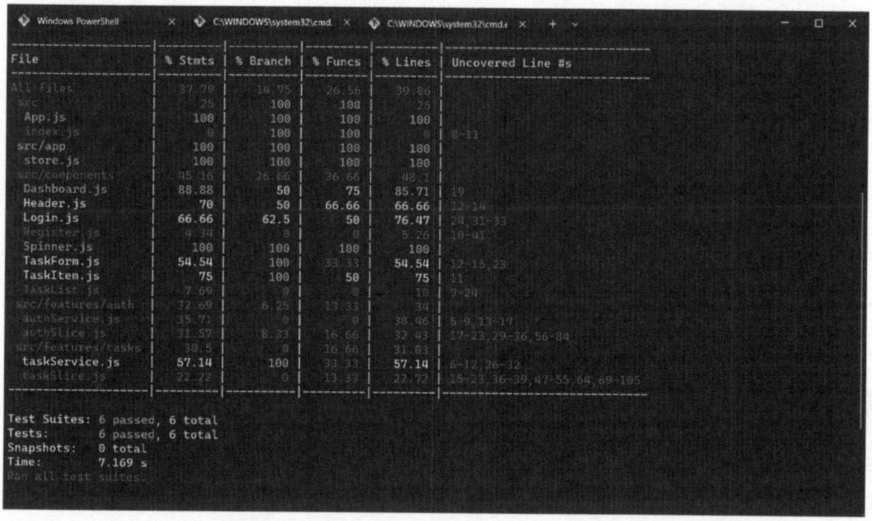

Figure 11.26: *Checking coverage of files*

We can also see the coverage in a nice html file. A **coverage** folder will be created in our frontend app. So, open it and then the **lcov-report** folder inside it. Here, we will find an **index.html** file, which contains all of our reports of coverage.

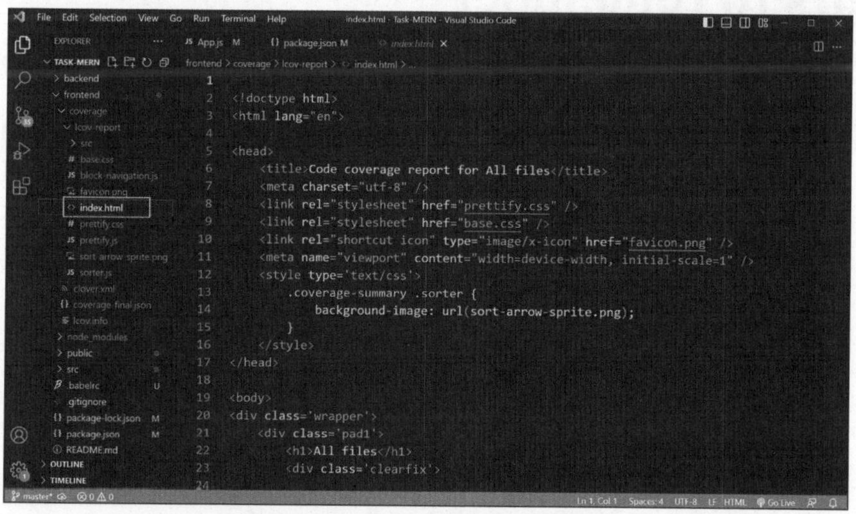

Figure 11.27: HTML *file for coverage*

Now, on opening the **index.html** file in the browser we will see the coverage of the major files in a nice graphical format.

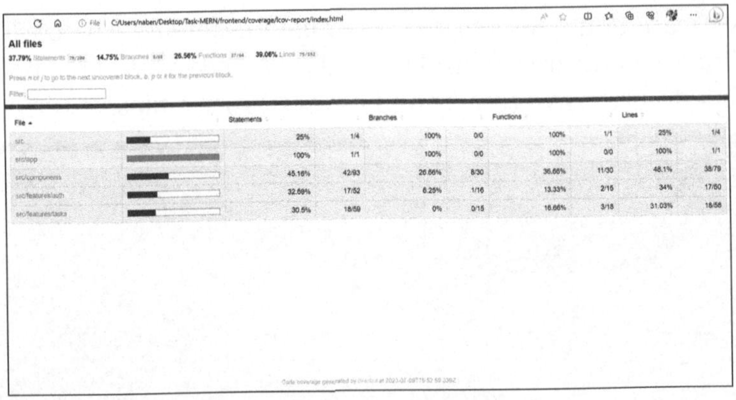

Figure 11.28: *Coverage in a browser*

Conclusion

In this chapter, we have learned to test our frontend code written in React. We have used the in-built libraries of Jest and React testing library to unit test our various components.

In the next chapter, we will test the backend built in NodeJS using Jest and Supertest.

Points to remember

- To write tests we need to target an element. Sometimes we don't have a unique field, and we can use data-testid for the same.
- We don't want to call the real API endpoint in testing. So, we add mocking capabilities in testing.
- We can also mock data, services, and functions, and through it, write complex tests to cover all scenarios.
- Once we are done with testing, we need to check the coverage for all test cases.

CHAPTER 12
Backend Testing

Introduction

This chapter covers the testing of our backend using Jest. This library is not in built into NodeJS, but we have to install it manually, as with most things related to NodeJS.

Structure

In this chapter, we will cover the following topics:

- Setting up testing in the backend
- Testing Register User controller
- Testing **`getTasks`** and **`setTask`** controllers
- Testing Update Task controller

Setting up testing in the backend

We need to do all the setup for testing, as the NodeJS app doesn't come with any testing installed. So, first change to the backend directory and then open it with VS Code with the **`code .`** command.

Figure 12.1: *Switching to the Backend*

Head over to https://jestjs.io/docs/getting-started site and copy the command to install Jest in your code.

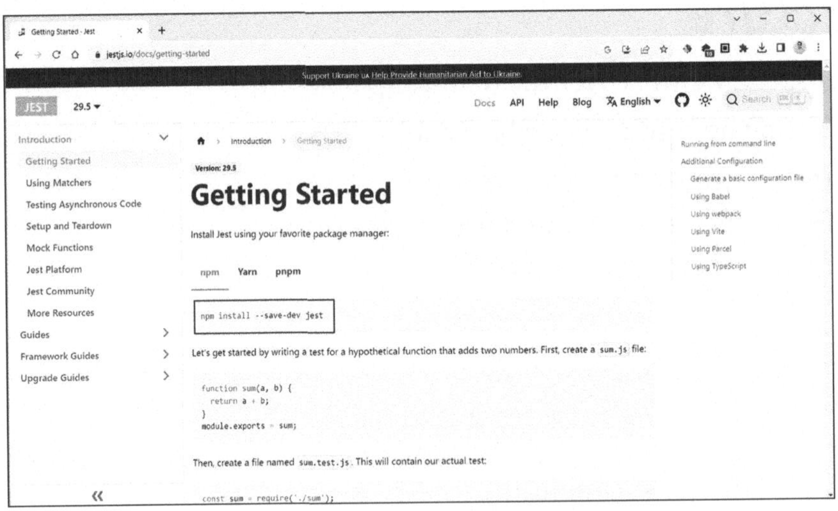

Figure 12.2: Jest Docs

In the backend folder from the terminal, we will give the following command. Notice that we are installing jest as dev dependent since we don't require it in production.

```
npm install --save-dev jest
```

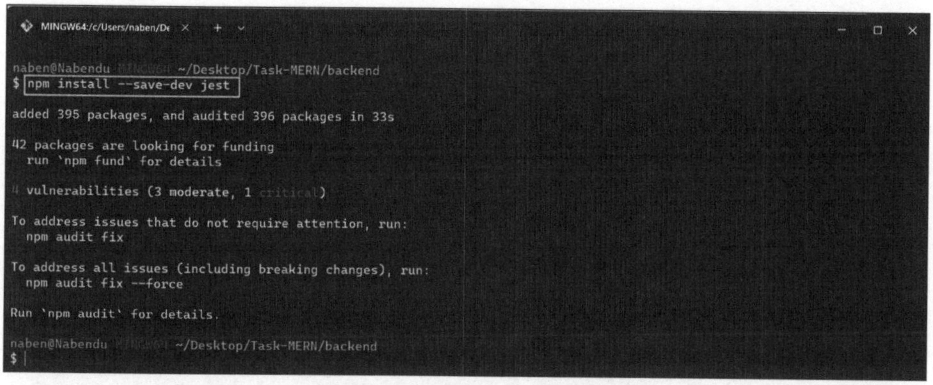

Figure 12.3: *Installing Jest*

Copy the **jest.config.js**, from the code at the end of this chapter. Here, make sure that the **`testMatch`** file is not commented on.

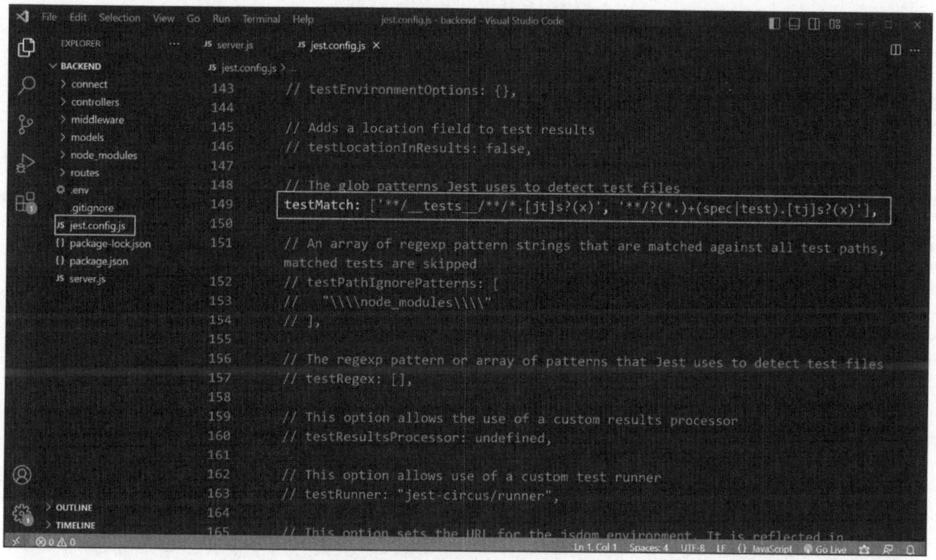

Figure 12.4: *Configuring Jest*

Finally, we will update the **package.json** file to have a script called test, which will call **`jest`**.

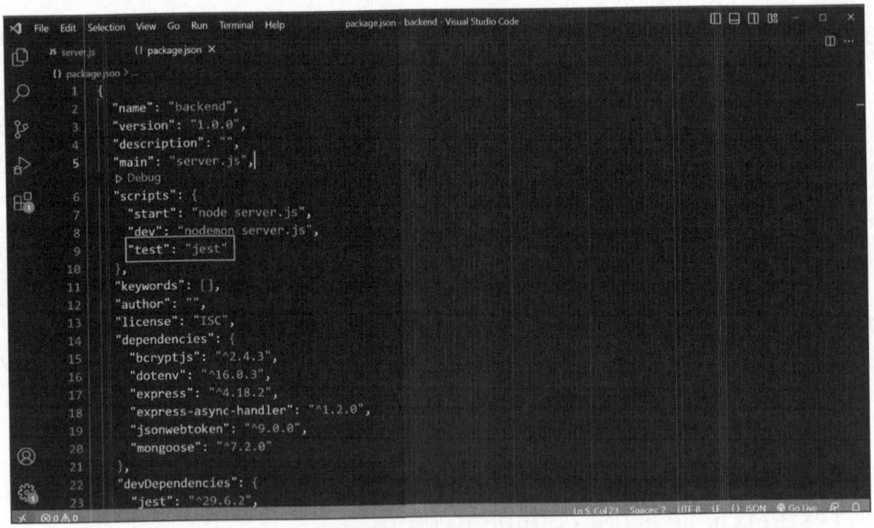

Figure 12.5: *Adding Jest*

Testing registerUser controller

We will test the **`registerUser`** controller now. It is called when we hit the / route with a post call. In the **userRoutes.js** file we call the **`registerUser`** function through a **`router.post()`**.

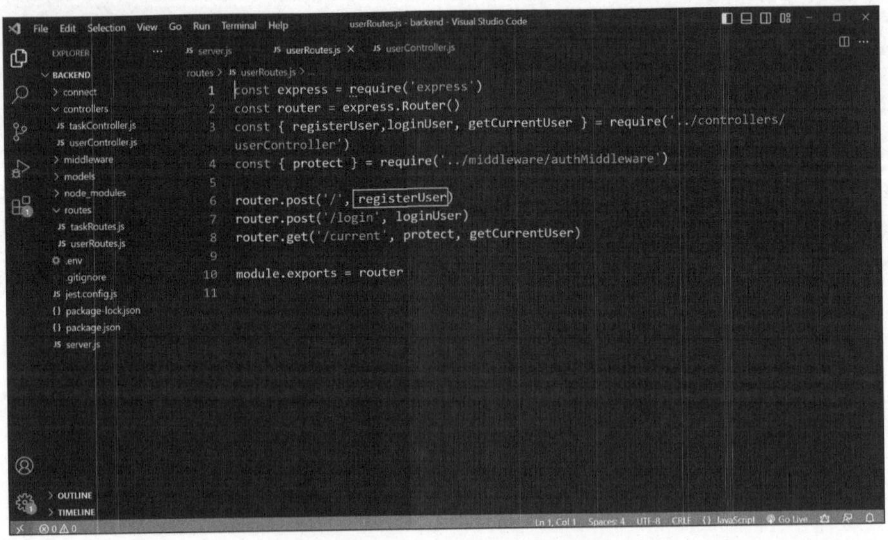

Figure 12.6: *Calling Controller*

The **`registerUser`** function in the **userController.js** file is as follows, which we created in earlier chapters. Here, we get the **`name`**, **`email`**, and **`password`** from the body. After validating all fields, we also check if the email exists with **findOne()**. If it exists, we are throwing an error.

We also encrypt the password with **bcrypt** before saving it in the database with **bcrypt**. Finally, we send a status of **201** and **_id**, **name**, and **email** back.

```
const registerUser = asyncHandler(async (req, res) => {
        const { name, email, password } = req.body
        if (!name || !email || !password) {
        res.status(400)
        throw new Error('All fields are mandatory')
        }

        const userExists = await User.findOne({ email })
        if (userExists) {
        res.status(400)
        throw new Error('User Exists')
        }

        const salt = await bcrypt.genSalt(10)
        const hashedPassword = await bcrypt.hash(password, salt)
        const user = await User.create({ name, email, password:
hashedPassword })
        if (user) {
        res.status(201).json({ _id: user.id, name: user.name, email:
user.email, token: generateJWTtoken(user._id) })
        } else {
        res.status(400)
        throw new Error('Invalid user data')
        }
})
```

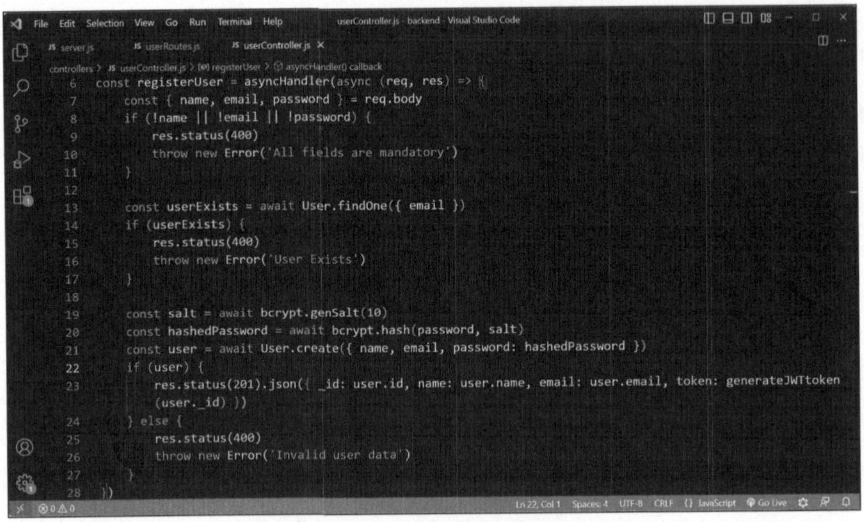

Figure 12.7: *Register User Controller*

We will write the test for this file. So, create a **__tests__** folder in the root directory and a **userController.test.js** file inside it. Here, we first import the **registerUser** from the **userController.js** file.

In **jest.mock()**, we pass the path to **userModel** as the first parameter and the arrow function as the second parameter. Inside the arrow function, we have created a variable of **mockUser** which is an object containing **_id**, **name**, and **email**.

Then, we return the mocked function of **findOne** and **create** from it. Next, we again use the **jest.mock()** and mock the sign function from the **userController.js** file.

Finally, we use **bcrypt** to mock the **genSalt** and hash functions used in the **userController.js** file.

```
const { registerUser } = require('../controllers/userController');

// Mock User model functions
jest.mock('../models/userModel', () => {
        // Mock User model
        const mockUser = {
        _id: 'user-id',
        name: 'John Doe',
```

```
        email: ‘johndoe@example.com’,
        };

        return {
        findOne: jest.fn().mockResolvedValue(null),
        create: jest.fn().mockResolvedValue(mockUser),
        };
});
// Mock JWT and bcrypt
jest.mock(‘jsonwebtoken’, () => ({
        sign: jest.fn().mockReturnValue(‘mock-token’),
}));
const bcrypt = require(‘bcryptjs’);
bcrypt.genSalt = jest.fn().mockResolvedValue(‘mock-salt’);
bcrypt.hash = jest.fn().mockResolvedValue(‘mock-hashed-password’);
```

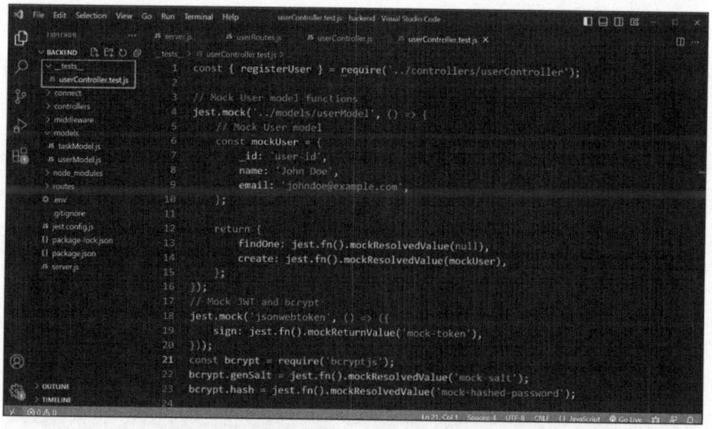

Figure 12.8: *Register User Test setup*

After the initial configuration, we will write the first test. Here, inside the test function from jest, we have two parameters. The first parameter is a string, which will be displayed when we run the test.

The second parameter is an arrow function, which will contain our whole test logic. Here, we have created a variable of req first, which is an object. This object contains a key of the body, which contains a value as an object. This object contains the name, email and password data.

In the next res object, we contain two values of status and json which are mock of status and json function from register function.

We call the **registerUser** function with the **req** and **res** using await. Then we expect the status to be 201 in this success scenario.

```
// Test
test('should register a new user', async () => {
  const req = {
      body: {
      name: 'John Doe',
      email: 'johndoe@example.com',
      password: 'password',
      },
  };

  const res = {
      status: jest.fn().mockReturnThis(),
      json: jest.fn(),
  };

  await registerUser(req, res);
  expect(res.status).toHaveBeenCalledWith(201);
});
```

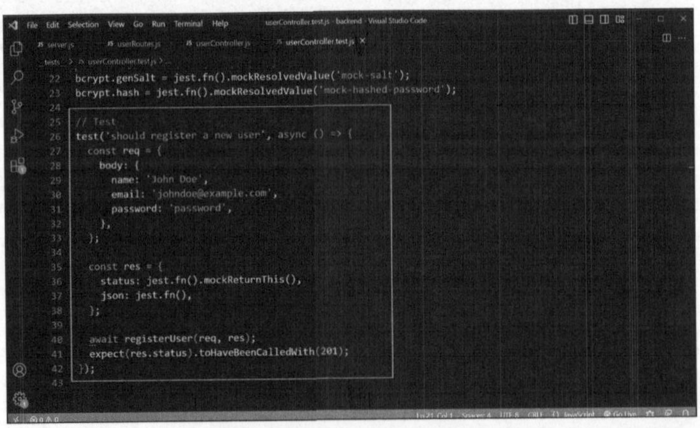

Figure 12.9: Register User First Test

Now, in the terminal from the backend folder, run the command **`npm run test`** and we will see the test has been passed. Also, notice that the name of the test which we have given "should register a new user" is being displayed.

***Figure 12.10**: Register User Test run*

We write the test case for an error in a missing field. Again, we have used the test method from jest but given it a different name. The **`req`** and the **`res`** are almost similar to our earlier test, but in the **`req`**, we are missing the email field.

After that, we call the **`registerUser`** through an expect, but it will throw an error because of the missing field. So, we chain it with rejects and **`toThrow`** from jest where we pass the "**`All fields are mandatory`**" message. Note that this message is the same as the message in the register function inside the **userController.js** file.

Lastly, we also check whether the status of 400 will be received because of the failed scenario.

```
test('should return a 400 error if any field is missing', async () => {
      const req = {
      body: {
      name: 'John Doe',
      email: '', // Missing email field intentionally
      password: 'password',
      },
      };

      const res = {
      status: jest.fn().mockReturnThis(),
      json: jest.fn(),
```

```
    };

    await expect(registerUser(req, res)).rejects.toThrow('All fields are mandatory');
    expect(res.status).toHaveBeenCalledWith(400);
});
```

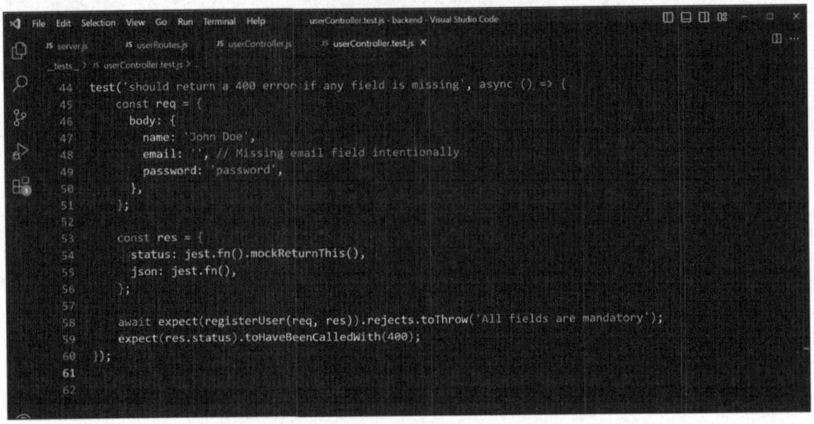

Figure 12.11: *Register User Second Test*

Again, from the terminal run the command **`npm run test`** and we will see the new test has been passed.

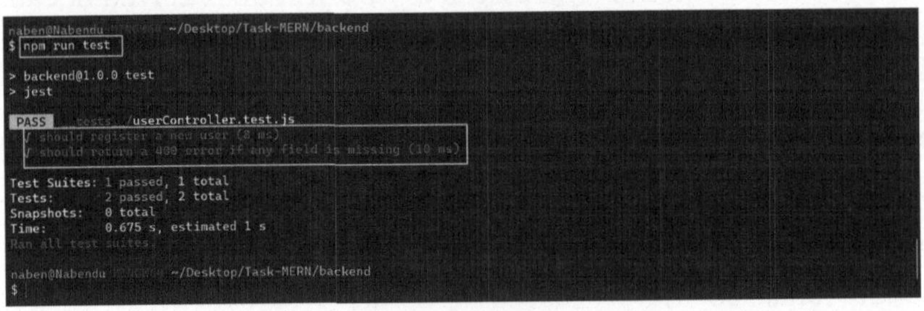

Figure 12.12: *Register User Test run*

Testing getTasks and setTask controller

We will now test the **`getTasks`** and **`setTask`** functions from the **taskController.js** file, which we created in earlier chapters.

These are simple functions which are used to get the task and add a new task in the database. In the **`getTasks`** we find the task with the find() method in which we pass the user id.

In the **setTask**, we first check if the text is present and throw an error if it is not present. After that, we use the **create()** method to send the text and user id to the database and save it. Finally, we send back a status of 200 along with the task to the browser.

```
const getTasks = asyncHandler(async (req, res) => {
        const tasks = await Task.find({ user: req.user.id })
        res.status(200).json(tasks);
})


const setTask = asyncHandler(async (req, res) => {
        if(!req.body.text){
        res.status(400)
        throw new Error('Please enter a task')
        }


        const task = await Task.create({ text: req.body.text, user: req.
user.id })
        res.status(200).json(task);
})
```

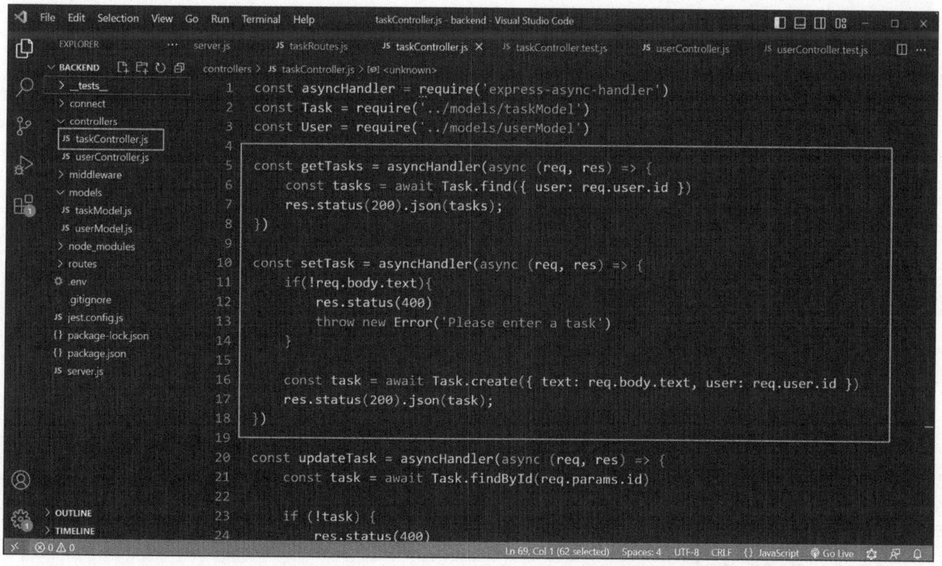

Figure 12.13: *Get Task and Set Task Controllers*

Now, we will create a file **taskController.test.js** in the **__tests__** folder. Here, we first import the **getTasks** and **setTask** from the **taskController.js** file. After that, we import task from the models and also mock the task model with **jest.mock()**.

We write our first test which is to get a task. Here, our req variable is an object with a user key which contains a value of the object. This object has an id as a key and a user-id as a value.

Then, we mock the tasks, which is an array of objects. Now, each object contains a _id, text and user. Next, we mock the find() method in the **getTasks()** method inside the **taskController.js** file.

Our res object contains the status and json as key and the respective **jest.fn()** for mocking them. Next, we call the **getTasks()** with req and res.

Finally, we write the expect statements where we check the **res.status** to be **200** and also the **res.json** to contain the tasks.

```
const { getTasks, setTask, updateTask } =
require('../controllers/taskController');
const Task = require('../models/taskModel');
jest.mock('../models/taskModel');


test('should get tasks for a user', async () => {
  const req = { user: { id: <user-id> } };
  // Mocking tasks for the user
  const tasks = [
      { _id: 'task-id-1', text: 'Task 1', user: 'user-id' },
      { _id: 'task-id-2', text: 'Task 2', user: 'user-id' },
  ];
  // Mocking the find method to return tasks for the user
  Task.find.mockResolvedValue(tasks);

  const res = {
      status: jest.fn().mockReturnThis(),
      json: jest.fn(),
  };
```

```
  await getTasks(req, res);
  // Ensure that the response contains the expected tasks
  expect(res.status).toHaveBeenCalledWith(200);
  expect(res.json).toHaveBeenCalledWith(tasks);
});
```

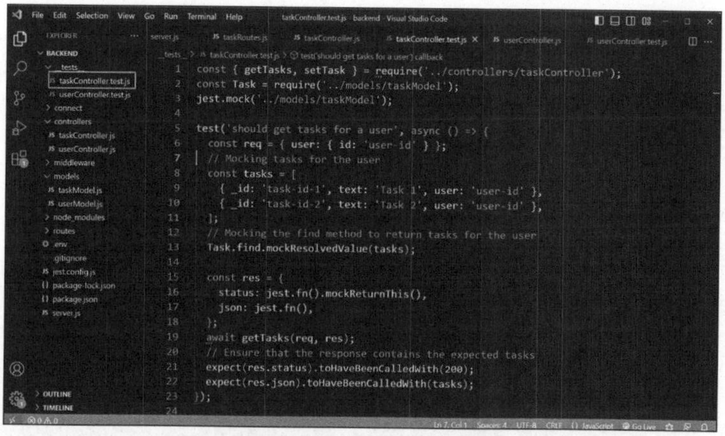

***Figure 12.14**: Get Task Test*

The next test is for setting a task and it is almost similar to the previous test for getting a task. Here again, first we have a **req** object.

Then, we mock the task object. Note that it is different from our earlier test in which we have a task array. Next, we mock the **create()** method in the **setTask()** method inside the **taskController.js** file.

Our res object contains the status and json as key and is similar to the earlier test. Next, we call the **setTask** with the **req** and **res**.

We have written the expect statements where we check the **res.status** to be 200. Also, the **res.json** to contain the task.

```
test('should set a new task for a user', async () => {
  const req = { user: { id: ‹user-id› }, body: { text: ‹New Task› } };

  // Mocking the created task
  const task = { _id: ‹new-task-id›, text: ‹New Task›, user: ‹user-id› };

  // Mocking the create method to return the new task
```

```
  Task.create.mockResolvedValue(task);

  const res = {
     status: jest.fn().mockReturnThis(),
     json: jest.fn(),
  };

  await setTask(req, res);

  // Ensure that the response contains the new task
  expect(res.status).toHaveBeenCalledWith(200);
  expect(res.json).toHaveBeenCalledWith(task);
});
```

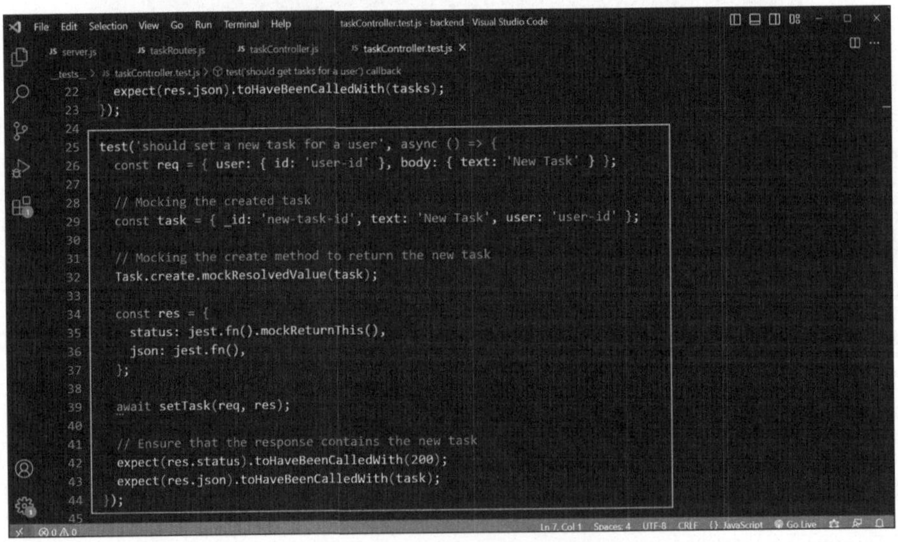

Figure 12.15: Set Task Test

We write the test for the error, when we have a missing task text. Here again, we have a **`req`** object but we have been given an empty body.

Next, the res object has status and json keys which have mock values with **`jest.fn()`**. After that, we call the **`setTask`** through an expect, but it will throw an error because of the missing field. So, we chain it with rejects and **`toThrow`** from jest where we pass the "**`Please enter a task`**" message.

Note that this message is the same as the message in the **`setTask`** function inside the **taskController.js** file. Lastly, we also check whether the status of 400 will be received because of the failed scenario.

```
test('should return a 400 error for missing task text', async () => {
  const req = { user: { id: 'user-id' }, body: {} }; // Missing the "text"
field

  const res = {
       status: jest.fn().mockReturnThis(),
       json: jest.fn(),
  };

  await expect(setTask(req, res)).rejects.toThrow('Please enter a task');
  expect(res.status).toHaveBeenCalledWith(400);
});
```

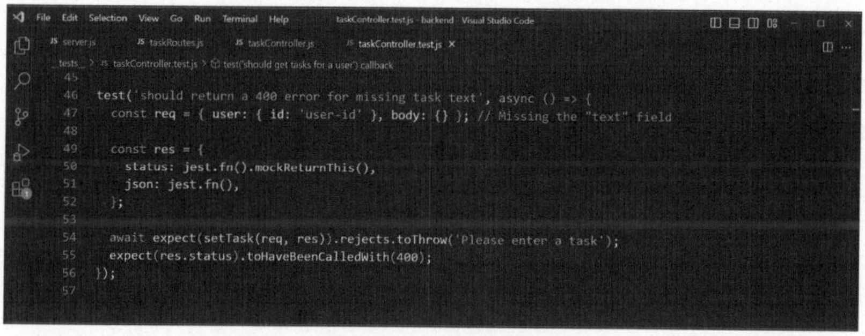

Figure 12.16: *Set Task Error Test*

We will run the **`npm run test`** from the terminal and our new tests in the **taskController.test.js** file passes.

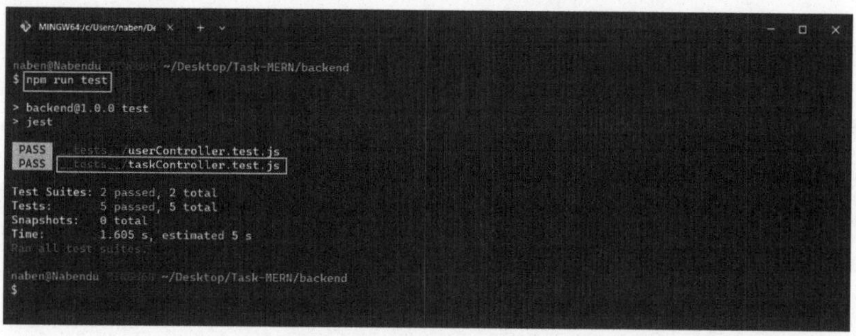

Figure 12.17: *Running Tests*

Testing updateTask controller

We will now test the update task controller from the **taskController.js** file. Here, we first find the task with the `findById` method by passing the id. Next, we check if the task is present. If it is not present, we throw an error of "`Task not found`".

We also find the user with `findById` and pass the user id. Again, if the user is not found we throw the error "`No such user found`".

Next, the test is for checking if the task's user id and user's id are the same. If they are not the same, we throw the error "User is not authorized to update".

Finally, we update the task with the method of `findByIdAndUpdate` by passing the task id and `thereq.body`. We also send back a status of 200, along with the updated task to the sender.

```
const updateTask = asyncHandler(async (req, res) => {
      const task = await Task.findById(req.params.id)

      if (!task) {
      res.status(400)
      throw new Error('Task not found')
      }

      const user = await User.findById(req.user.id)

      if(!user){
      res.status(401)
      throw new Error('No such user found')
      }

      if (task.user.toString() !== user.id) {
      res.status(401)
      throw new Error('User is not authorized to update')
      }
```

```
        const updatedTask = await Task.findByIdAndUpdate(req.params.id, 
req.body, { new: true })
        res.status(200).json(updatedTask)
})
```

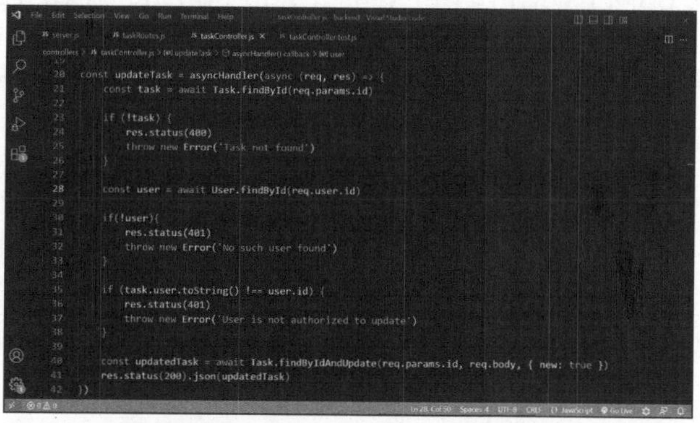

Figure 12.18: *Update Task Controller*

Back in the **taskController.test.js** file, we have to update our imports first. We first import the `updateTask` from the controllers. Next, we also import the user model and also mock the user model with `jest.mock()`.

```
const { getTasks, setTask, updateTask } = 
require('../controllers/taskController');
const Task = require('../models/taskModel');
const User = require('../models/userModel');
jest.mock('../models/taskModel');
jest.mock('../models/userModel');
```

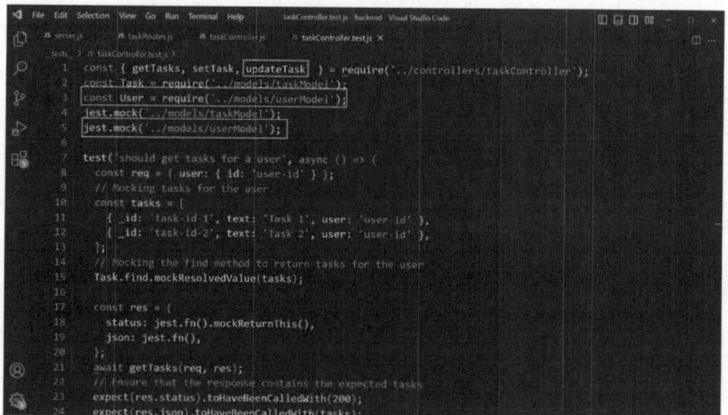

Figure 12.19: *Importing user models*

Now, we will write our first test for the update task in the **taskController.test.js** file. Here, we check if we are getting the 401 error if the user is not found. First, we have created a variable of `taskId` and `userId`.

We created a `req` object with params, user and body as keys. Each one of them contains an object as the value. The params object has a key-value pair of `id` and `taskId`. Then the user object has a key-value pair of id and `userId` and the body object has a key-value pair of text and 'Updated Task'.

We create a variable of **taskToUpdate** which is an object. It contains the keys of _id, text and user with respective values.

We mock the task `findById` to return the mocked task of **taskToUpdate.** Similarly, we also mock the user `findById` and return a null which tells the user is not found.

Our res object contains status and json with respective mock functions. After that, we call the **updateTask** through an expect, but it will throw an error because of the missing user. So, we chain it with rejects and `toThrow` from jest where we are passing the "No such user found" message.

Note that this message is the same as the message in the `updateTask` function inside the **taskController.js** file. Lastly, we also check whether the status of 401 will be received because of the failed scenario.

```
test('should return a 401 error if user is not found', async () => {
      const taskId = 'task-id-1';
      const userId = 'non-existent-user-id';
      const req = { params: { id: taskId }, user: { id: userId }, body:
{ text: 'Updated Task' } };

      // Mocking the task to be updated
      const taskToUpdate = { _id: taskId, text: 'Original Task', user:
'user-id' };

      // Mocking the findById method to return the task to be updated
      Task.findById.mockResolvedValue(taskToUpdate);

      // Mocking the findById method to return null, indicating user not
found
      User.findById.mockResolvedValue(null);
```

```
        const res = {
        status: jest.fn().mockReturnThis(),
        json: jest.fn(),
        };


        await expect(updateTask(req, res)).rejects.toThrow('No such user found');
        expect(res.status).toHaveBeenCalledWith(401);
    });
```

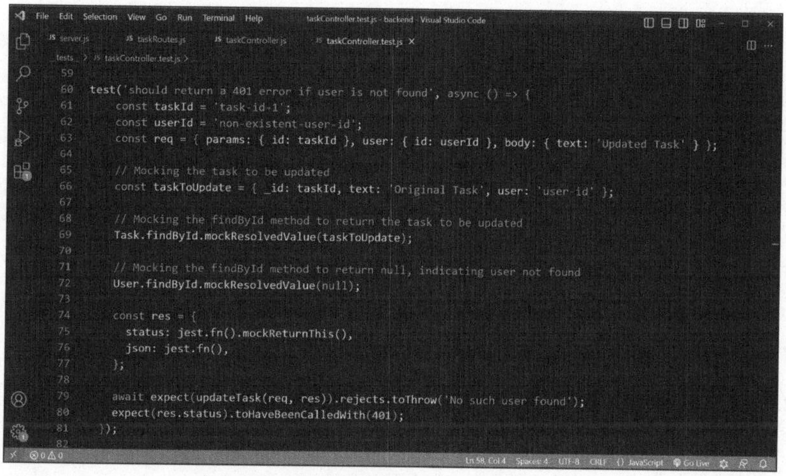

Figure 12.20: *User not found error test*

The next test we have for the user is not authorized to update the task. Here again, we have a **taskId** and **userId** variable. After that, we have a **req** object exactly similar to our previous test.

Our **taskToUpdate** also has a similar structure as the previous test. But notice here that the user value is different from the owner's. After that, we are mocking the task **findById** which will return the task to be updated.

We mock the user **findById**, which will return our authorized user with the id of **user-id-2**. Again, our res object contains status and json with respective mock functions.

We call the **updateTask** through an expect, but it will throw an error because of the unauthorized user. So, we chain it with rejects and **toThrow** from jest where we pass the "**User is not authorized to update**" message.

Lastly, we also check whether the status of **401** will be received because of the failed scenario.

```
  test('should return a 401 error if user is not authorized to update the task', async () => {
        const taskId = 'task-id-1';
        const userId = 'user-id-2'; // Different user ID from the task owner
        const req = { params: { id: taskId }, user: { id: userId }, body: { text: 'Updated Task' } };

        // Mocking the task to be updated, owned by a different user
        const taskToUpdate = { _id: taskId, text: 'Original Task', user: 'user-id-1' };

        // Mocking the findById method to return the task to be updated
        Task.findById.mockResolvedValue(taskToUpdate);

        // Mocking the findById method to return the user
        User.findById.mockResolvedValue({ _id: userId });

        const res = {
        status: jest.fn().mockReturnThis(),
        json: jest.fn(),
        };

        await expect(updateTask(req, res)).rejects.toThrow('User is not authorized to update');
        expect(res.status).toHaveBeenCalledWith(401);
  });
```

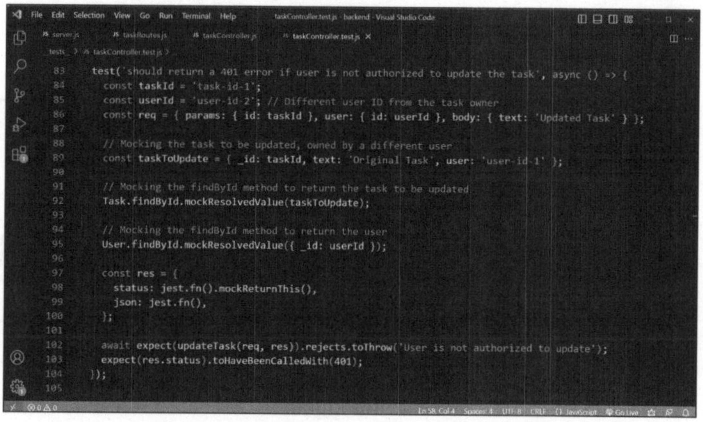

Figure 12.21: *User not authorized error test*

We will again run the **`npm run test`** from the terminal and all the new tests will also pass.

Figure 12.22: *Running Tests*

Conclusion

In this chapter, we have learned to test our backend code written in NodeJS. We have used the popular libraries of jest to unit test our various components.

In the final chapter, we will deploy both our frontend and backend code separately.

Points to remember

- Configuring jest from the start for a NodeJS application
- Adding mocking capabilities for testing
- Writing complex tests using mock data and services
- Writing tests for common backend scenarios of get task, set task and update task

Chapter 13
Deployment

Introduction

This chapter covers the deployment of both our frontend and backend code. We will use it with freely available services. This includes deploying the front end with Netlify and the back end with Back4app.

Structure

In this chapter, we will discuss the following topics:

- Frontend code repo creation
- Backend code repo creation
- Backend deployment in Back4app
- Backend integration with frontend
- Frontend deployment in Netlify
- Fixing CORS errors and final deployments

Frontend code repo creation

We will first create a repository for our frontend code in GitHub. For this, you need to have a GitHub account and also Git installed on your Windows machine. By default, Mac and Linux machines have Git installed.

First login to your GitHub account at https://github.com/.

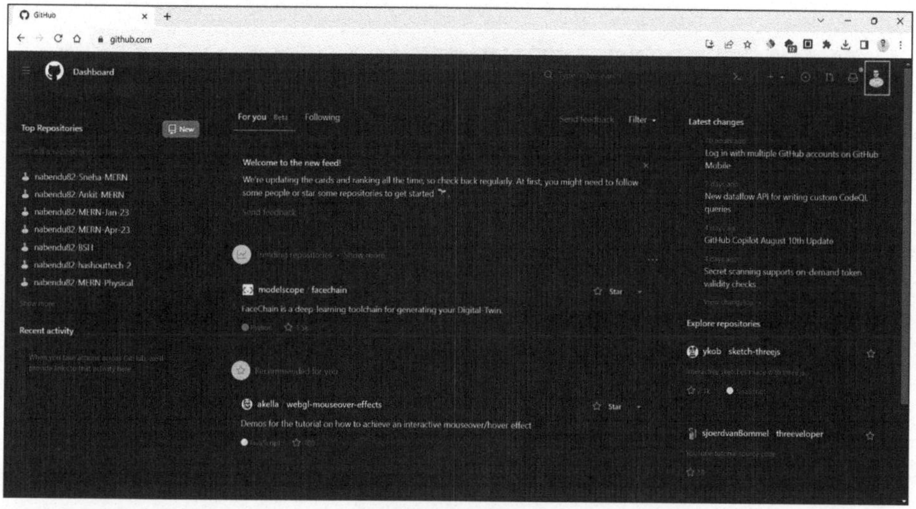

Figure 13.1: GitHub

Now, click on the Plus sign (+) in the top right corner. And then in the dropdown, click on **`New repository`**.

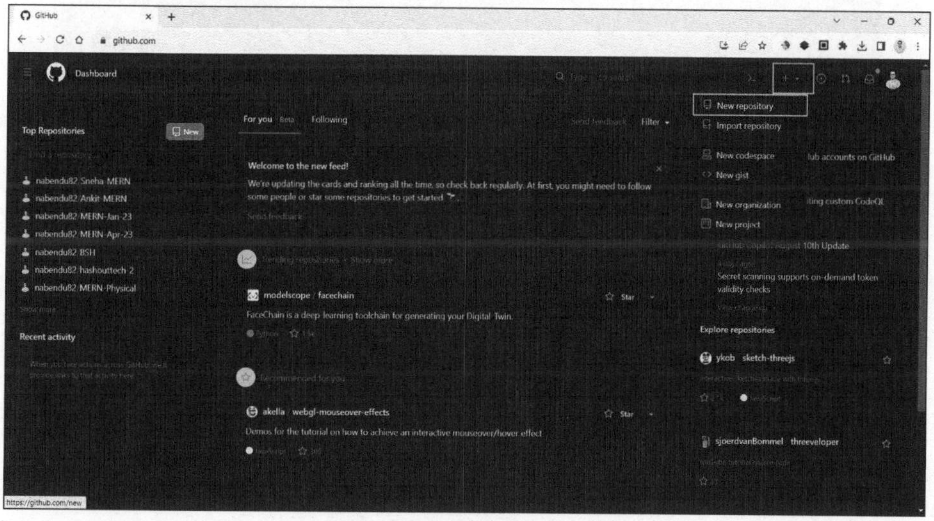

Figure 13.2: New repository

In the next screen give the repo a name like **`task-mern-frontend`**. Also, give a nice description. Make sure the repo is public and then click on the **`Create repository`** button.

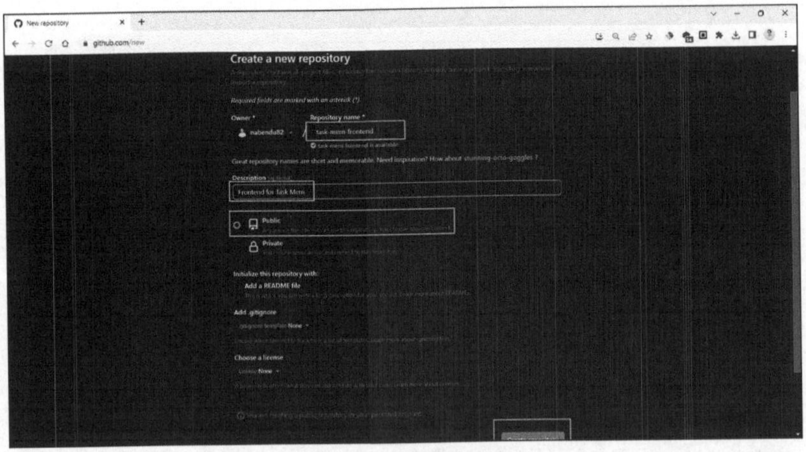

Figure 13.3: *Creating a New repository*

In the next screen, we will get all the commands to create a repo. Then, push the code to GitHub.

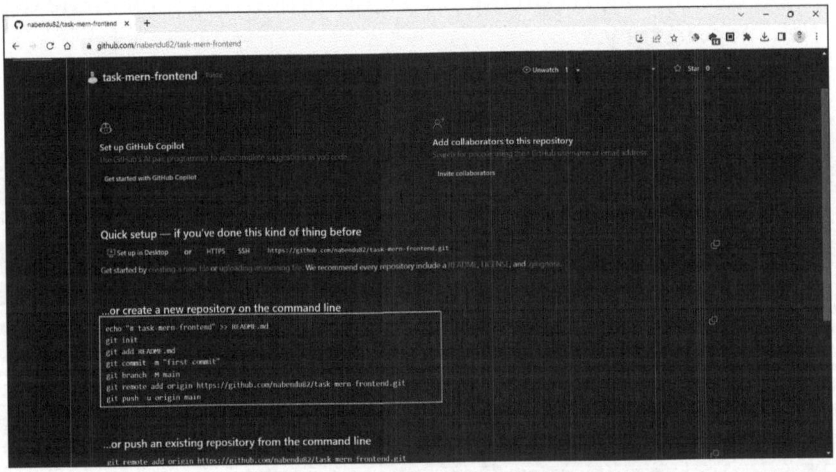

Figure 13.4: *Commands for the New repository*

Now, from the terminal (Windows, Mac or Linux), first go to the folder where our frontend code is located. After that, enter the following commands. Here, the first command is creating a new git repository.

The second command is adding all the files to the staging area. Note that both the commands can be found in the preceding screenshot, although a bit modified.

```
git init
git add.
```

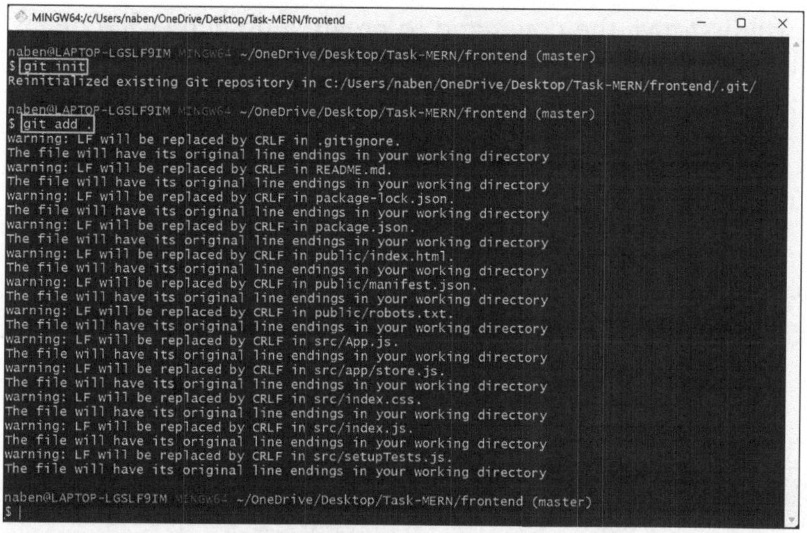

***Figure 13.5**: git init and add*

Next, we will run the command to **`commit`** the code in the staging area to the commit area. Notice, here we can give any message and we have given a **`Deployment commit`**.

```
git commit -m "Deployment commit"
```

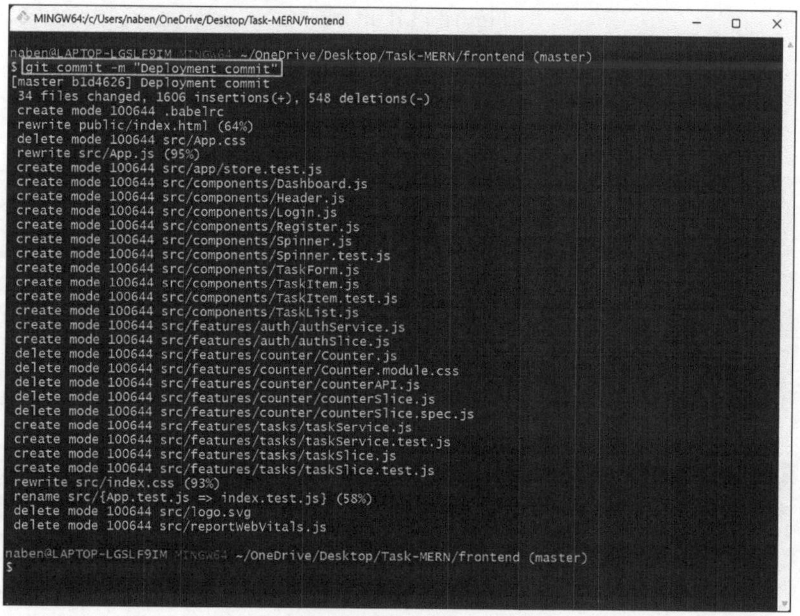

***Figure 13.6**: git commit*

Next, we will first give the command to create a branch called main. The next command will add the unique remote path given to us by GitHub. The last push command will push our code from the local system to GitHub.

Note that all of these commands are exactly the same as what we have got from our GitHub command list earlier.

```
git branch -m main
git remote add origin https://github.com/nabendu82/task-mern-frontend.git
git push -u origin main
```

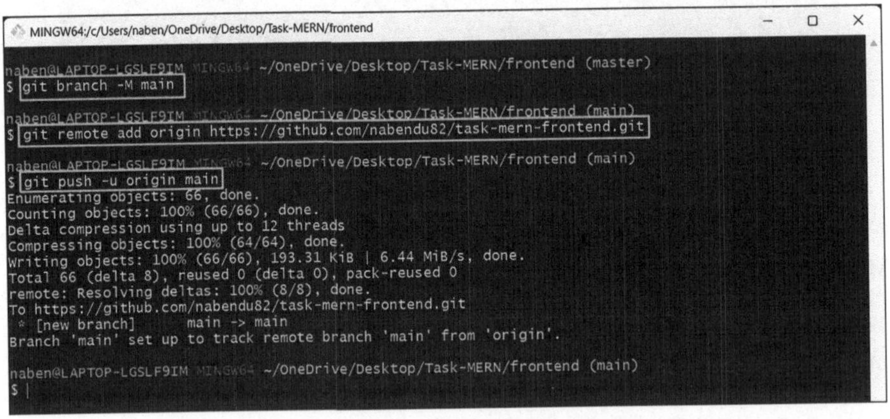

Figure 13.7: *git push*

Back in GitHub, we will find all of our code being uploaded in our repo.

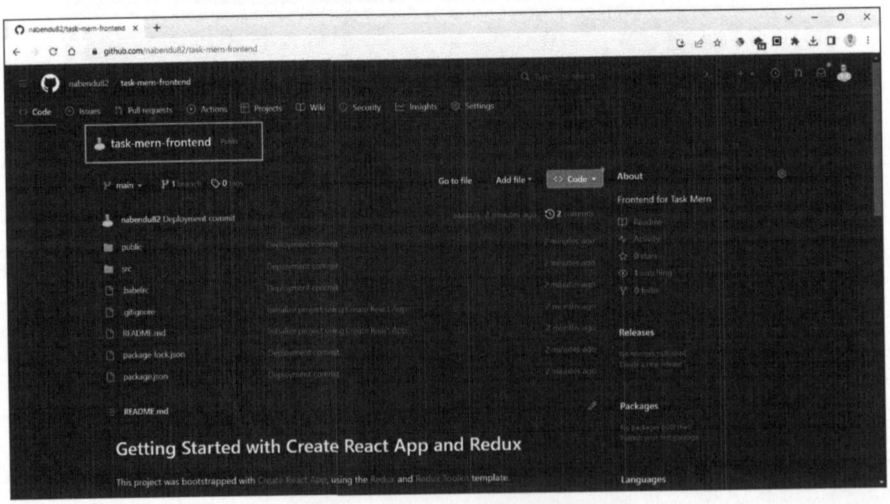

Figure 13.8: *Frontend repo*

Backend code repo creation

We will now create a repo for our backend code and transfer all code from the local computer to this remote GitHub repository. The steps will be exactly the same as the Frontend part.

Now, to create a new repo, we will again click on the plus(+) sign and then the **`New repository`**.

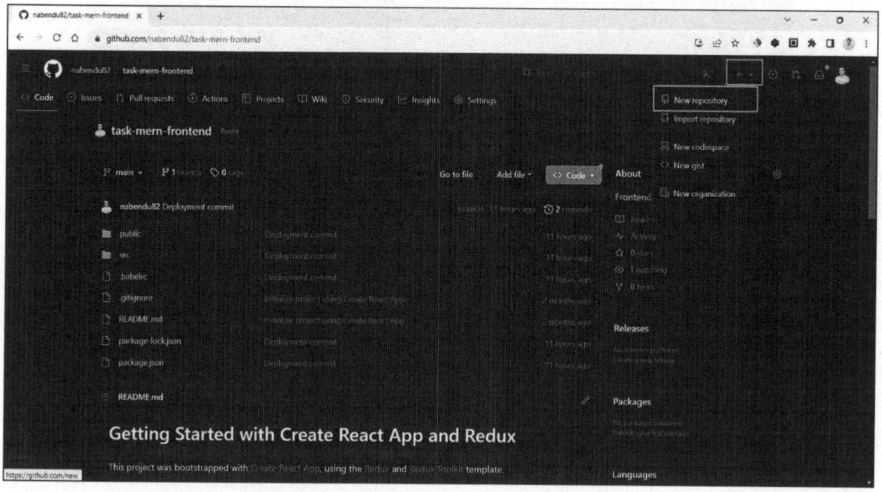

Figure 13.9: *New repository*

In the next screen, we will give the repository a name and description and then click on the **`Create repository`** button.

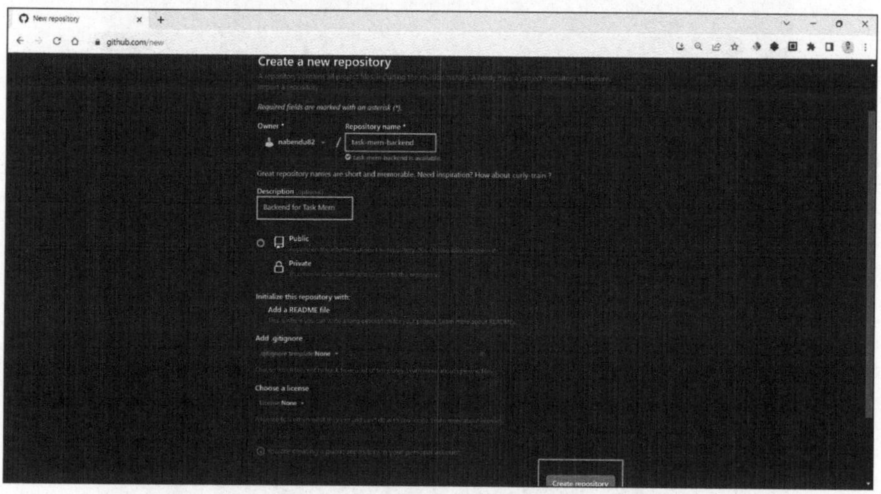

Figure 13.10: *Backend repository*

In the next screen, we will again get the set of commands to be given in the terminal. Note that here the path is different in the remote command with a unique link.

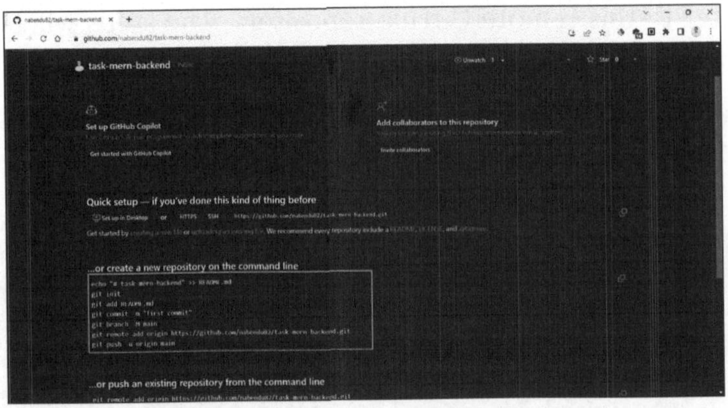

Figure 13.11: *Backend repository commands*

Again, we will enter the following three commands first. The first one is to initialize a Git repo, the second is to put the files in the staging area, and the third is to put the files in the commit area.

```
git init
git add .
git commit -m "Deployment commit"
```

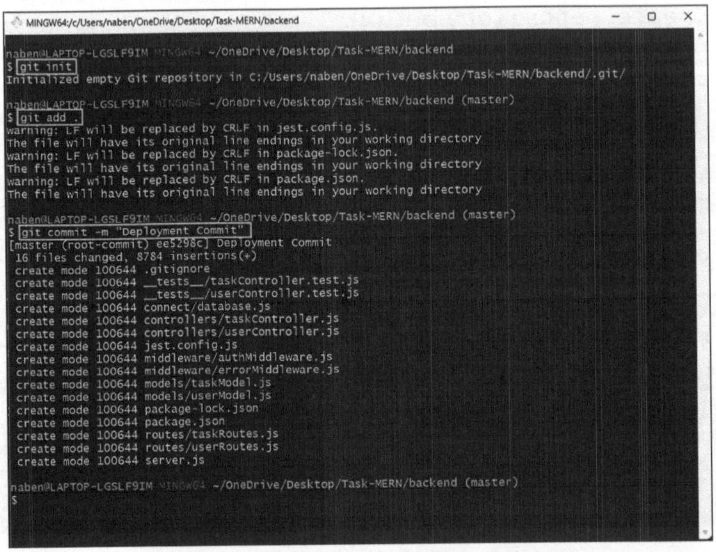

Figure 13.12: *git init, add and commit*

The next three commands will be to create a branch, adding a remote path and pushing the code from the local computer to GitHub.

```
git branch -m main
git remote add origin https://github.com/nabendu82/task-mern-backend.git
git push -u origin main
```

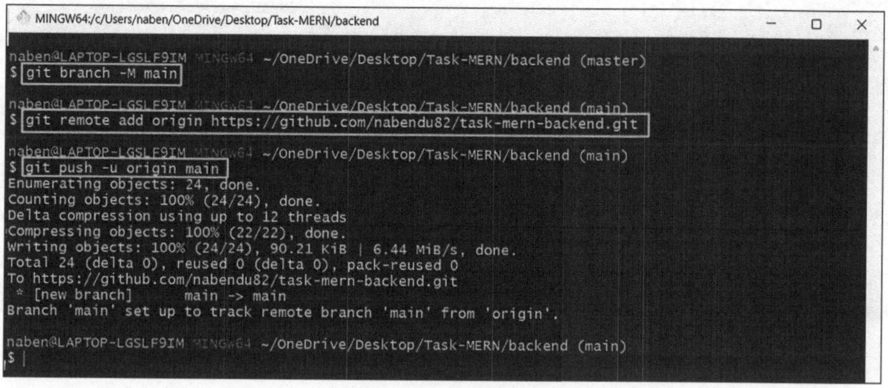

Figure 13.13: *Git push*

Now, our backend code is also deployed successfully in GitHub.

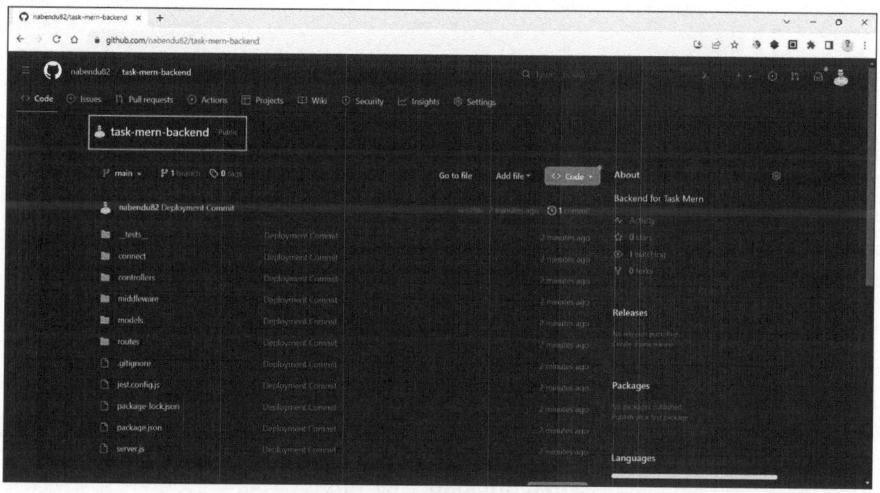

Figure 13.14: *Backend repository*

Backend deployment in Back4app

We will first deploy our backend code to an awesome free service called Back4app. So, first, head over to https://www.back4app.com/ and `Sign up` with Google.

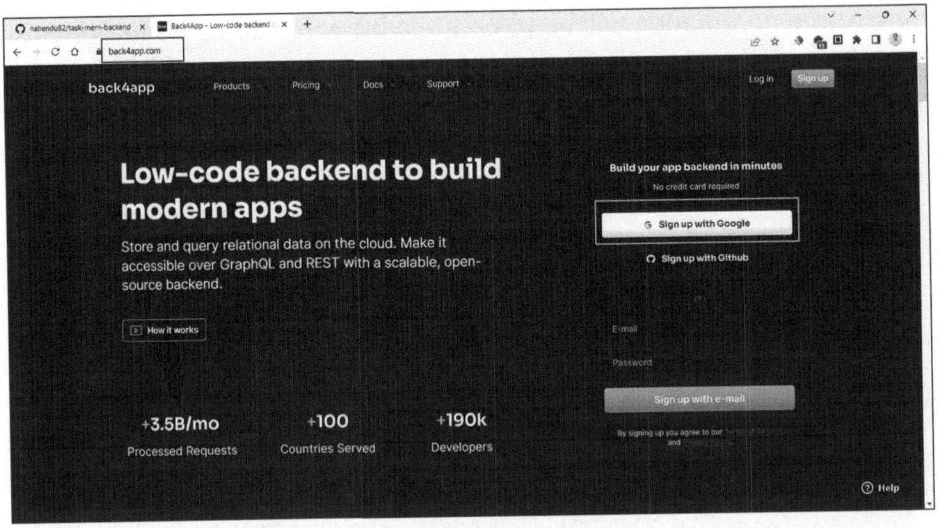

Figure 13.15: *Back4app*

Next, click on the **`NEW APP`** button in the top right corner.

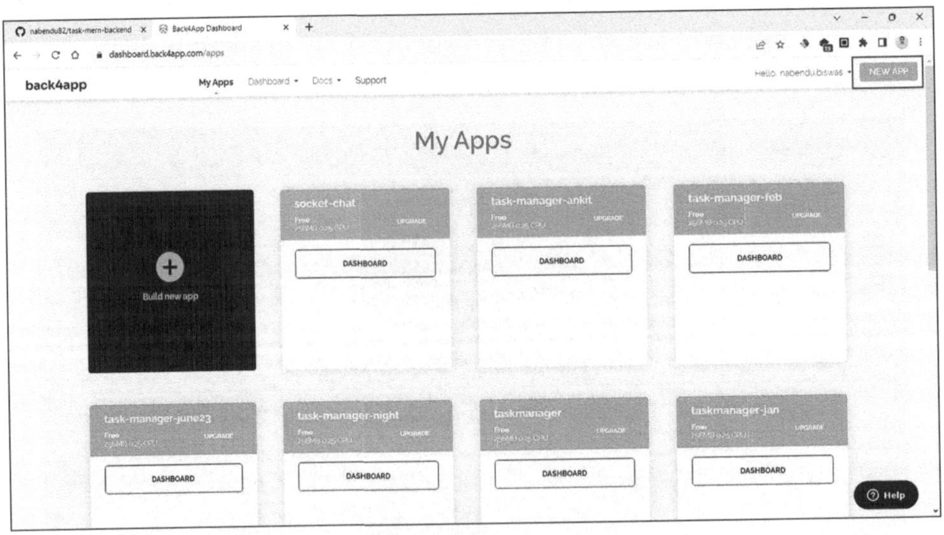

Figure 13.16: *New app*

In the next screen, click on **`Containers as a Service`** banner.

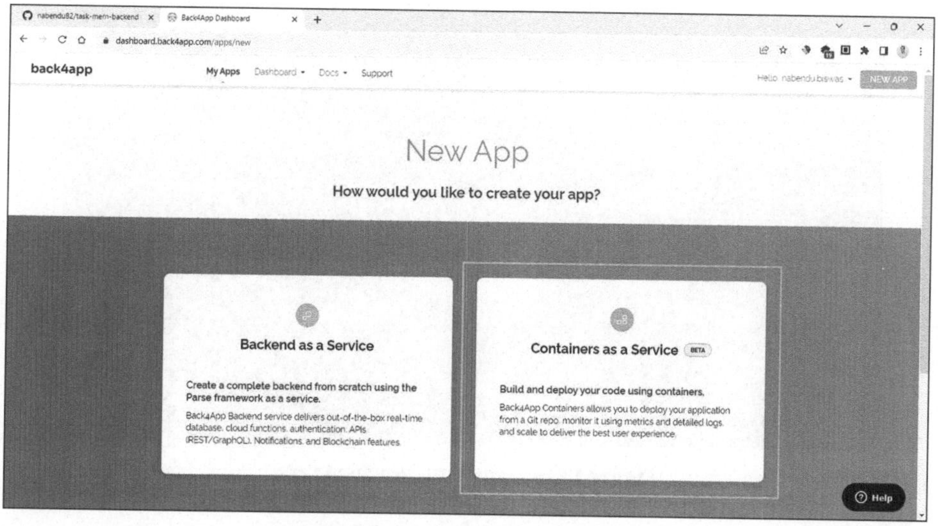

Figure 13.17: *Containers as a Service*

It will now ask us to select a Git repository containing our code.

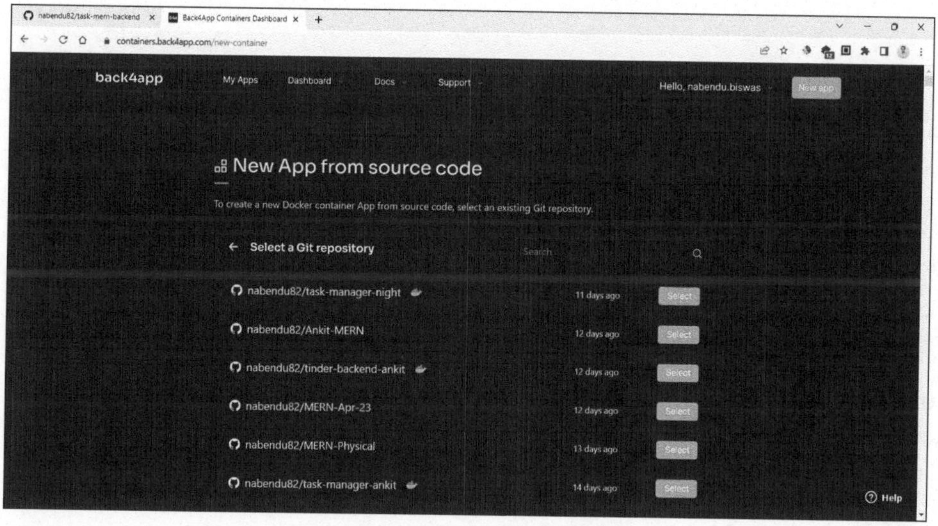

Figure 13.18: *New repo addition*

Now, we will search for our backend repository by typing task-mern. But since the permission is not given, we will not find it. Also, notice that a message of Dockerfile is mandatory is shown.

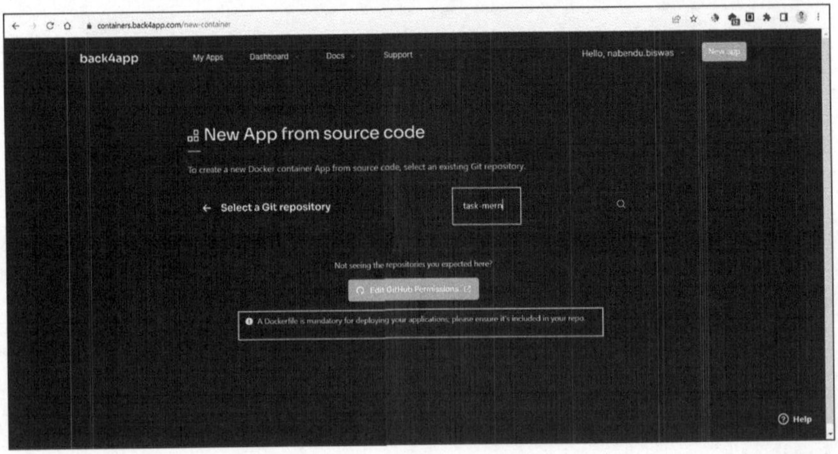

***Figure 13.19**: Searching for new repo*

So, we need to first go back to our backend code and add a file **Dockerfile** in the root directory. Add the below content to it. Note that it should expose the correct port on which our backend code is running.

```
# Use the official Node.js image as the base image
FROM node:18

# Set the working directory in the container
WORKDIR /app

# Copy the application files into the working directory
COPY . /app

# Install the application dependencies
RUN npm install

EXPOSE 8000
# Define the entry point for the container
CMD ["npm", "start"]
```

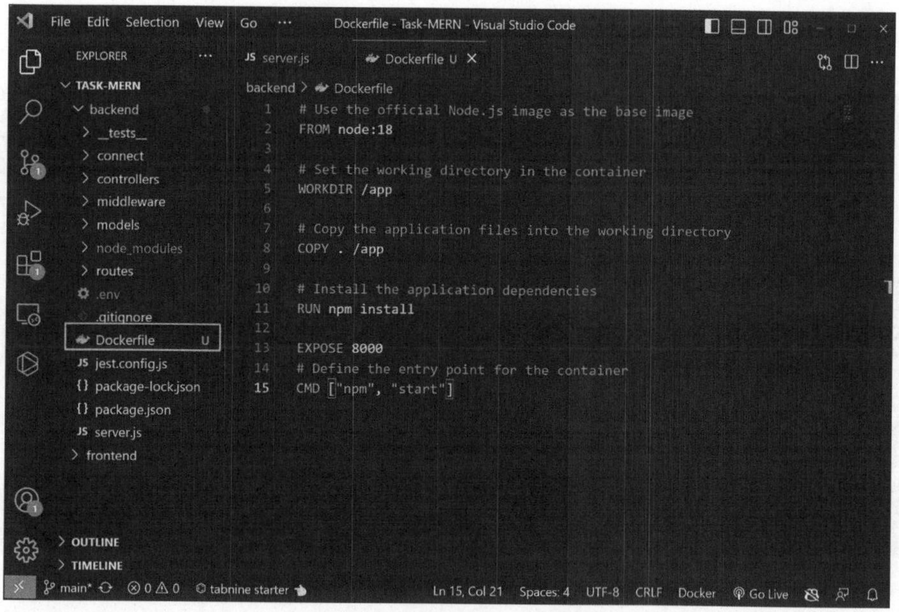

Figure 13.20: *Adding Dockerfile*

Since we have added a new file in our backend code, we need to push again this changed code to our GitHub repo. So, again we need to give the add, commit and push commands.

```
git add .
git commit -m "Dockerfile added"
git push
```

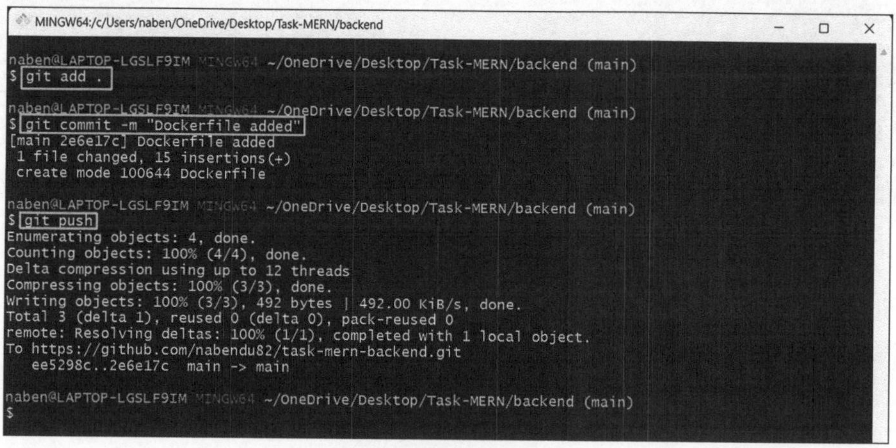

Figure 13.21: *git push*

Now, in GitHub for our backend code, we will find the **`Dockerfile`**.

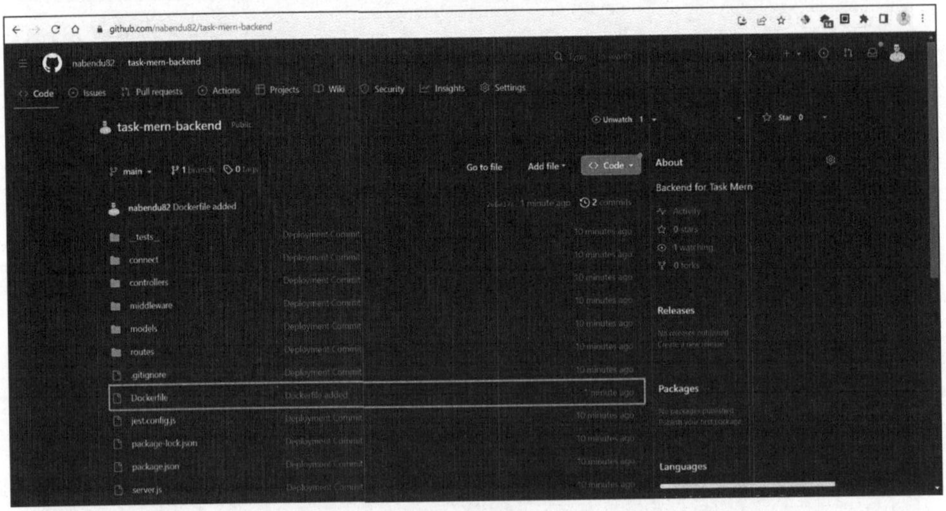

Figure 13.22: *Dockerfile in GitHub*

Back in Back4app, click on the **`Edit GitHub Permissions`** button.

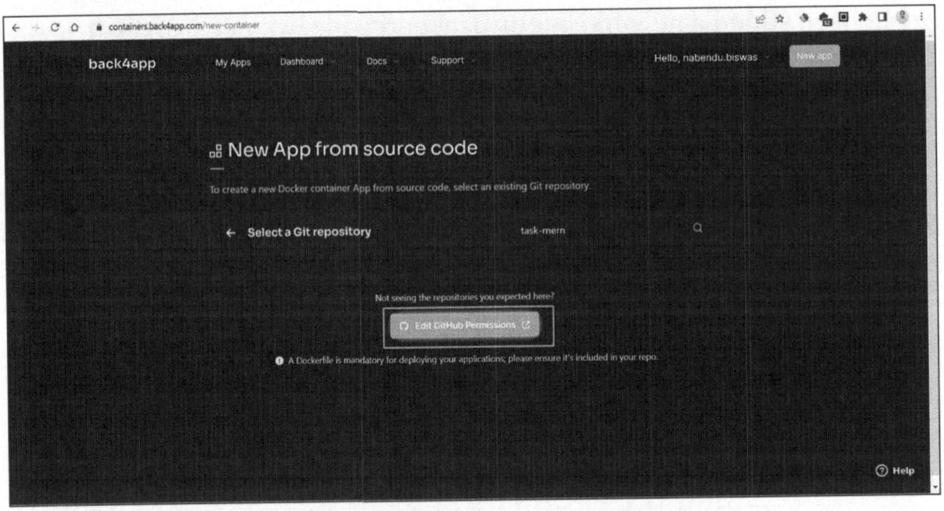

Figure 13.23: *Adding backend code*

We will get a pop-up in which we need to select the right account.

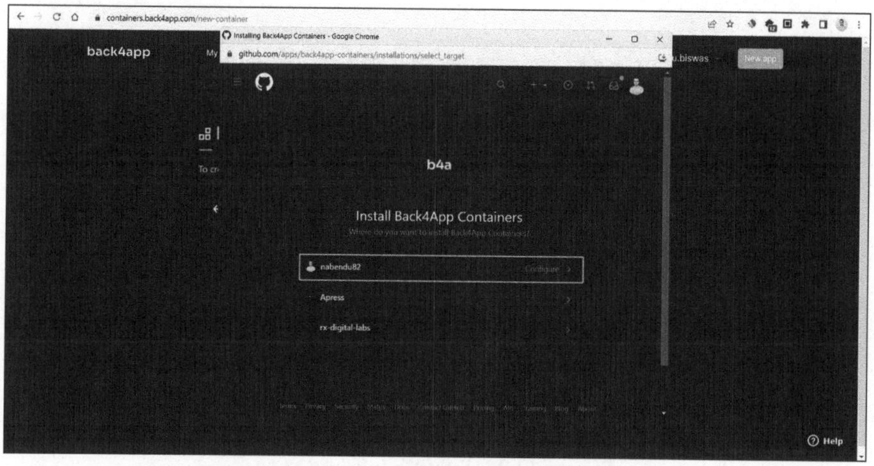

***Figure 13.24**: Selecting the GitHub account*

In the next screen, we will select our backend repository of **task-mern-backend**.

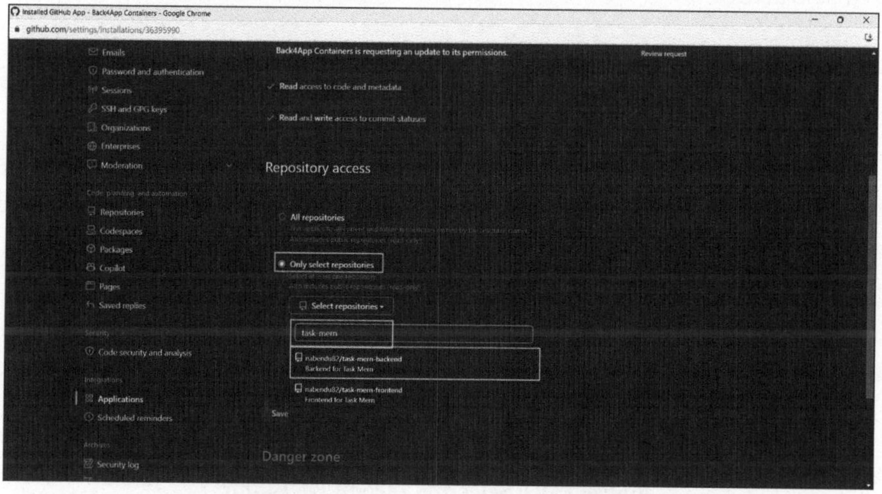

***Figure 13.25**: Adding backend repo*

Next, click on the **Save** button.

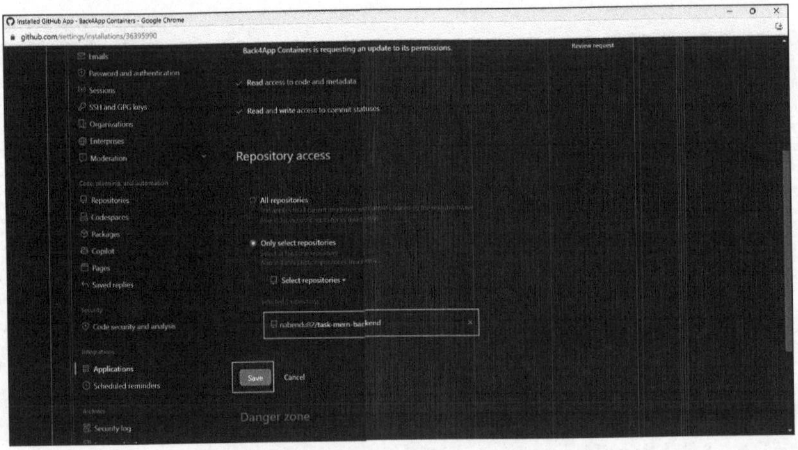

Figure 13.26: *Saving backend repo*

We will get back to Back4app and now we will see our repository. Here, click on the **`Select`** button.

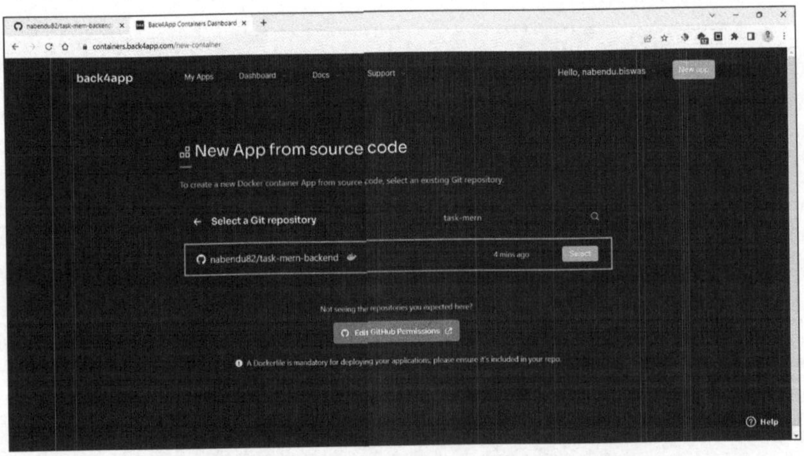

Figure 13.27: *Selecting repo in Back4app*

Since, our backend code also contains environment variables in the **.env** file, we need to give them in the next screen.

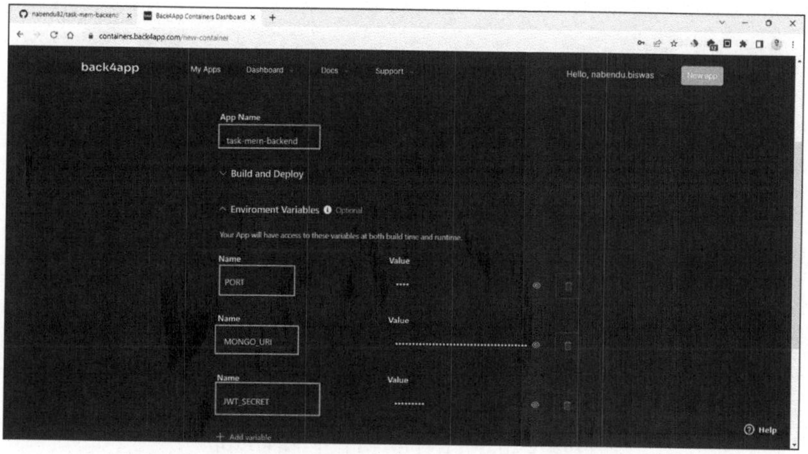

Figure 13.28: *Adding environment variables*

After that, scroll down and click on the **`Create App`** button.

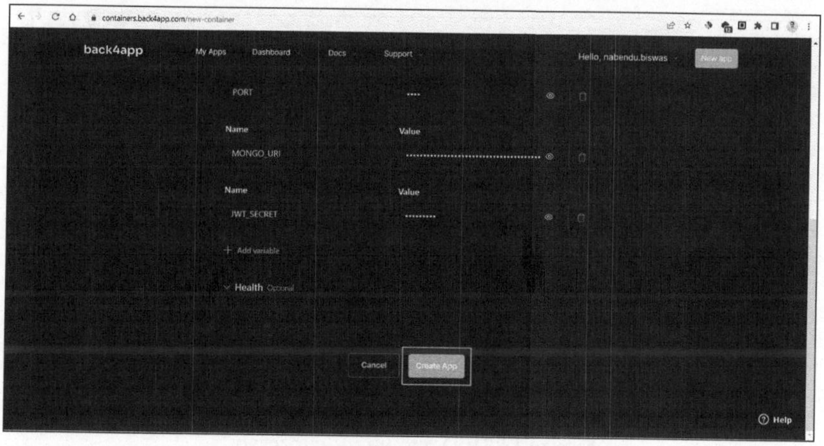

Figure 13.29: *Create App*

In the next screen, we will see all the logs when the deployment happens.

Figure 13.30: *Deploying in Back4app*

After some time, we will get the **`DEPLOYMENT READY`** message on the logs. We will also get the link to the deployment on the left side.

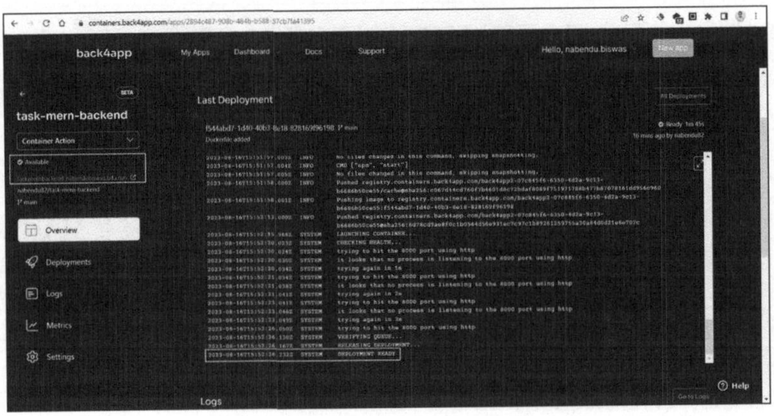

Figure 13.31: *Deployment successful*

Backend integration with frontend

We will now do the backend integration with the front end. But first, take the newly created backend endpoint and test the **`Register User`** route in Postman.

Here, we are able to use this route to create new users.

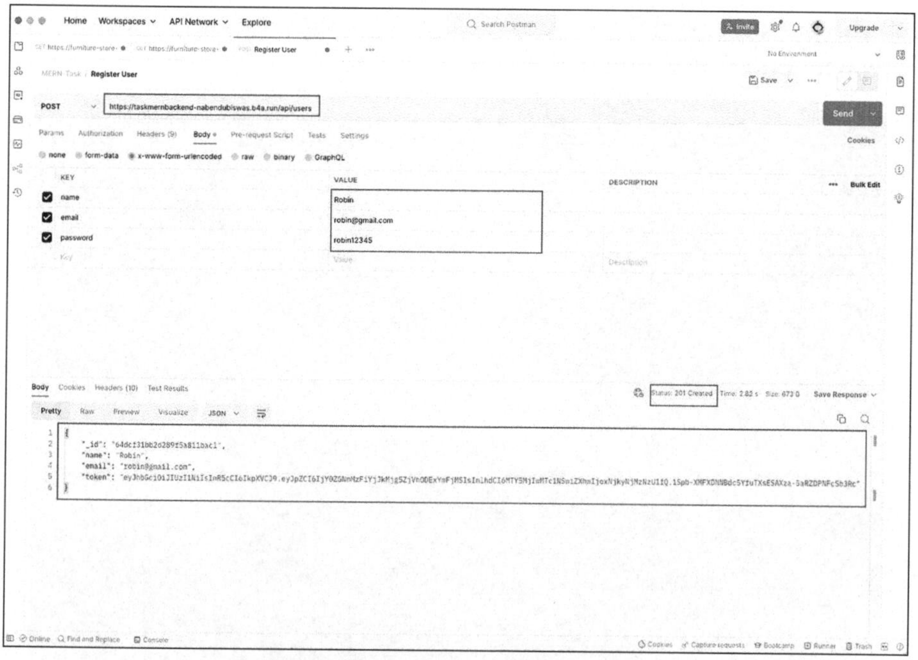

Figure 13.32: *Register user in Postman*

We are also able to log in with this newly created user in the login route.

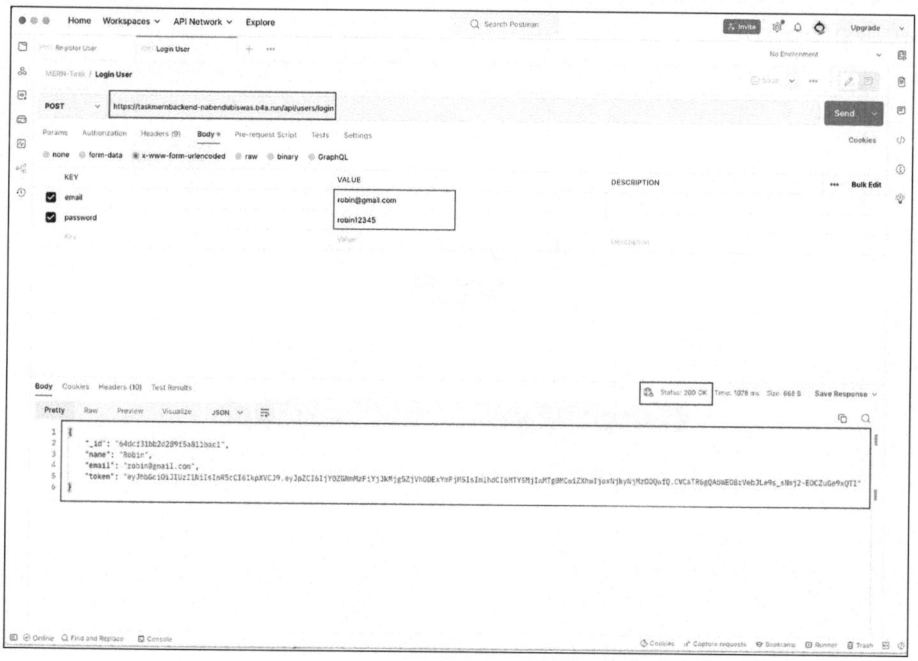

Figure 13.33: *Login user in Postman*

Now, in the **package.json** file in proxy, we will change the earlier localhost route with this backend route. Again, don't give / at the end.

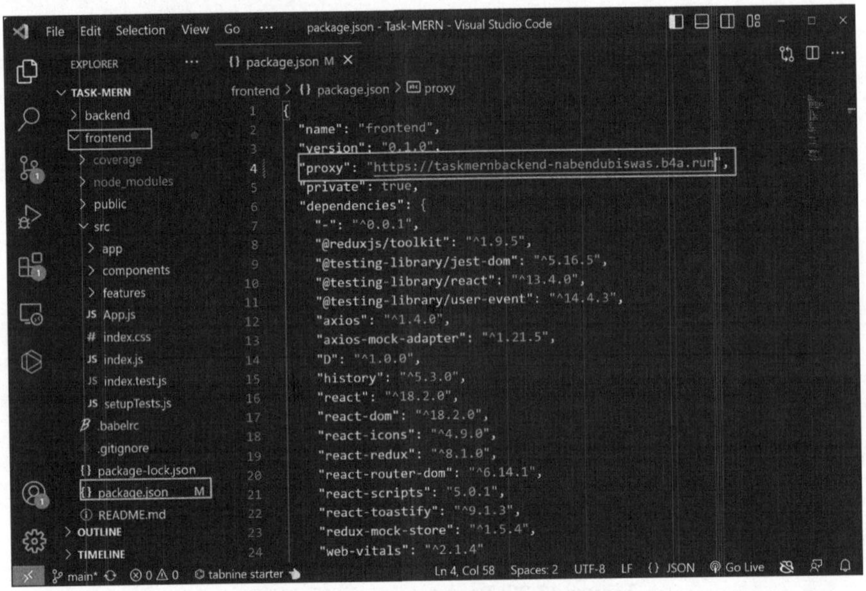

Figure 13.34: *Proxy in package.json*

Now in http://localhost:3000/, we will log in with the newly created user and it will work properly.

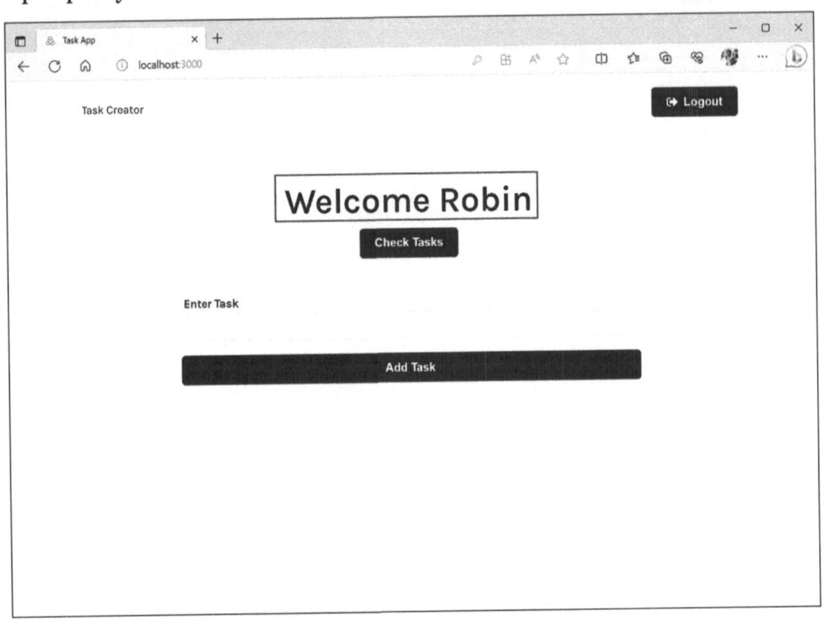

Figure 13.35: *Login to frontend*

Since we have made changes in the frontend code, we will stage, commit, and push this code to GitHub.

```
git add .
git commit -m "Backend integrated"
git push
```

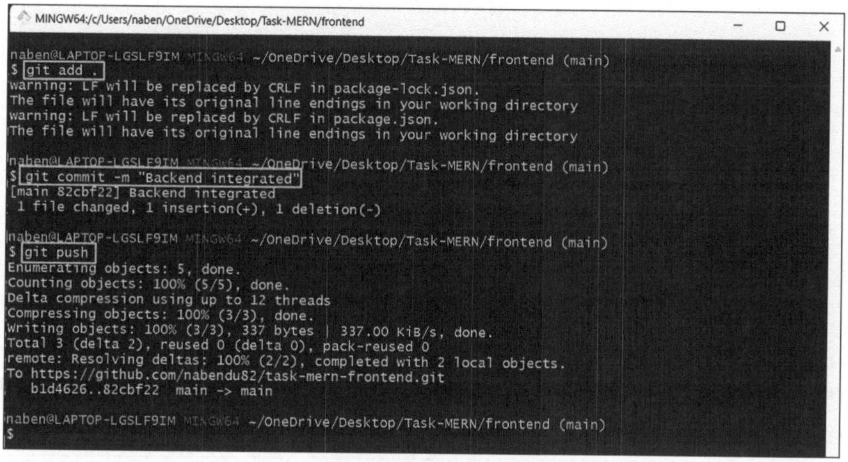

Figure 13.36: *git push*

Frontend deployment in Netlify

We will now deploy our project in Netlify. So, open Netlify at https://www.netlify.com/ and click on the **`Sign up`** button, if you don't have an account.

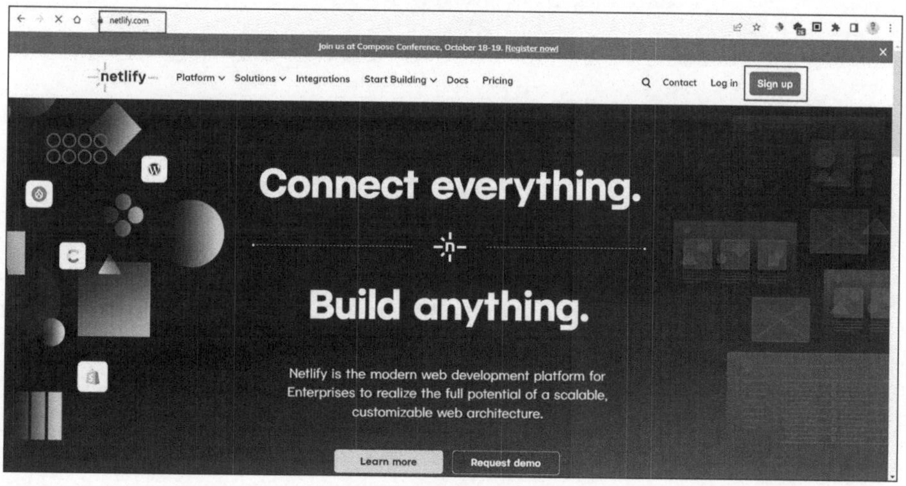

Figure 13.37: *Netlify*

Netlify requires you to Sign up or log in with any Git cloud account like GitHub Gitlab and Bitbucket. **`Login with GitHub`**, since our code is in GitHub.

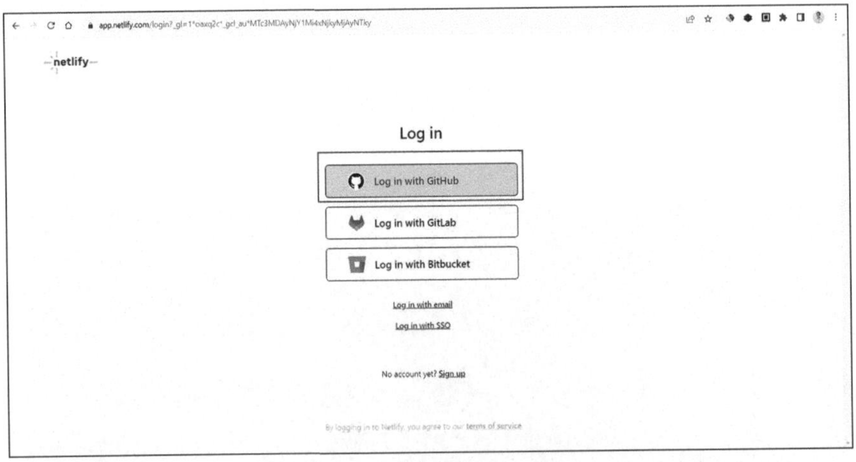

***Figure 13.38**: Netlify login*

Since we have a lot of deployed projects, it will show all the sites. If you don't have any, it will show blank.

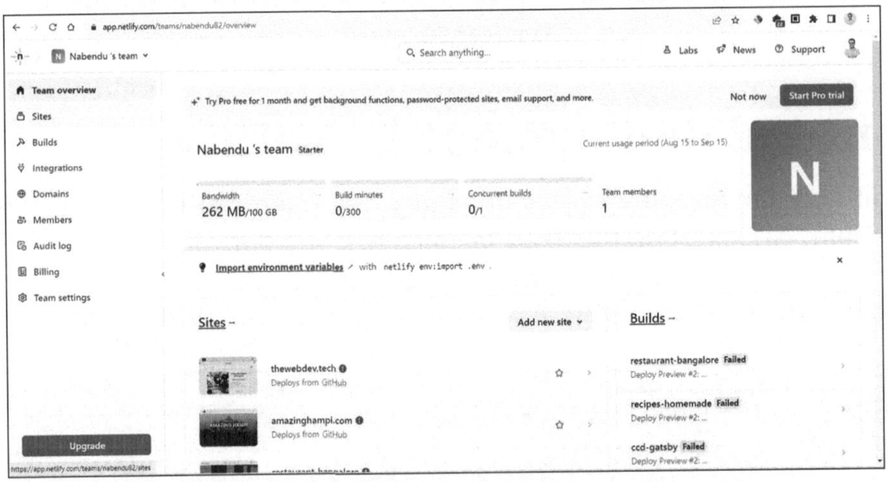

***Figure 13.39**: Netlify dashboard*

Now, click on **`Sites`** first and then the **`Add new site`** button on the top-right. Here, from the drop-down menu, click on **`Import an existing project`**.

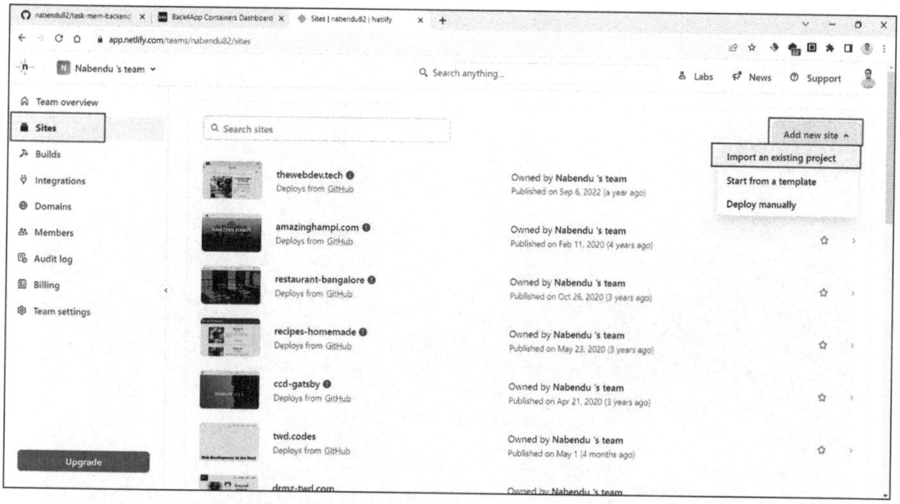

Figure 13.40: *Import existing project*

In the next screen click on **`Deploy with GitHub`** button.

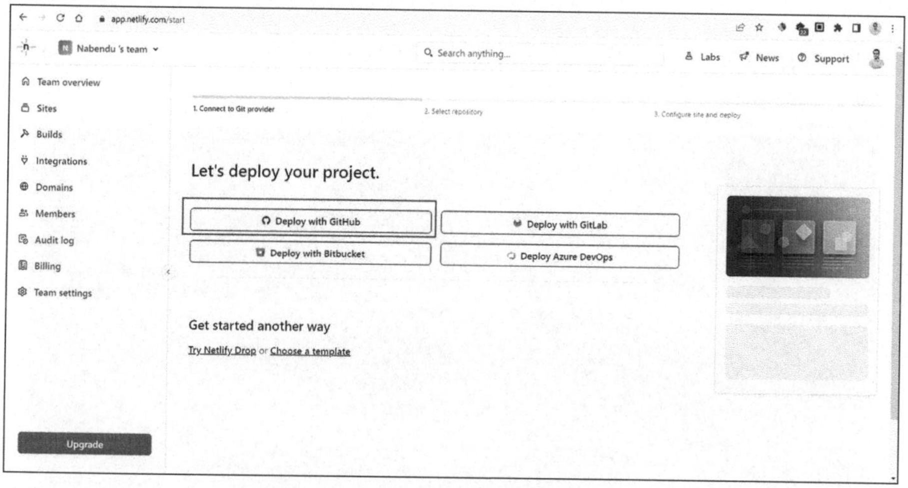

Figure 13.41: *Deploy with GitHub*

Now, in the GitHub access screen, we will select the **`task-mern-frontend`** after clicking on the **`Only select repository`**.

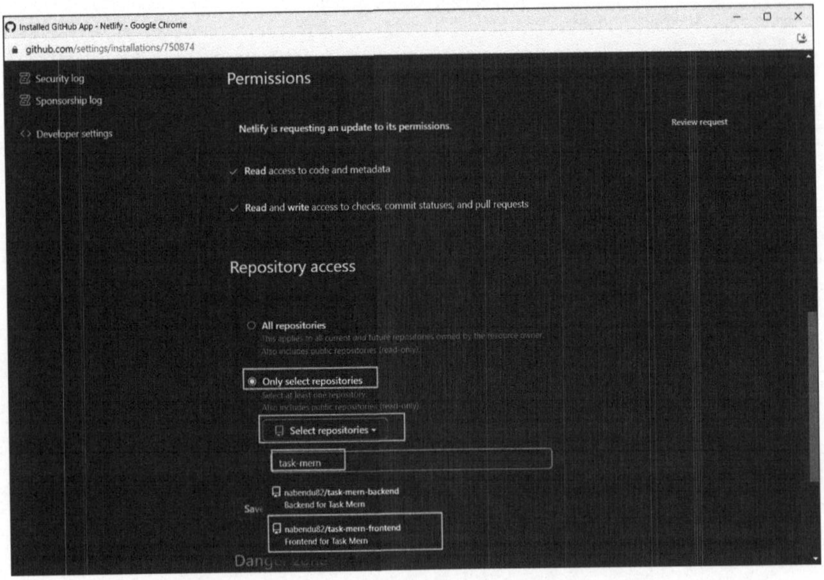

***Figure 13.42**: Selecting in GitHub*

After selecting the repository, click on the **Save** button.

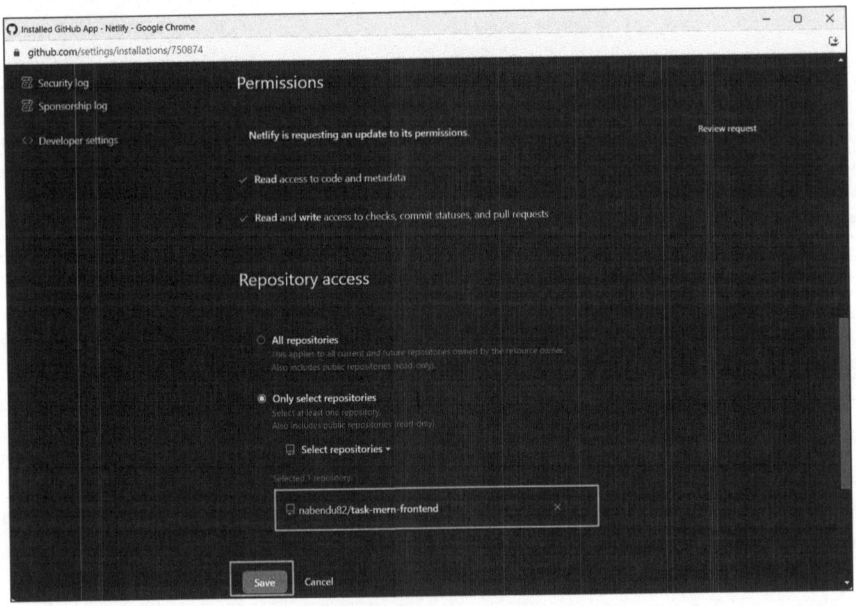

***Figure 13.43**: Access in GitHub*

Again, it will ask the permission to install the repository. Click on the **Install** button next.

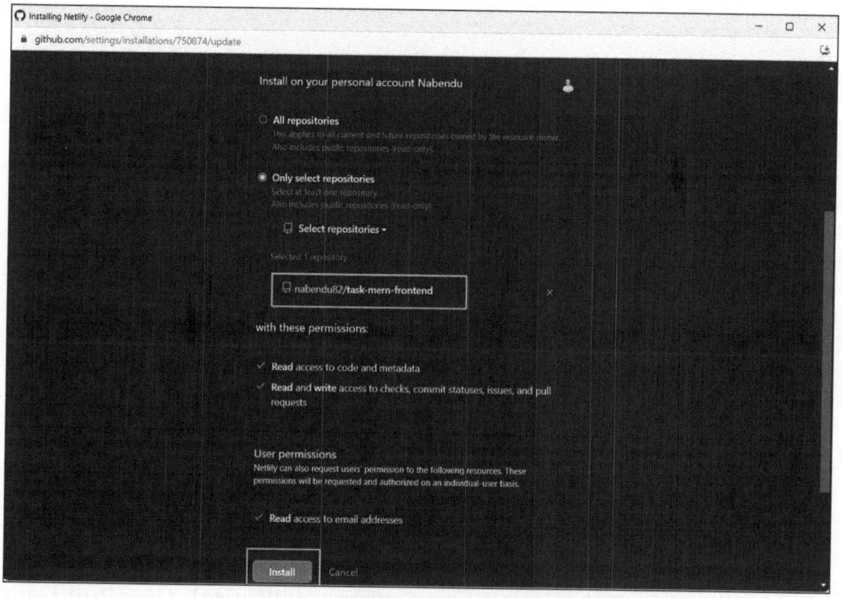

Figure 13.44: *Install in GitHub*

We will now get back to the Netlify screen. Here, we will now see the new repository. Click on the new repository.

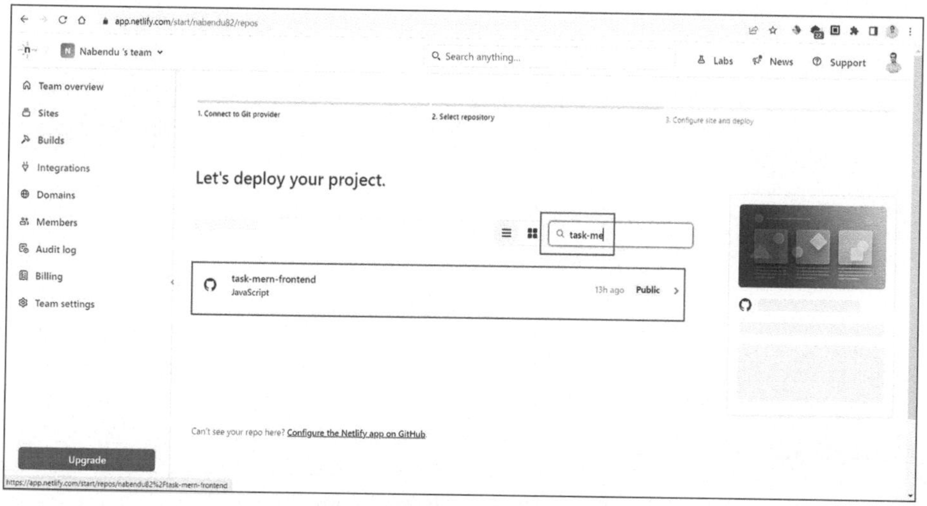

Figure 13.45: *Selecting GitHub in Netlify*

In the next screen, we will see the branch for deploying the project. Here, make sure it's the main branch.

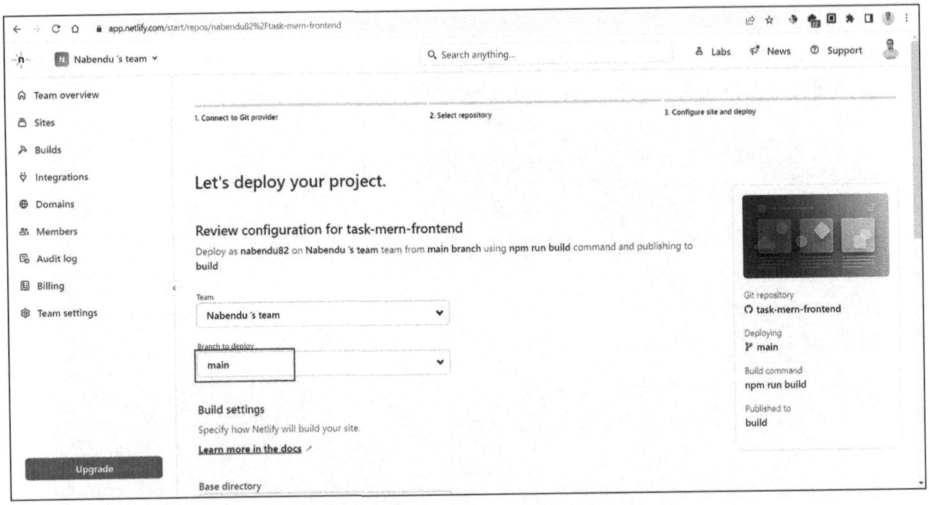

Figure 13.46: *Branch of GitHub*

On scrolling down on the same screen we will find the Build command and the publish directory. Both of them are right, so click on the **`Deploy task-mean-frontend`** button.

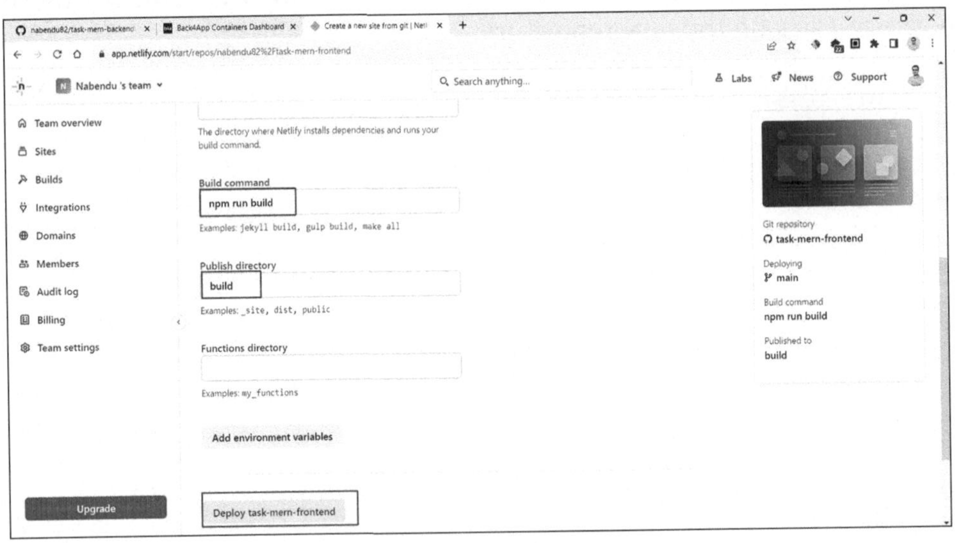

Figure 13.47: *Built commands*

In the next screen, we will see the site deploy in progress.

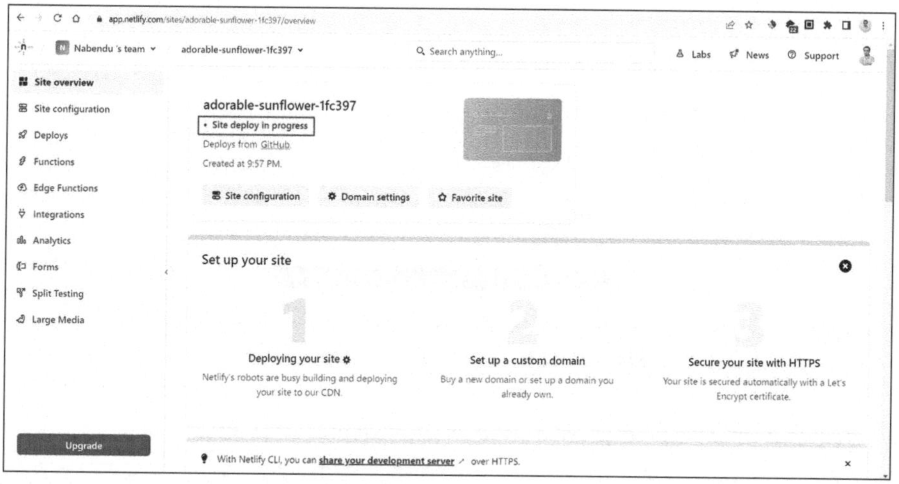

Figure 13.48: *Deploy in progress*

Once the site deployment is successful, click on the **`Open production deploy`** button.

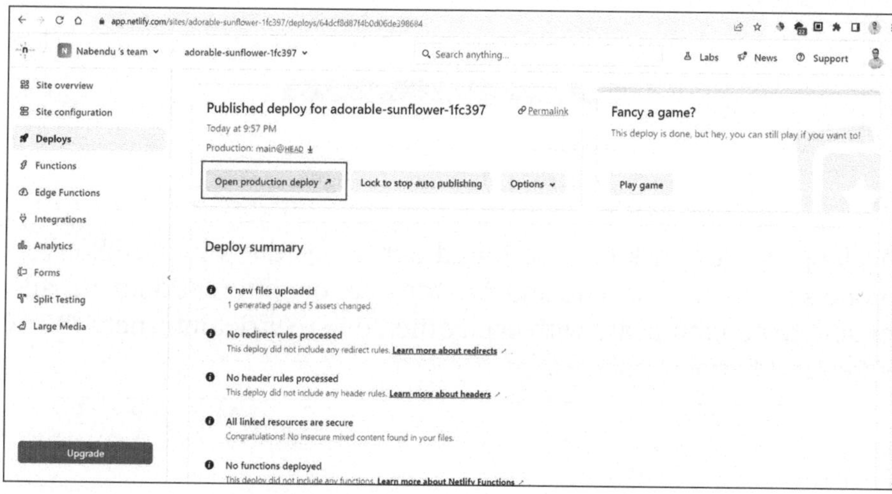

Figure 13.49: *Deployment successful*

Fixing CORS errors and final deployments

We will now try to log in with the credentials created earlier in the deployed site.

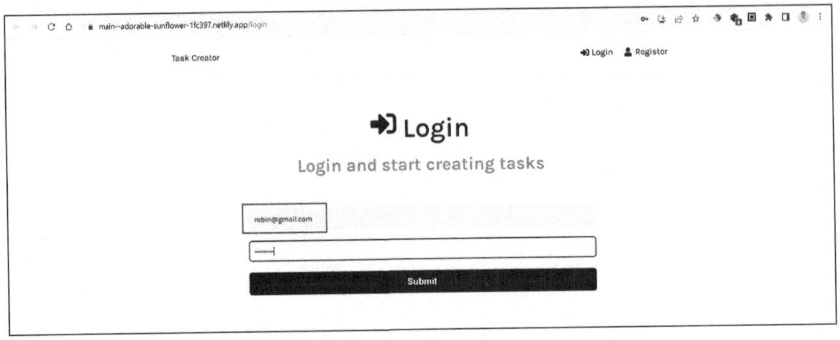

Figure 13.50: *Login to the deployed site*

But we got the error of Request failed with status code **404**.

Figure 13.51: *Failure to Login*

On checking the network tab, we found out it was due to a CORS error. This error comes when our backend and frontend are on different domains and they are not able to communicate with each other, due to strict internet CORS(Cross Origin Request Service) policies.

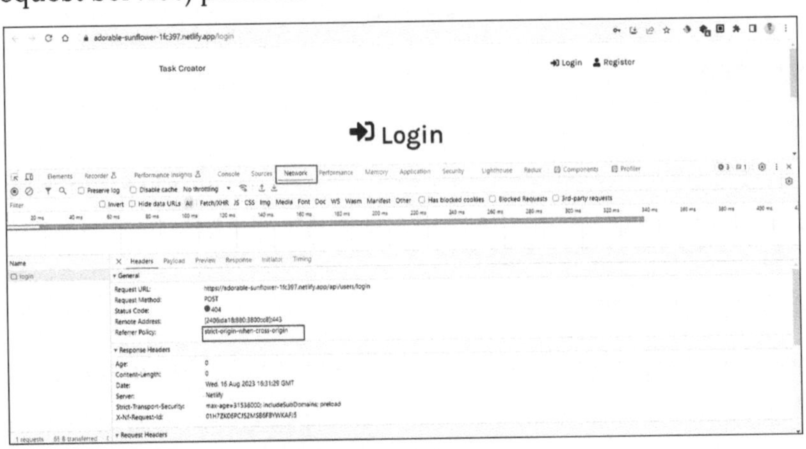

Figure 13.52: CORS *error*

To fix this issue, we need to first install the **`Cors`** package in the backend folder. We are doing the same by giving the **`npm i cors`** command in the integrated terminal.

We also need to import and use it in the **server.js** file.

```
const Cors = require('cors');
app.use(Cors());
```

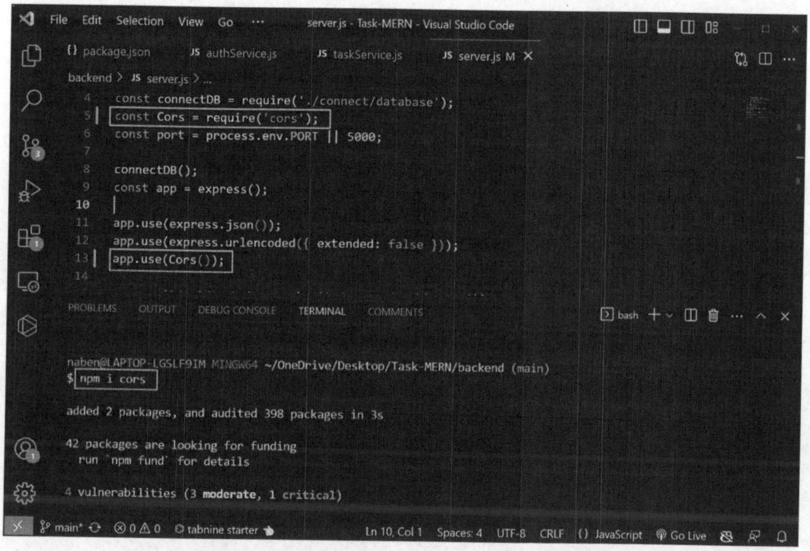

***Figure 13.53**: Adding CORS in the backend*

Since we made changes in the backend code, we need to **`add`**, **`commit`**, and **`push`** the code through the familiar git commands.

```
git add .
git commit -m "Cors Added"
git push
```

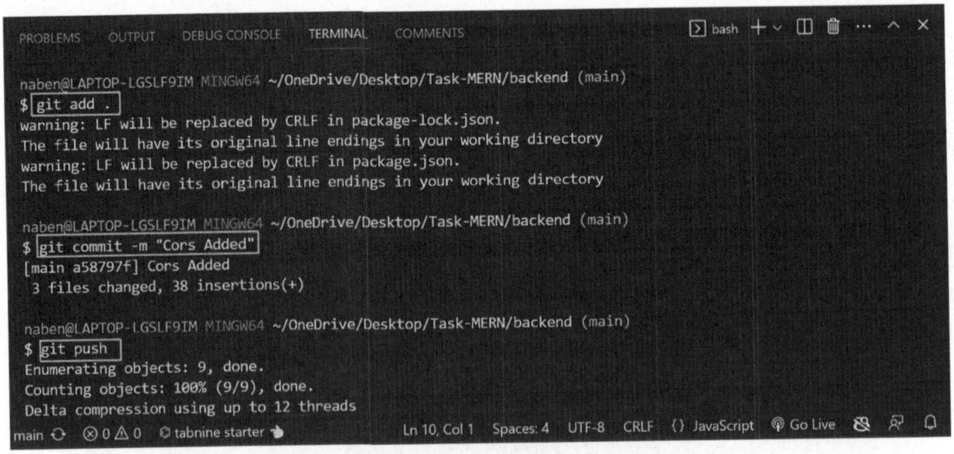

Figure 13.54: *git push*

We also need to delete the proxy code from the **package.json** file of the client.

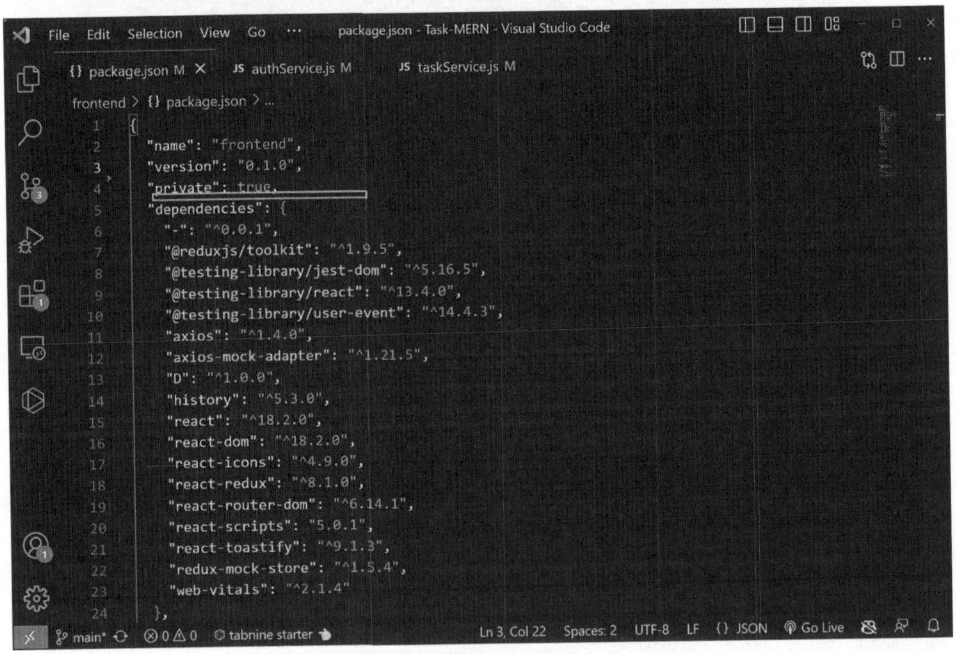

Figure 13.55: *Deleting proxy*

Next, we will update our **authService.js** file to contain the full backend URL.

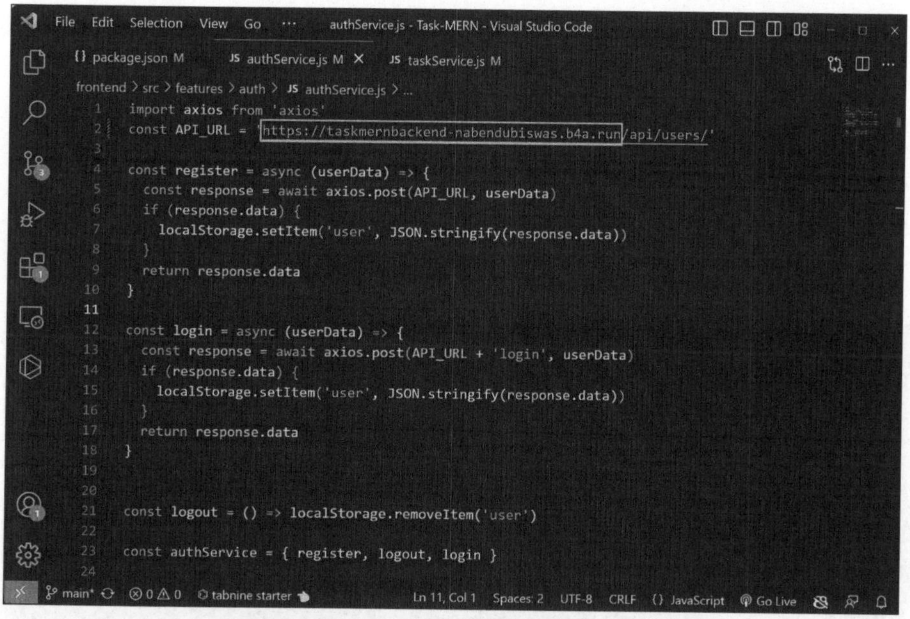

Figure 13.56: *Deployed link in authService.js*

We will also do the same in the **taskService.js** file.

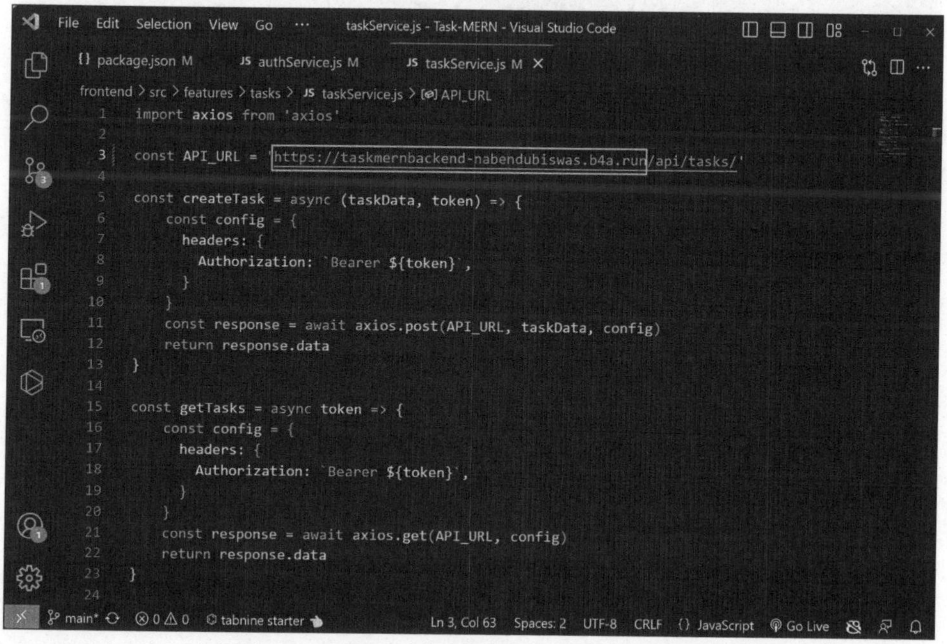

Figure 13.57: *Deployed link in taskService.js*

Since we made changes in the frontend code, we need to **add**, **commit**, and **push** the code through the familiar git commands.

```
git add .
git commit -m "Cors Added"
git push
```

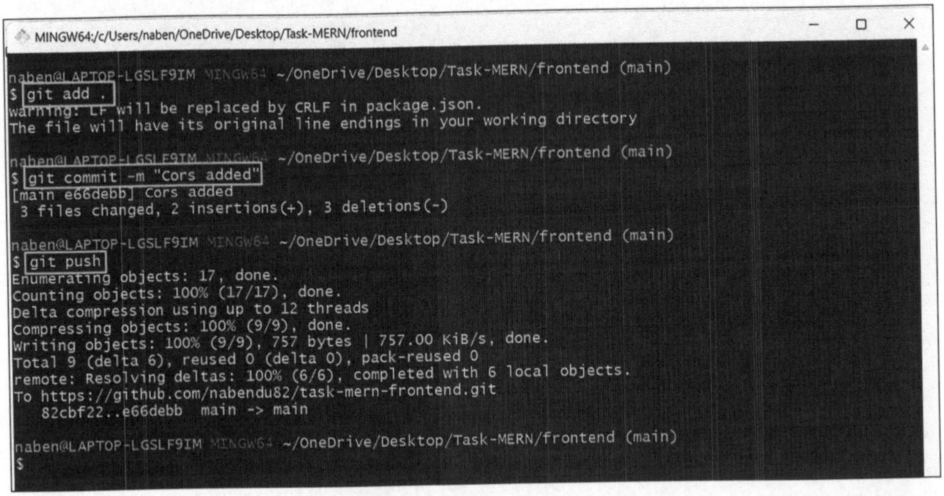

Figure 13.58: *git push*

Once we push the code to GitHub, it will automatically deploy to the front end. Now, when we go to our deployed app, everything will work perfectly.

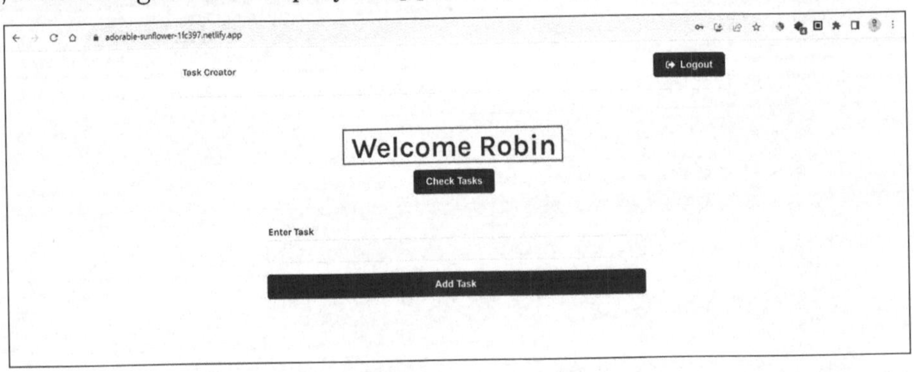

Figure 13.59: *Successful deployment*

Conclusion

In this final chapter, we have learned to deploy both the frontend and backend code. We deployed the frontend code using the service of Netlify. And deployed the backend code using the service of Back4app.

Points to remember

- Uploading code from the local machine to GitHub using the command line
- Deploying backend code in Back4app
- Deploying frontend code in Netlify
- Solving CORS issue which occurs due to frontend and backend on different URLs

Index

A

B

C

D

E

F

G

H

J

L

M

N